Travels with Baby

The Ultimate Guide for Planning Trips with Babies, Toddlers, and Preschool-Age Children

Shelly Rivoli

www.travelswithbaby.com

ISBN 978-0-615-15925-6

First Edition / Second Printing

Important Note to Readers

While every effort has been made to offer current and accurate information, this edition may contain reference to certain policies, standards, and regulations that may change over time. Always confirm critical information and seek professional advice when appropriate. Each child is unique and this book is not intended to substitute for the advice of your child's physician, your parent's intuition, or your own good judgment. Read all labels of medications and health products before use and seek professional advice if there is any confusion or indication of an emergency. Exercise common sense when using products and equipment for children, and always follow the manufacturer's instructions for use.

Special Sales

Special discounts are available for bulk purchases of this book. Special editions, including personalized covers, excerpts or select content, and corporate imprints can be created in large quantities for special needs. For more information, write to sales@travelswithbaby.com or Travels with Baby, P.O. Box 7696, Berkeley, CA 94707.

TABLE OF CONTENTS

Preface

Before crossing the Pacific with our firstborn, we had braced ourselves for the worst, half-expecting a long-haul exercise in torture we would boldly endure to reach our destination: Thailand. To our surprise, flying overseas with our 7-month-old was much more fun than any overseas flight we'd ever experienced. Instead of checking our watches as the airplane icon inched its way across the movie screen in between showings of second-run films, we were simply hanging out with our favorite little person in the world, having meals prepared for us and delivered right to our seats, watching movies which, for obvious reasons, we hadn't made it to the theater to see yet. We quickly realized that we were already on vacation—free to enjoy our daughter's wonderful smiles and share her fascination with the reading lights and passenger safety brochures, free to cuddle her and cat nap at leisure with nary a load of laundry to fold, free to agree with the flight attendants and fellow passengers that yes, she is absolutely adorable. Even when she cries.

Whether you are gearing up for your trip because you *have* to travel with your baby, toddler, or preschooler, or because you simply *have to travel* and are ready to try it with your child, this book will help you lay the groundwork for successful travel of any kind: weekend getaways, lengthy road trips, international treks, family reunions, and virtually every reason you might have for packing up and heading out with the newest member of your family. Rest assured, it is written by someone who has been there— inventing songs no one should ever sing in the eleventh hour on the road, pleading with the manager of the general store to let a helpless infant (and her numb-knuckled mother) come inside to warm up before opening hours, and sprinting behind the train caboose through the rain shouting, "Stop! You have our car seat!!!"

As you might suspect, there have been moments when even I have had to ask myself, "Who in her right mind travels with a baby?" But I will be honest with you; after trotting the globe with a small child in tow, the good times have by far outweighed the more challenging moments. Yes, by far. And much like the birthing of a child, I suspect you will find that even the roughest moments look much rosier in retrospect—and have all proven to be well worth the effort.

Now don't get me wrong, I'm not saying that traveling with your baby or toddler will be easy. In fact, I can pretty much guarantee that, as with any trip you might take, with or without children, you will have some difficult moments. Yet, while many parents opt to wait to vacation until their children are older, or are old enough to be left behind with grandparents or friends, they are—sometimes literally—missing the boat. New parents need vacations. New families need bonding time. New people need stimulation, fresh air and scenery, and happy parents. Leaving the house together, if only for a day, can work wonders for a family.

As I stroll along our "wall of travel," the collage of travel snapshots plastering our hallway at home, I am often overwhelmed by feelings of nostalgia and a longing to not just go back to many of the wonderful places we've visited, but to feel the weight once more of our eldest daughter still in her sling as we visited the elephant farm, to hear the clatter of her stroller wheels on the cobblestones of Provence, to feel her small hand squeeze mine the first time she realized what it really meant to take-off in the airplane as she shouted to all the passengers, "Big Daddy Ay-pane! Up!"

Traveling with a baby, a toddler, a baby *and* a toddler, and now with a toddler and a preschooler, has certainly kept us on our toes. As our tenth wedding anniversary approached, friends kept asking, "So, are the Rivolis finally going on a trip *without* the kids?" My husband explained, "We could, but it wouldn't be nearly as much fun." Sure, the nature of travel has changed for us somewhat after having two kids. Mostly, it's more expensive. There are more people to please as well. Cultural odysseys are generally bypassed in favor of beach vacations and camping trips. When possible, flights are dismissed in favor of road trips and travel by train. The concept of cruising, something that had never entered our minds to do in our pre-parent lives, has become especially enticing.

We count ourselves so lucky to have had these chances to see so much of the world already, from the sandy shores of Santa Cruz to the markets of Tunisia. But wherever our adventures take us, be it the backyard or abroad, I count myself luckiest for the chance to see it through the eyes of my children. Here's wishing your family many safe, memorable, and pleasant journeys.

Shelly Rivoli

Acknowledgments

T his book would not have been possible without the help of my mother, who gave so generously of her time, patience, love, and cooking for our family throughout the gestation of *Travels with Baby*. Because of you, I am lucky beyond words. Thank you.

Also, special thanks to Rona Renner, R.N., for introducing me to the field of Temperament and The Preventive Ounce project, and for taking the time to address my questions on temperament as applied to travel, as well as discussing her own inspiring adventures as a mother traveling overseas.

Additional thanks to my friends and family who provided helpful feedback on earlier drafts and incarnations of *Travels with Baby*: Susan Bumps, Amy Kang, Cinzia Solari, Davide Cis, Connie Anderson, and Polly Packard. And exponential gratitude to my husband and travel companion Tim, who logged countless miles of his commute with my manuscript pages in his hands, giving essential input and support for this project.

A hearty thanks also goes out to Captain Jon and Barbara Rivoli for their airport anecdotes that are included in this book, to Linda Geiser for the "McDrive," to Melissa Colby who helped Ziploc bags take up permanent residence in my suitcase, and to the numerous parents who have shared their travel wisdom and experiences with me through surveys, interviews, emails, chats in airport restrooms and café cars, and in contributions to TravelswithBaby.com.

Finally, I thank my family for living this book—and for letting me finish it, even when there were plenty of other things to be done: Tim, who agreed that you *can* take a baby to Thailand; Angelina, who showed us the way; and Rosalyn, who continues to remind us that each child is her own adventure. I dedicate this book to you.

"Today is your day! Your mountain is waiting. So... get on your way."

- Theodor Seuss Geisel (Dr. Seuss),

from *Oh, the Places You'll Go!*

PART I
GOOD CHOICES MAKE GOOD JOURNEYS

- *Chapter 1* -
Deciding When to Go

THE CASE FOR TRAVELING WITH BABIES

Who could use a vacation more than a couple in the trenches of new parenthood? Sleep deprivation, mounting laundry, visits from gift-bearing guests, and a return to the workplace can leave Mom and Dad with little energy or time to enjoy the marvel of the newest twig on the family tree. But when you travel with your child, far afield or close to home, it allows for a refreshing change of scenery for both you and your child. Better yet, it is an escape from the other responsibilities of home that too often get in the way of enjoying quality time together. So why wait?

As we prepared for our first getaway as a family, a weekend camping trip, it seemed much less overwhelming when I realized this: For the next few days, I will change just as many diapers, stop for just as many feedings, and sleep just as many (or few) hours, whether I'm at home or not. So why not do it all somewhere incredibly beautiful? And so I found myself nursing our infant daughter under a canopy of redwood trees, her little eyes shining up at the patches of bright sky overhead, her little ears perked for the sounds of birds and the trickles of a nearby stream.

I began to rest in a way I had not been able to at home, with the never-ending laundry, thank-you notes still to write, and other hovering responsibilities on top of the simple biological rigors of new motherhood. And as my husband took over meal preparation (a vacation in itself for me) and the details of our camp, I was free to focus entirely on our daughter and the wonder of her presence in our lives. We came home from that long weekend refreshed and recharged, and with a renewed sense of confidence in ourselves as parents, and as partners.

Traveling with a child younger than 6 months old may sound overwhelming at first, especially when you are a first-time parent and are as new to the world of parenthood as your child is to the world around him. What do you pack? How do you plan? How do you physically transport the child? Where will he sleep? How will you deal with all of those diapers—and how many will you pack, and in what? What about exposure to germs? What if he catches a cold?

Many doctors advise against flying with newborns in their first two weeks as they adjust to life outside the uterus, and some airlines simply won't allow it (see Airlines' Minimum Age Policies, page 234). Yet, once your child has made the transition and gets your doctor's go-ahead for travel, there are really no reasons you shouldn't travel with your infant, provided that the baby is in good health, that you are feeling well enough and are in good health yourself, and that you are reasonably comfortable with the idea of traveling with your child. In fact, there are many health and safety advantages to traveling with your child while she is still an infant as opposed to waiting until she's older, dexterous—and mobile.

The infant is better protected from germs and illness than older babies, toddlers, and preschoolers, because she has very limited access to foreign objects (including the railings, turnstiles, arm rests, and other things older travelers encounter) and she puts far fewer things in her mouth than do her mobile counterparts. You have control over virtually everything that comes in contact with her, and so long as you keep your own hands clean and washed frequently, you'll have a tremendous advantage over offending germs. If she is breastfeeding, she has additional immunity benefits from her mother's milk, which includes white blood cells (leukocytes) activated by microbes the mother is exposed to (see Breastfeeding for Healthy Travels, page 116).

In all honesty, traveling with your child may seldom be as easy as it is in the months before he eats solid foods or crawls. The infant's needs may be frequent, but they are few. The infant still spends a good deal of time napping—while you may do what you please (strolling museums, eating in restaurants, flying overseas, or driving down the coast). They infant is also easier to feed on the go than are older babies and toddlers, without the need to pack along strained or finger foods, or deal with the inevitable mess generated by each meal. Breastfed infants are, of course, especially easy to feed while traveling, though it may take a little time to master the "public feeding" with grace (see Nine Tips for Nursing on the Go, page 74).

The infant is also incredibly portable. Infant carrier car seats make it possible to transport baby from taxi to stroller frame without disturbing her sleep—and give you a convenient place to set her while eating in restaurants. Slings and frontpack carriers also let you travel with ease even through stroller-prohibitive terrain such as many subway stations and more rustic locales.

Top 3 Reasons to Travel While Your Child is Still a Baby

1. You can choose a destination and activities that interest you. For now, your child is equally content to visit MOMA as the aquarium or zoo, so long as she's with you. In a couple of years, however, you can bet that you'll all be finding Nemo.

2. Jetlag won't faze you with your already sporadic sleeping routine. Or more importantly, your baby adapts to new time zones more easily when she still sleeps multiple times per 24-hour day. Later on, when she naps only once a day or not at all, it may take

longer to adjust to a difference in time zones. For now, you can also look forward to her naps to help catch extra winks during your vacation, should you need them.

3. Your child will never be cheaper to travel with (hurry!). Your heart may skip a beat the first time you price airfare for THREE to your extended family's festivities or your favorite vacation spot. Until she turns 2 years, however, your child can fly free on your lap for domestic flights or for 10% of your ticket on international flights, or for 50% in her own seat with many airlines (more details in Chapter 14). Plus, some cruise lines, all-inclusive resorts, and tour operators will not charge fees for infants—though they will for "children," which is sometimes defined as 1 year or, most often, 2 years and older.

ANTICIPATING AGES AND STAGES

As the saying goes, there is a time and place for everything. For example, a trip to the Big Apple may be much easier while your child can still travel in her infant carrier car seat, popping in and out of taxis and a lightweight stroller frame. And a beach vacation may be much more relaxing once your child knows not to eat the sand or run headlong into the surf. But predicting the right time and place for trips with your child can be a tricky business. Especially since each child marches, crawls, and rolls over to the beat of his own drummer.

What could be a delightful adventure with your child riding along in the sling or frontpack may become frustrating for you both by the time she wants to practice her new walking skills—and there's no telling when that will be. Even the child who once rode along happily in his stroller may at some point decide he's too grown up for such trifles and insist on walking along side of you (until his legs wear out). And the lengthy road trip will be vastly easier when your child still naps more than once a day, or later on when he is old enough to appreciate the passing scenery and help entertain himself. But spend too many days on the road with a non-napping toddler and you may all be ready to trade in the family car for airline tickets home.

While keeping in mind that each child will develop at his own perfect pace, and with his own distinct temperament (don't miss Temperaments in Transit, beginning on page 81), here are some general guidelines for the various ages and stages of development your child may experience from birth through four years, and tips for how you might best plan your travels together.

Birth to 3 Months

Once you begin to feel you have your sea legs as parents, it may do you a world of good to get out of the house. Weekenders not too far from home, or visits with family and friends can be a great place to begin. Since your baby sleeps more now than she will in the months to come, it's an ideal time for trips that require long hours spent in the car seat. She also requires little space for sleeping, and may be fine sleeping next to you or in a space-saving infant travel bed (as opposed to the portacrib you may long for on trips later on), so you still have many options for lodgings, including smaller and more economical hotel rooms, economy train sleeper compartments (roomettes), or basic cruise ship cabins. Gear and feeding needs are minimal, though you will want to take into consideration that she'll need to feed and be diapered frequently. The travel wardrobe couldn't be simpler. No shirt, no shoes, no problem — just pack plenty of footed cotton playsuits, and some extra layers for warmth.

Best bet vacations: Visits to family and friends, urban adventures, car trips, train trips, short cruises.

3 to 6 Months

Your baby is in his prime for riding (and napping) contentedly on laps and in an infant carrier or sling, while sharing early smiles, all making travel together a true delight. He takes a new interest in his surroundings, and enjoys seeing the sights from the comfort of your sling or frontpack carrier—where he still has the comfort of staying close to the people he knows best. You are still relatively free to choose a destination and schedule the itinerary to suit your adult selves, but because your child's skin is still very thin and sensitive, sunscreen and repellents are not recommended (see Having Fun In [Spite Of] The Sun, page 111, and Managing Mosquitoes, page 113). Consequently, you may lean toward destinations where extreme sun and biting insects are not a concern. Urban adventures in cultural capitols may provide the right amount of stimulation for all of you (MOMA for mom, baby swings in Central Park for Junior), balanced with climate controlled interiors when and where needed. His sleeping arrangements may require more attention as he becomes more active, quite possibly rolling over at some point and perhaps even doing some version of crawling. A travel bassinet or infant travel trundle will give him a comfy place to snooze and play with his toys, or a portacrib may also be available on request at your hotel or in your cruise ship cabin. Most children in this range do not yet eat solid foods, which helps keep things simple and relatively tidy in transit. In particular, you won't need a complete clothing change after every meal as you may in the following few months.

Best bet vacations: Urban adventures, overseas travel, car trips.

6 to 12 Months

Baby becomes an accomplished explorer in virtually any room as long-distance rolling, scooting, crawling, cruising, and possibly walking become part of her physical repertoire. It will be much easier to manage a long-haul flight before your child starts walking well, so you may want to plan an overseas trip during this window. Since the floor is where it's at during this stage, and everything goes in the mouth, choose your accommodations accordingly. You'll want to plan a trip that includes a suitable space and time each day where she can exercise and explore in a safe environment. You may find it well worth paying the upgrade for a larger room or to stay somewhere you are confident will be clean. Consider bringing or renting any gear she is especially fond of at this time if it could make a tremendous difference in her enjoyment of the vacation (and yours). Bring a play mat or baby quilt for play time on the floor. Also, a "jumper" that mounts in an open doorway (possibly your bathroom's or a closet's) will easily fit in most suitcases and can help keep her out of harm's way while you ready yourselves for the day. Consider exotic and under-developed destinations carefully as you may have to pack along your entire supply of diapers and jarred baby food. Urban adventures, on the other hand, allow you to pick up your baby essentials at markets and pharmacies as needed.

Best bet vacations: Urban adventures, overseas travel, car trips.

12 to 18 Months

Your child may look more like a "staggerer" than a toddler through much of this phase, and even though he is on his feet, he may be very unsteady and prone to falls. He will likely want to spend every chance he gets perfecting his walking skills, whether he is still cruising from object to object or sprinting off in sheer delight, and he may also be reaching new heights as a climber. If you hope to relax on your vacation, it may be more important than ever to look for destinations and lodgings that are prepared—and safe—for small children. Rethink exotic resorts with hard tile floors, or sleek hotels with "edgy" furnishings. Look for a family-friendly hotel or vacation rental that anticipates small children, where you won't have to spend all the time in your room distracting your child from the furnace or AC controls, or steering him away from the glass coffee table (see the Checking-In Safety Checklist, page 138). If he will still nap in the stroller, this may provide you with opportunities to enjoy some attractions and activities during his naps that he might lose patience with in his waking hours. He may now be eating more of the foods you do, which could help simplify things so long as there are not concerns of food or water safety for your destination (if there are, see page 120).

Best bet vacations: Camping trips, beach resorts, shorter trips by airplane.

18 to 24 Months

These are the final months your child will be able to fly as a lap child — free on domestic flights and for 10 % of your ticket price on international flights. On very long flights, however, you may prefer purchase a seat for him, and some airlines will provide a special discount for infants in seats (you'll find them beginning on page 187). Your child may not have much patience for long hours spent in transit, especially in the car seat, so it will be important to break up long drives when possible, and walk laps around the airplane together. Train travel, which allows for greater physical freedom and more face time with Mom and Dad, may be preferred. Talk about your trip plans ahead of time so that the events and activities will come as less of a surprise. It's an ideal time for camping trips or beach vacations close to home, but be careful in choosing campsites as your child is highly mobile but does not yet understand dangers such as campfires, creeks, or wildlife, or the problem with poison oak.

Best bet vacations: Beach vacations, camping trips, train trips.

2 to 3 Years

You will have to pay your child's way for most travel now, including domestic flights, most cruises, rail travel in the U.S. and Canada, and stays at some hotels and resorts, though discounted rates may apply. Some points of interest, especially those geared toward children, will charge a child's admission as well. We all have our favorites, and that goes for your child now, too. She begins to express her own opinions about everything from food, to wardrobe, to activities, to whether or not she approves of getting into the car seat. The more involved and empowered you can help her feel through this phase, the more smoothly your travels are likely to go. Small steps along the way, like choosing which books to put in the carry-on, or which pajamas to wear at Grandma's house, could help her feel much more in control of the changing situation. Tantrums, for even the best-behaved little travelers, may strike from time to time; you may all be happiest in vacation settings where these can be managed as safely and effectively as possible—and avoided as much as possible! A vacation that allows for flexible daily schedules, regular meal times and snacks, and physical freedom and activity for your child can be critical at this stage, so most beach vacations and camping trips will fit the bill nicely. This could also be a great year to travel by train, with your child free to explore the train cars with you, not constrained in a car seat. Since she rides trains for half the adult fare in the U.S. and Canada, and for free in Europe, it may be less expensive for your family to travel by train than by airplane on some routes (see Part VI of this book for "Travels by Train"). Also, potty training will likely become an issue this year, so be sure to plan your itinerary accordingly. Longer flights become a little easier as the year passes and your child's attention span allows for more reading time, some basic games, coloring, and other pastimes.

Best bet vacations: Beach vacations, camping trips, train travel

3 to 4 Years

For many families, this is the year when travel becomes significantly easier, especially with the completion of potty training and the child's improved ability to express himself. Your preschool-age child may also crave more social interaction than ever before, so trips to campgrounds that are popular with families and stops at playgrounds and parks where other children may be can help provide this outlet. Also, "3 years and out of diapers" is often the magic formula for children to qualify for most kid's programs, clubs, and activities at many family resorts and on cruise ships, giving them supervised creative playtime with their peers while you get a chance to snorkel, shop, visit a museum, or take a nap by the pool. Although art museums are most likely out and amusement/theme parks may still be overwhelming (few children this age have the patience to wait in one line after the next), your child will likely enjoy visits to aquariums, natural history or science museums with children's displays, and zoos. Your load lightens as less gear is needed, though you may end up having to carry an exhausted child if he begins to refuse his stroller this year.

Best bet vacations: Cruises, beach vacations, camping trips, urban adventures.

4 to 5 Years

Your child becomes more of a travel partner at this stage. He's able to better grasp the concept of your trip from start to finish, and has the patience required at times for sitting still or standing in lines. He may take pride in packing his own suitcase and may also enjoy being in charge of his own camera (a disposable one should do nicely). Gear needs are at a minimum now, enabling you to travel lighter than you have since becoming a parent. Your child may be ready for his first trip to the big amusement park this year, but make sure he understands he will spend some time waiting in lines for rides, and forewarn him about minimum height and age requirements that may prevent him from enjoying some "big kid rides." He is also reaching an age of awareness where some background may be appreciated when traveling to or through areas of interest (e.g. when the pilgrims came here a long time ago…). For travel abroad, he may enjoy learning some words or phrases ahead of time to use at your destination, and may also take more of an interest in the local customs and modes of transportation. Collecting souvenirs as you travel (pine cones, coasters, wildflowers, ticket stubs…) and creating a travel scrapbook for your trip may be a fun project and creative outlet for your child.

Best bet vacations: Urban adventures, overseas travel, beach vacations.

- *Chapter 2* -
Deciding Where to Go

BEACH VACATIONS

Bring sun block, a blanket, a bucket of toys, and you're set for days and days of fun. It can be well worth it to choose a hotel, resort, or vacation rental that is walking distance to the beach to avoid the hassle of loading and unloading your car on each end, each day, and finding parking. Depending on your destination, the higher price for a beachfront resort may also make up for the cost of a rental car and gas. When choosing your beach destination, keep in mind what your little beachcomber might find in the sand; some beaches are much more likely to have litter or fishing hooks, for example. Also, consider the shoreline carefully—will it be relatively safe for splashing and wading, and if not, will you be able to relax and watch the waves or will you have to spend most of your time keeping your child out of the surf? Pop-up shade tents are excellent for beach vacations, providing shade for napping babies and even privacy for nursing, and they stay fun for children well through the preschool years.

With infants and babies – Hit the beach during naptimes and, with baby lounging in the shade, you can enjoy a good book, a snooze, or taking turns with your partner dipping in the surf. Infants are easy to keep clean and well-shaded with help from a pop-up shade tent. Older babies thrill at their first discovery of sand—and miles and miles of it. In your child's earliest days of mobility, once you can no longer confine her to the beach blanket, some beaches may prove more frustrating than fun. With crawlers and early walkers, aim for beaches where odds are the sand won't be littered with trash from picnickers and partiers, and try to avoid rocky or pebbled shores for now as they may feel to you more like miles on end of choking hazards at this stage. Also, be wary of destinations popular with sailors and windsurfers as the winds and waves they favor may be unfavorable to your family. Since most beaches feature little or no sources of shade, you may favor beachfront resorts or private beaches that provide sun umbrellas for added comfort and protection.

Naptime: Push a couple of seaside lounges together under a shade umbrella.

With toddlers – Beaches are one of the few vacation destinations that can completely appease the desires of a toddler: exploration, discovery, exercise, fresh air, and loads and loads of sand. The secret to planning your beach vacation is finding a shore with a gentle surf and favorable water temperature. Look to destinations like Cape Cod, the Caribbean, or sandy-shored lakes, and beaches along seas rather than the vast oceans. For exploration at the water's edge, invest in a good life jacket or swim vest that will last through the preschool years, and for extremely sunny locations, consider UV-protective swim attire as an extra measure of protection. Some swimsuits that are made to look like surfer suits have special appeal for small kids and cover them to their knees, which is also helpful in keeping sand out of the diaper zone. To help further avoid the "sandpaper syndrome" that results from rubbing baby wipes on sandy behinds, keep an extra water bottle handy for rinsing off. The bicycling and sports variety that you squeeze and squirt are ideal.

With preschoolers – Sand castles become more complex, treasure hunts for shells and tidbits can become all consuming, and tide pools capture the preschooler's imagination. Bring a kite to windy beaches, or a small boogie board to gentler shores if your child is interested and ready. Short boat trips for whale watching and visits to lighthouses can also be quite exciting and memorable for the preschooler. Let him bring his own (disposable) camera to preserve the memories from his perspective.

CAMPING TRIPS

Babies could stare up at tree leaves and limbs against the sky for hours, and toddlers could spend just as long studying what's on the ground below: twigs, pine cones, frogs, beetles, lichen, rocks, and more (and let us not forget the thrill of the occasional chipmunk sighting). Camping, whether by car or by backpack, can be one of the most satisfying, and affordable, vacations for families with babies and small children. Getting back to nature for many of us also means getting back to our roots, and if some of your best childhood memories revolve around the campground, sharing the experience with your child will have even greater significance.

With infants and babies – Your biggest concern may be camping when and where the nighttime temperatures will not dip too low, since infants and babies can't snuggle down with their faces into their sleeping bags like the rest of us. Take care if you attempt co-sleeping with your infant or baby in your sleeping bag or on an air mattress. A safer practice could be making a tent within your tent by using a travel bassinet or play yard that can be safely draped with a light blanket to hold the warmer air around your baby, but leaving a gap for good ventilation. The Peapod travel bed (as shown) pops up like a mini tent with a zip-tight screen and may be quite useful both inside your tent and out (more details in Travel Beds, page 54). If you have a large enough tent, you can use a play yard with a fitted mosquito net to help (nets are available to fit standard models). Remember that it is not advised to use DEET-containing insect repellant or sunscreen on babies younger than 6 months, so chose destinations and seasons with more favorable conditions, and bring good sun hats and protective clothing (see tips for Managing Mosquitoes on page 113). A play yard or bouncer seat can be helpful outside of your tent as a safe, clean place for baby to play while you set up camp, prepare meals, and play cards or strum your guitar. Back-country camping will be easiest before your child begins eating solid foods, and while it is still comfortable to wear her in a frontpack (in addition to your backpack!).

A Peapod travel bed may be useful indoors and out.

With toddlers – When choosing a campsite, make safety a top concern. You'll want to keep your little explorer a comfortable distance from the water's edge or other hazards so you can relax as much as possible at camp. Campfires are fascinating at this stage, but with little comprehension of the danger, so you may want to wait until after dinner clean-up to build yours, when you can sit down and enjoy it together. Toy trucks or train cars, sand toys, and children's garden tools can all be good toys to bring along from home. If you have room, a six-panel Superyard keeps toddlers corralled while you set up and break down your camp or cook. Also, a pop-up sun tent gives your toddler his own tent to play and nap in.

With preschoolers – Time for first fishing trips (a la Fisher Price, perhaps), nature walks, and boat rides. Your preschooler will have more of an appreciation for nature than ever before, ready to catch frogs and fireflies, observe chipmunks, and learn to identify a few flowers and trees. Even if your child is potty trained, you may be glad to have a training potty in the tent when nature calls at night, or if the camp facilities are a little crude or unnerving for your child (e.g. ye olde pit toilet).

Tips for Back-Country Camping with Babies and Toddlers

Car camping allows you to bring many helpful comforts along: an ice chest, more toys, more gear, a bigger tent, camp chairs, the play yard... But back-country camping is also possible with babies, toddlers, and preschoolers, with good planning and a few modifications.

1. **Breastfeed.** Nothing to pack, mix, wash, or sterilize for baby to drink. With the frontpack or sling adjusted just right, you can even do it as you hike!

2. **Bring shelf-stable boxed milk** for weaned toddlers and preschoolers. It isn't always easy to find, but cow's milk can be purchased in individual serving boxes that need no refrigeration, packaged with straws like juice boxes. Real Fresh is a brand of boxed whole milk you may be able to find in the baking aisle of your grocery store, or Horizon also offers organic cow's milk in these packs in some health food stores (and in some Starbuck's cafes if you're really having a hard time finding it). Many children are just as happy with boxed soy or rice milk for the trip, which may be easier to come by. This is a great option for shorter trips and trips where the water supply may be questionable or taste unpleasant.

3. **Mix evaporated milk with powdered milk,** if you go that route instead. Powdered milk is typically skim (or .05% milk fat at best), and you will still need the water to mix with it. Evaporated milk (whole milk with 50% of the water removed from it) can be added to improve the flavor and consistency.

4. **Go light on baby food.** This is no time to weigh down your pack with glass jars of pureed foods. Shelf-stable packaged applesauce and mixed "berry sauce" servings and baby foods packaged in plastic tubs are a much lighter weight alternative. Bring along some rice cereal flakes or other grain cereal in a baggie to serve up straight or mix in with other food for extra nutrition and substance. Freeze-dried fruit and veggie puffs made for babies and toddlers are quite helpful, too.

5. **Don't skimp on clothes.** In your pre-parent life, it was easier to calculate the bare necessities you might need for your trip. But chances are that didn't account for the occasional diaper blowout, spit-up, potty training accident, or spontaneous romp in the stream. One puffy thermal suit for your baby won't be enough if her diaper leaks and soaks it your first night. So be sure to figure out a back up as you pack up.

6. **Choose destinations accessible by jogging stroller.** With babies and toddlers, it may be easier to carry your child on your back and

put your pack and gear in the stroller. Once you arrive at your campsite, the stroller works as a make-shift bouncer seat, dining booster, and camp chair. With a weather shield, it also becomes your child's rain gear!

7. **Invest in a good backpack carrier.** If you will spend much time hiking with your child on your back—plus some gear, you'll need a very sturdy, supportive backpack carrier like the higher end models by Kelty. Attachable sun/rain/wind hoods can be especially helpful, and a fitted mosquito net is also available.

8. **Start small.** Even for the accomplished backpacker, backcountry camping with kids may present new and unanticipated challenges. Start with shorter treks close to home where the weather and climate are easy to predict. You may even want to plan a "reconnaissance mission" ahead of time—a daytrip to check out the trails and site before you stay overnight. A site that offers potable water and garbage service will help keep things simple as well. The National Park Service Web site, www.nps.gov, gives helpful descriptions of trails and backcountry campsites for its parks. Your state and regional park services may offer this information as well.

9. **Divide and conquer.** Camping with a group may help all of you lighten your loads as some food and gear can be shared, particularly for cooking. If your group has other babies and small children, the kids will keep each other entertained and one lucky adult can carry the designated "diaper pack."

10. **Diaper details.** If you'll be packing out dirty diapers, consider your trip length carefully. Seal away soiled diapers in a large slide-lock storage bag, with one designated for each day. At day's end, squeeze out all the excess air and add it to your garbage sack.

11. **Update your first-aid kit.** Make sure you have appropriate contents for your child and your trip, including child-size bandages, infant or child pain reliever/fever reducer, and antihistamine (in case of a bee sting).

12. **Simplify.** The fewer pots and pans and dishes to pack and wash and carry… the more you'll be able to relax and enjoy the journey and time with your child. If you can, splurge on the freeze-dried meals you simply add boiled water to in a sack. Single-serving applesauce and puddings are an easy treat for all ages and need no

refrigeration. Instant oatmeal is an easy breakfast for babies accustomed to thicker textures as well as their parents; add raisins or dried cranberries for extra appeal for those who can chew them.

URBAN ADVENTURES

An overdose of the Teletubbies? Elmo on the brain? Look to the "the big city" for emergency CPR (cranial parental resuscitation). Whether it's a short drive from home or a long flight overseas, an urban adventure can provide the enlivening and enlightening experiences you crave, with plenty of stimulation for your child as well.

But do keep your wits, and wallets, about you. The parent struggling with a stroller on a crowded street, juggling an upset toddler while consulting a guidebook, or taking 236 pictures of his child chasing pigeons may appear to the unscrupulous an easy target for pick pocketing. Carry only the things you'll need with you (cash, I.D., a credit card) in a slim travel wallet you can wear beneath your shirt or trousers so you can focus on keeping track of your child and enjoying your vacation.

Choose a city with great public transportation—subway, light rail, efficient buses—and a centrally located hotel, and you've even got the makings of a car-seat free vacation. Hop on/Hop off bus service is available in most major cities around the world, and is a fantastic option for families with babies and small children in tow. With a simple pass (24 hours or 48 hours), your family can ride this dedicated bus route around to most of the major attractions at your own pace, getting off when and where you please without need of a car seat or climbing up and down subway steps.

If you need to catch some grown up opera or theater while you're in town, ask your hotel if they provide babysitting or babysitter referrals, or visit www.gocitykids.com to find childcare referrals for major cities across the United States. If you'd like to stay a week or more, consider renting an apartment with all the amenities of home (see Condos and Vacation Rentals, page 39).

With infants and babies – Bring a frontpack or sling (or both for variety) for wearing your child on and off public transportation, and consider a good travel stroller with a carrying strap or handle to keep things simple as you climb up and down subway steps or board buses (I prefer a stroller with a shoulder strap so I can keep both of my hands free). Let your baby snooze, reclined in the stroller as you take in a museum, and help fend-off his fussies at evening time with a walk through the city park. If baby has an early bedtime, take advantage of room service a night or two, or order a pizza to enjoy by the romantic glow of the nightlight while she sleeps.

Who says art and infants don't mix?

With toddlers – If you are lucky, your child will still take one good nap each day (some toddlers still take two!). So be sure to bring a comfortable stroller (preferably a travel stroller with a nice recline) so he can nap well while you do other things. In his waking hours, be sure to visit sites that will have some appeal to him, like natural history museums with dinosaur bones and bugs, or aquariums (what toddler isn't thrilled by the sight of life-size dinosaurs or sharks?). But most toddlers unaccustomed to city life will find much to marvel at just being out and about—like pigeons, mimes, street musicians, elevators, and streetcars. Make sure to plan breaks for some freedom and exercise, whether that means a romp in the park or practice climbing the stairs of the hotel.

With preschoolers – Choose a city with many attractions that will excite both you and your child. Consider historic monuments with tours (and even guides in costume), Children's Discovery Museums (like in Denver, New York, and the Bay Area), planetariums, aquariums, and zoos. Also, investigate special opportunities like carriage rides or short cruises and boat rides. And don't overlook ice skating rinks for those ready to give it a try!

CHOOSING YOUR ACCOMMODATIONS

Small Hotels and Inns

Although they are generally more charming and more economical than larger chain hotels, small hotels and inns can present some challenges for the family traveling with a baby or small child. Rooms are generally smaller, prohibiting the use of a portacrib and limiting play space—and where to park the stroller? Walls are often thinner, making rough nights with your child rough nights for everyone on your hall (this is why few Bed & Breakfasts take children under age 12). And childproofing may be much more of a concern, where furnishings are home spun (or otherwise "unique") and heaters or air conditioning units are a hazard to curious children.

On the up side, it's often the smaller hotel or inn where you'll find the best advice for local attractions and restaurants to visit with children. And you're much more likely to get a taste of the "local flavor" when staying somewhere owned and operated by locals, who are often a family as well. Before making a reservation, it is wise to check for traveler reviews of the property (try www.tripadvisor.com) and to contact the innkeeper directly to ensure suitability for your family. Here are some helpful resources for finding smaller hotels and inns online:

- www.tripadvisor.com
- www.venere.com
- www.virtualcities.com

Large Hotels and Resorts

If your child has trouble napping on the go (in the stroller, in the car), you may want to choose a resort that include as much of your entertainment and recreation as possible—especially if you may end up taking turns with your partner while one stays with the child and the other hits the pool or sauna, or gets a much-needed massage. Having a restaurant (or several) on site, though it is rarely a bargain, can also help to keep things simple at the end of long days.

If your child goes to bed much earlier than you and your partner or tends to sleep through your dinner time, it may prove very practical to take some meals in your room. Room service may also come to the rescue if dinner at the diner was not all your child had expected, or if jet lag finds your family awake and hungry at an inconvenient hour.

Many large resorts now offer children's clubs as well, where children (usually 3 years minimum and out of diapers) can be registered for group activities and events to enjoy while Mom and Dad gear up for scuba lessons or trek to the tops of magnificent ruins. Private in-room babysitting is also often available for babies and toddlers on request, usually with minimum 24-hour notice. Check the hotel's Web site and/or call for details if this is a deal-breaker for your trip.

With any luck your hotel room will have a mini-refrigerator that, in spite of being fully stocked with overpriced treats and refreshments, will have enough space left for your leftovers or snacks and, perhaps, a bottle or a sippy-cup. But there are some stages when travel with a child is much easier if you can just have a kitchen of your own (see next section).

Although the specific amenities will vary by hotel property, here are a few of the major hotel and resort chains where you will likely find family-friendly perks and conveniences.

Disneyland Resort Hotels, California

All three hotels provide free cribs and in-room refrigerators, plus themed swimming pools and restaurants, and children's play areas. Children 5 years to 12 years can attend Pinocchio's Workshop with special activities offered evenings from 5 p.m. to midnight at Disney's Grand Californian

Hotel at a rate of $13/hour per child, optional dinner included for $5. In-room babysitting is available for an additional fee (with signed waiver). http://disneyland.disney.go.com 1-714-520-5060.

Hilton Worldwide Resorts, International

Forty-nine of their international resorts are labeled as "family resorts," providing on-site nurseries, babysitting, cribs, children's activities, playgrounds, kiddie pools, children's menus, connecting rooms, and more. See the list of resorts recommended for families at www.hiltonworldresorts.com/type/f.html or call 1-800 -HILTONS.

Holiday Inn SunSpree Resorts, International

Children 12 years and younger stay and eat free in the hotel restaurants (with paid adult). Select Sunspree Resorts have supervised (drop-off) activities for ages 4 years and up. Many resorts have kiddie pools, play areas, and other special perks for children. www.sunspree.com or 1-888-465-4329.

Holiday Inn Full-Service Hotels & Resorts, International

All full-service hotels and resorts feature a swimming pool and full-service restaurant on site where children 12 years and younger eat free from the children's menu (with paid adult). www.holidayinn.com or 1-888-465-4329.

Hyatt Resorts, International

Numerous resorts worldwide feature kiddie pools and restaurants with children's menus. Camp Hyatt is available for an additional fee at many resorts worldwide, with supervised activities for potty trained children from 3 years to 12 years. Partial day, full-day, and some evening sessions may be available, depending on the destination. www.hyatt.com or 1-800-233-1234.

Hotel Suites with Kitchenettes

Booking a room with a kitchenette could save you money and possibly your sanity. But think twice if your child is at a stage where an un-childproofed kitchen may be more of a nuisance than a convenience. As well, ask yourself: How much of your vacation time do you really want to spend in the kitchen? And how much will you spend on groceries? And how much might you end up eating out anyway?

Yet there are times the advantages will far outweigh the luxury of eating out. For example, would it make a tremendous difference to have access to a carton of milk and other essentials all hours of the day or night? Would formula preparation and bottle washing be more manageable with a kitchen of your own? Does eating in restaurants with your child at this stage wear you out—or over stimulate your child? Would the savings from not having to eat every meal in a restaurant more than make up for the cost of lodgings that include a kitchen? Is your child a picky eater, or will you be staying somewhere that food safety is a concern?

One-bedroom suites also give the advantage of a separation of space, which can also make a tremendous difference for families when a child needs naps or goes to bed much earlier than the parents would like to. Often, parents enjoying a one-bedroom suite will put the child to bed in the bedroom, then enjoy the rest of the suite for themselves. When ready to retire, they can tiptoe into the bedroom.

Here are some hotels where you can expect to find suites with kitchenettes or kitchens, and some other family-friendly amenities.

AmeriSuites All-suite hotels found in 32 of the United States, with microwaves and refrigerators in every room. Complimentary hot buffet breakfast daily. Children up to 17 always stay free. Cribs are provided on request, sleeper sofas in every suite. www.amerisuites.com or 1-800-833-1516.

Crossland Economy Studios Hotel rooms with fully equipped kitchens. Self-service laundry facilities on site. Children under 17 stay free. www.crosslandstudios.com or 1-800-805-3724.

Extended Stay America Suites include fully equipped kitchens ("economy studio suites" have a mini refrigerator, 1-bedroom suites have a full-size refrigerator). Children under 17 years stay free.
www.extendedstayhotels.com or 1-800-805-3724.

Georgetown Suites Studio and 1-bedroom suites in Washington, D.C., have fully equipped kitchens (including full-size refrigerators, oven/range, and dishwashers). Children under 12 years stay free. Self-service laundry, free crib on request. Complimentary continental breakfast bar daily.
www.georgetownsuites.com or 1-800-348-7203.

Hawthorn Suites Spacious studio, 1-bedroom, and 2-bedroom suites available. Convenience store and swimming pool on site. Children up to 17 stay free. Complimentary hot buffet breakfast daily. www.hawthorn.com or 1-800-833-1516.

All-Inclusive Family Resorts

All-inclusive resorts can also help keep things simple—you never have to wonder where you'll eat or how much it will cost you. If you're vacationing with a toddler or preschooler, be sure the resort offers children's menus and/or buffet items of interest. Some all-inclusive resorts offer dining in restaurants that—by the way—won't serve children under a certain age; good to know before you sentence yourselves to a week of dining at the resort snack bar.

Check the fine print of what is actually included at any all-inclusive you consider, as the perks for families with small children can vary widely. Some will let children under a certain age stay free with two paid adults, whereas others will charge the same rate for any additional people in the room, regardless of age. And where some all-inclusive resorts offer free children's programs and childcare—even private nannies (see following recommendations), others will charge for any and all children's activities, and may not offer any type of care for children in diapers. Another cost savings for families can be inclusive air transfers, where everyone's ride to and from the airport is covered in the price (most shuttle services charge per person, regardless of age).

Keep in mind, however, that an all-inclusive resort may not be the best value for your family if you plan to use it only as a base for sightseeing, or if your child is a very light (or picky) eater that may as well share from your plate at meal times. And if you don't want to gorge yourself on unlimited foods all week or plan to drink your weight in rum or tequila, it may be more cost-effective to stay at a regular hotel or resort, or get a vacation rental instead. These all-inclusive resorts provide a good value for most families with small children.

Beaches All-inclusive Family Resorts, Jamaica and Turks & Caicos

Includes daily childcare by professionally certified nannies in the price of your vacation. Newborns through toddlers of 23 months are cared for in the nursery, and 2- to 5-year-old children attend the daily Kids Kamp. Nannies are available for additional childcare after hours at around $10/hour (varies by resort). www.beaches.com or 1-888-BEACHES.

FDR Pebbles Resort and Franklyn D. Resort, Jamaica

Includes a personal "Vacation Nanny" assigned exclusively to your family who will help look after your children each day from 9:00 a.m. to 4:40 p.m. She is also available after hours if needed at around $4 / hour. The guest to staff ratio is 1 to 1, and children under 2 years may also attend the daily children's activities with their vacation nannies. Children under 6 years old stay free. www.fdrholidays.com or 1-800-654-1FDR.

Club Med Resorts, destinations worldwide

Includes group childcare and activities for children 4 years and older. For an additional fee, certain Club Med resorts also offer care for children ages 2 years to 3 years, and a handful of the resorts also offer care for children 4 months and older. www.clubmed.com or 1-888-932-2582.

Condos and Other Vacation Rentals

For many parents, a vacation rental is the ideal home away from home. Many not only include a helpful separation of space in the form of bedrooms and common areas, but they also include kitchens and often other homey amenities. For weekly rates that are usually comparable to that of nearby hotels, you may have access to laundry, a yard, a kitchen, and parking (where hotels may charge extra), depending on the property.

If your child is very mobile, beware of properties that may pose more risks than the average hotel room: including stairs, decks, porches, kitchens, additional bathrooms, or easily accessible swimming pools and/or Jacuzzis.

If a week is longer than you'd like to stay, some vacation properties offer "short breaks" (a.k.a. long weekends), especially in the low seasons. Here are some sites to get you started in your search for the ideal vacation rental.

Euro Relais – Properties throughout Europe. www.eurorelais.com

Internet Holiday Ads – Worldwide vacation rentals. www.iha.com

Rentalo.com – Properties worldwide. www.rentalo.com

Trip Homes – Properties worldwide.www.triphomes.com

Vacation Rentals by Owner – Properties worldwide. www.vrbo.com

Bed & Breakfasts

So few bed and breakfasts will accept children, particularly those under 5 years old, that it is scarcely worth mentioning here. However, if you are looking for a more intimate-sized retreat in a unique setting, you may want to visit Virtual Cities' 1st Travelers Choice Travel & Lodging Directory, where you can browse a range of child-friendly bed and breakfasts, country inns, hotels and vacation rentals at destinations throughout the United States, Canada, and Mexico. Most listings include a minimum age for children, so you can search for something appropriate. Find them at www.virtualcities.com, and follow the links to "Children Welcome."

STAYING (SAFE AND SANE) WITH FRIENDS AND FAMILY

Staying in the home of friends or relatives is by far the most common trip new parents make with their child, and for many, it's likely to be a repeat occurrence through the baby, toddler, and preschool years. Yes, having access to all the comforts of home, including a full kitchen, laundry facilities, separate quarters for your napping child, and of course, the loving presence (a.k.a. help) of your friends or family, can be a wonderful, relaxing way to vacation with your child. It *can* be, in many cases, with some good planning.

First, you will need to get grounded in reality. As a guest in someone else's home, you will be obliged to observe their daily rhythms and routines. Enthusiastic pets, light-saber-wielding children, steep staircases, toxic houseplants, precariously perched lamps, Hummel collections, and more may await your little family at the home away from home. Just establishing a safe place for your child to sleep or play during your visit could prove challenging. Add to that the possibility of delayed bed times, extended meal times, and noisy visiting hours and you may find yourself wishing for a night off at the local motel.

As well, take your hosts' lifestyles into consideration—in spite of their best intentions, would having a baby or small child under their roof full time prove a major inconvenience to them? Try to get your hosts on the same page before you arrive in their home. Describe a typical day with your child at home, when he usually rises, naps, how often he eats, and what his sacred rituals are. Tell them how much you are looking forward to seeing them, but be honest about your concerns—including upsetting their own routines (like, perhaps, sleeping). Share your ideas of how you can help with childproofing concerns and other details about having a baby or small child in their home. Especially where friends and family are concerned, it could be well worth spending a little more to stay nearby and come for visits if it means safeguarding the integrity of your relationship.

That said, here are some friendly suggestions for how to avoid some common pitfalls and have a safe, sane visit with those who are near and dear to your heart.

Dining

Your hosts may not be as prepared as they think they are for dealing with the thrills and spills associated with baby and toddler dining. If your child is using a portable dining booster, ask your hosts for an extra bath towel you might use to protect their chair from any overboard spills or splats. Pack a vinyl tablecloth (like those used outdoors) to spread beneath your child's seat to protect your host's floor during meal times. Afterward, you can simply shake off the crumbs and wipe the surface clean. Also, bring along your child's own plate or bowl to save your host from searching for suitable dishes or risking breakage of their own.

Diapering

As Benjamin Franklin said, "Guests, like fish, begin to smell after three days." Guests in diapers, however, may smell upon arrival. Be sure to check with your hosts early on to see where they keep their outdoor trash so that you may use it when needed. Bring your own supply of plastic bags and export any stink bombs straight away. Also, be thoughtful on disposing wet diapers; some people bristle at the sight of perfectly harmless puffy Pampers in their bathroom wastebasket. It may be simplest to bring your own sack or trash bag for collecting these in your quarters rather than filling up your hosts' wastebaskets.

Sleeping

I'll say it until I'm blue in the face: Earplugs can make a thoughtful and a humorous hostess gift. If your child isn't likely to make it through the night without a vocal interlude, give your hosts fair warning. They can take any precautions to help ensure a restful night for themselves (using aforementioned ear plugs, closing their doors, indulging in a nightcap, and so on). This will also help prevent them from worrying if your child is feeling well or if you need their assistance or intervention—Uncle Larry's get-happy clown dance could prove disastrous at three a.m.

Household Hazards for Young Children

Anywhere you stay (a hotel, a campsite, a sleeper car) you will have to size up potential dangers to your child and deal with them the best you can. But when you stay in someone else's home, the number of potential dangers may actually increase. In addition to the more easily anticipated risks like stair steps, sharp corners, and electrical outlets, you may also face a few surprises that come with staying in an active household of friendly folks who may not be accustomed to playing "What's Under Grandpa's Easy Chair?" or, with toddlers, "Look What I Found in the Kitchen Trash!" Just make sure you don't overlook these potential hazards while in the throes of visiting.

- Pet foods, snacks, and grooming supplies
- Excitable or aggressive pets
- Prescription drugs and other medications, including those not kept in childproof canisters like ointments or drops
- Craft projects and knitting baskets
- Candy dishes and nut bowls
- Decorative fountains
- Holiday ornaments and decorations
- Floor lamps and cords
- Table lamps within reach
- Unsuitable toys from older children
- Party favors or decorations (including latex balloons, which can be a choking hazard)
- The "junk drawer"

Child Hazards to the Household

Also, don't overlook the hazards your child might pose to your host's home. Other adults may not be as tuned in to the potential consequences of leaving some items within a child's reach, or the lightning speed with which a child can perform magic tricks with table cloths (swoosh!) and car keys (flush!). Especially if you'll be visiting with a curious toddler, you will need to stay two steps ahead of your child where these items may be accessed.

- Purses with pens and lipstick inside
- Books and magazines
- Cell phones or regular phones

- Stereos and entertainment equipment
- Remote controls
- Car keys (especially with remote control key fobs)
- Cameras
- Computers and PDAs
- Toilet paper
- Music CDs and DVDs
- Musical instruments
- Table cloths

- Chapter 3 -
Deciding What to Bring

Your Child's Travel Kit

Your child's travel kit is more than what simply goes into the diaper bag or carry-on. These are basic products and items that can help your child through a wide range of difficulties that might crop up in your travels, but could be hard to come by while en route, on a day trip, late at night, or in faraway destinations.

You may want to keep these items in a clear plastic slide-lock food storage bag that will contain any leaks and make it easy to find items inside. And keep in mind that those cute little travel-size tins you may see with certain ointments for babies are not necessarily great for traveling—they can be virtually impossible to open at sea level once they've been used in an airplane or at very high elevations due to the change in air pressure.

- **Saline nasal spray** (non-medicated) – For infants, just a drop or two in each nostril can help clear passages, soothe dryness (especially from flying), or loosen debris for removal with the aspirator.
- **Aspirator with guard** – The guard not only helps parents use these with confidence but it can be a bit safer when in motion on airplanes, in trains—and while tending to an animated child.

- **Emery board or nail clippers**
- **Thermometer** – A digital thermometer can be used at your child's armpit and can be used for Mom and Dad, too, if needed.
- **Quicklist of current dosages** – A quick reference list of your child's current correct dosage for any over-the-counter remedies you may need to use during your trip, some of which follow here. Your doctor's office can provide this info at your appointment or possibly over the phone.
- **Acetaminophen drops** (e.g. Infant's or Children's Tylenol) – Helpful for teething and reducing fevers when they strike. Confirm current dosage with your child's doctor.
- **Antihistamine drops** (e.g. Children's Benadryl) – Helpful for spring allergy-type symptoms as well as some allergic reactions like bee stings. Confirm indications for use and correct dosage for your child with his doctor.
- **Tummy drops** (e.g. Mylicon) – To soothe upset tummies and relieve gas.
- **Measuring dropper/medicine spoon** – You may prefer to use one purchased independently of the medicine that is easier to use and wash.
- **Baby vapor rub** (e.g. Vick's Baby Rub) – This kinder, gentler version of the vapor ointments for adults can be rubbed on your child's chest and neck to help her breathe easier during bouts of congestion. If there is a safe place to leave the open jar near your child's bedside (but where he cannot access it) it can also work as a makeshift vaporizer at night.
- **Antibiotic ointment** (e.g. Neosporin) – Treat scrapes, scratches, nicks, and cuts right away—and that goes for all the travelers in the family. Cover scrapes with a bandage to keep clean and protected, and to help prevent babies from ingesting the ointment.
- **Band-Aids** – Bring a variety of sizes. You needn't pack too many if you can purchase more if needed at your destination.
- **Tea tree oil or other antiseptic** – Cleans scrapes and wounds.
- **Protective skin cream or balm** – A mild, soothing cream for chapped cheeks and tender bottoms (particularly those due to sandy swim diapers). Burt's Baby Bee or similar product works well.

CLOTHING CONSIDERATIONS

When you travel with a baby or small child, there is no right number of onesies, socks, or this-and-that's for X number of days' vacation. Your travel trousseau will be as individual as your child, her age, and the trip. As you contemplate the variables for your upcoming adventure, it may be more helpful to meditate on these certain truths about types of children's clothing—and a few items of parents' apparel—as applied to travel.

Playsuits – Footed playsuits offer some definite advantages: no socks or booties will be lost along the way, ankles and lower legs will not be exposed to sun or cold as they might be with pant legs that can ride up, there is no elastic to bind at the waist or trap heat, and they always match themselves. Those with numerous snaps to align and close can be a drag, however, especially when racing to board an airplane on time or get back to your seat before a bout of turbulence. For greater ease and speed of changing, look for those made with a zipper instead; you may be able to find some in cost-effective 3-packs by Gerber or Circo.

Two-piece outfits – Top or bottom? With babies and small children, you never know which will be the first to soil. One-piece outfits and playsuits require a total change either way, but a shirt is easy to replace in transit, as are pants when you're already changing a diaper. By only replacing one half at a time, you may also reduce your laundry load. There may even be times you elect to simply remove the shirt before feeding.

Overalls – For older babies and young toddlers, overalls provide one fantastic advantage over other two-piece outfits: the straps provide the perfect place to link a toy.

Shirts – It's hard to go wrong with a lightweight cotton, long-sleeve T-shirt. It's a great basic layer in changeable weather, adds warmth in cold climes, and provides lightweight, breathable sun protection in hot weather. Just remember that, unless your shirt specifies a level of SPF protection (as some do), it will not provide total sun protection in extreme situations.

Hats – A good hat protects its wearer from sun, rain, or cold weather, but a better hat does so while providing a strap to help keep it in place. While Mom and Dad need hands free to carry children, hold smaller hands, or push strollers, a gust could make off with either of their hats. And at some stages, children will simply try and remove their own hats themselves, unless they have that indispensable chin strap.

Shoes - Parents will want especially supportive, comfortable shoes for traveling if they'll be spending any amount of time carrying a child — especially if you'll be using a sling, frontpack carrier, or backpack carrier during sightseeing. Shoes for toddlers and older children should provide adequate protection from gravel, rocks, and pinecones if they'll be exploring that sort of territory.

Zipped jackets and sweaters – Parents who will be wearing children in frontpack carriers will want to avoid wearing jackets and sweaters with zippers that could scrape or irritate the child.

Hooded sweaters and jackets – These offer the built-in advantage of having no extra hat to keep (or lose) track of.

GREAT PRODUCTS AND GEAR FOR TRAVEL

Having the right products and gear for trips with your child can make all the difference between a relaxing, comfortable trip and, frankly, a logistical nightmare. If you err on the side of over-packing, you may be bogged down with too much gear and too many suitcases to fit in your taxi or rental car, or to make it through the airport without enlisting an army of skycaps. Pare down too much and you may suffer through every meal of your vacation with your child in your arms, or end up financing your chiropractor's next sailboat from having left your stroller behind.

Following are some of the best products and gear available to help streamline trips with babies and small children, from truly portable travel beds and safe alternatives to car seats, to mini waterless vaporizers and portable safety gates. Thanks to their lightweight properties, and space- and sanity-saving conveniences, many of these items may also be preferred for use at home. (You can also get a look at these at TravelswithBaby.com.)

Car Seats, Accessories, and Alternatives

Infant carrier car seat – Car seats for infants and babies that can snap in and out of a base in the car and can be carried by a handle. Many are designed to be used without the base during travel. Virtually all include a shade canopy and can also be used with a stroller as a "travel system," or with a Snap N' Go or universal-type stroller frame. Available from Graco, Peg Perego, and all the major car seat brands. Check for more travel-friendly and longer lasting models from Combi, Britax, and Compass.

Sit'n'Stroll – A car seat that converts to a stroller and buckles easily into airplane seats, taxis, and other vehicles (the seat belt goes around it, instead of under it). Rear-and forward-facing, from birth up to 40 lbs. The Sit'n'Stroll now comes standard with a (once optional) sun/rain canopy, which can also be quite helpful for keeping sun off your child in the car. The Sit'n'Stroll is especially well suited to cruise vacations, where space is at a premium, but a lightweight stroller, car seat, and dining booster (and just a safe seat for your child in the cabin) may all be quite helpful.

Tote 'N Go DX Safety Vest – This "wearable car seat" is an alternative to forward-facing toddler car seats, for children 25 lbs to 40 lbs. It weighs less than 4 lbs. and folds up to fit under your stroller or in your suitcase. Put it on your child at the hotel room, and he's ready to jump in the taxi at the curb—just buckle your seat belts and go. It is not recommended as a complete replacement for car seats or suitable for everyday use (no side impact protection), but it can be a great option for traveling and is certainly preferable to using no car seat at all. Not approved for use in aircraft.

Ride Safer Vest – The "wearable booster seat" that meets or exceeds all standards of the FMVSS 213 (Federal Motor Vehicle Safety Standard). Available in two sizes: Small, from 35 lbs to 60 lbs, or large, 50 lbs. to 80 lbs. It weighs less than 5 lbs and can be used with shoulder or lap-only belts (with upper tether). Unlike regular booster seats, this provides the protection of a 5-point safety harness. Like booster seats: it's not approved for use in aircraft.

Baby B'Air lap child safety vest – A flight safety vest for lap-held babies and toddlers that attaches to a parent's seat belt to help protect against turbulence. FAA-approved for use in flight, but not for use taxiing and take-off. Available in two sizes. (See photo on page 220.)

CARES safety device – The new FAA-approved flight harness for children over 1 year old and weighing 22 to 44 lbs. It attaches to both the airplane seat back and lap belt to help secure children in the adult-sized seat. Although it's convenient for flying, it is not approved for use in automobiles.

Backpack carrier for car seats – Attaches to your car seat for easy hands-free carrying of your car seat. Great for parents flying with seated toddlers and preschoolers. The Pac Back is widely available, which provides padded straps with extra support from hip and chest belts. Some other models include a cover for the entire car seat, like the J.L. Childress Ultimate Car Seat Carrier.

GoGo Kidz Universal TravelMate – Adds wheels and a height-adjustable handle to your car seat, making it possible to wheel your child clear to the gate and even down the aisle of larger aircraft in most major brand car seats (airplanes larger than a 737). You can leave it attached to your car seat while flying, but it must be removed before installing your car seat in an automobile.

Car seat shade canopy – If you've enjoyed the shade canopy on your infant carrier car seat, you know how nice it is to be able to adjust it and keep the sun off your child and out of her eyes. Happily, Combi makes a universal car seat canopy that attaches to most infant AND toddler car seats (those with side supports) and can be used rear- or forward-facing. The Sit'n'Stroll also has a sun canopy (now standard) that can be used in the car as well as when it's in stroller mode. Both canopies are adjustable and retract when not in use.

Strollers and Accessories

Snap n'Go or Universal infant carrier stroller frame – Far lighter than the strollers included in most so-called travel systems, these stroller frames work with your infant car seat to give you the benefits of a stroller with the convenience of keeping your child in her carrier. Models are available from Graco, Kolcraft, Combi, and Maclaren. Combi's offers the extra convenience of a shoulder carrying strap.

Umbrella strollers – Lightweight, inexpensive, and often the first consideration for travel, these bare-bones strollers fold compactly just as their name suggests. Since they offer little to no recline, they are usually not suitable for children younger than 6 months old, and even older babies and toddlers will often slump forward in these when napping. If you'll need your child to do much napping on the go, or if you plan to check your stroller or use it on challenging terrain (uneven sidewalks, curbs, cobblestones), you may prefer a travel stroller.

Travel strollers - Travel strollers are also designed to be lightweight and fold compactly, while better handling the needs of travelers and rigors of traveling. Seats may recline part-way for children 3 months and older, or recline completely for use with newborns or help with diaper changes. Other helpful extras may include a bumper bar (great for attaching toys or a travel tray), sun canopy with storage pockets, storage basket, or a carrying handle or strap. A few models are also compatible with infant car seats.

Good economical options can be found from One Step Ahead and Chicco. Other popular models are available from Combi, Maclaren, Zooper, Silver Cross, and Britax.

The Arc de Triomphe has 284 steps and zero parking for strollers. The Combi travel stroller has a shoulder strap and weighs a mere 11 lbs.

Stroller shade nets – They go over your stroller just like rain shields but offer UV protection and shade instead. Look for one with a UV-protective mesh for the best ventilation combined with UV protection, and one that also offers a snug fit for insect protection for the best value.

Stroller canopy shade extensions – Strap on to your stroller for wider coverage than what's provided by your stroller's canopy alone.

Stroller UPF parasol – These clip right on to your stroller side bar to provide additional sun protection from the front or sides, changing as needed. It can be very helpful with travel and umbrella strollers that have small canopies and leave little legs exposed. Bugaboo makes one that fits its models of strollers, and Eckert of Germany offers a universal stroller parasol with UPF 50 that is made to work with both strollers and joggers.

RayShade – An alternative to the parasol, the RayShade fits over your stroller's canopy to create a much larger shade canopy that extends further out above your child and offers some side protection as well. It blocks 99% of harmful UVA and UVB rays. Available for single and side-by-side twin strollers, both with small storage pockets (including one for a cup). Folds to 10" x 10" and fits in its own storage pouch.

Child Carriers, Wraps, and Slings

Slings and wraps – Most slings and wraps allow you to wear your child in multiple positions, and can be used from infancy into toddlerhood. Simple, across-the-body fabric slings like the New Native and Maya Wrap slip easily over the head with one hand, ensuring easy passage through airport security scanners (tips on clearing airport security begin on page 212). Others, like the PreMaxx Adventure or New Addition slings also include handy zipped storage pockets. The Moby Wrap is perhaps the most versatile of the wraps, allowing you to wear your child in a snug sling position (even twins, if you've got'em), and also forward-facing, outward-facing, or even on your back, plus it uses wide bands of fabric crossing both shoulders and your back to help distribute the weight—though it is no so easily removed for security screenings (see photo, page 54). All of these may also help mothers nurse discreetly on the go.

Frontpack carriers (frontpacks)- Most of these can be used with infants from their earliest weeks, provided they meet the minimum weight and length limits outlined by the manufacturer (Baby Björn specifies 8 lbs and 21" minimum), and are used following the instructions and using any extra inserts or leg straps for infants. With multi-position models, children may face inward with head and neck support until they are ready to face forward. Many brands are available now, with some models providing better back support for the parent, or enhanced ventilation for the child. Chicco makes a model with a sun/rain hood, and Body Glove even makes one of neoprene that can be worn in water. Keep in mind that these must be removed and run through the scanner at airport security, and heavier/quilted fabrics and dark colors can be very warm for children if you'll be visiting hot destinations. Average max weight for child is 25 lbs.

Framed backpack carriers - Most are created for children at least 6 months of age, who can sit up comfortably unassisted. A framed backpack carrier, like most Kelty or Sherpani models, can provide much-needed support for hours of carrying your child upon your back. Framed models range in quality and features from those designed for afternoon outings to week-long treks in the wild. Accordingly, many include optional add-ons like sun/rain hoods, comfort stirrups, storage bags, and removable daypacks. The Kelty Convertible actually comes with wheels and can switch between backpack and stroller mode, especially helpful in airports and anywhere you may find escalators or stairs. Average maximum load for these packs (child + toys + snacks + water + diapers, etc.) is 40 lbs., though the Sherpani Rumba Superlight goes up to 55 lbs., and the Rumba is rated up to 70 lbs. (though few parents may be).

Soft backpack carriers – If you won't be spending long, uninterrupted hours with your child on your back, you may be able to get by with a soft backpack carrier instead of a bulkier framed model. Soft backpacks usually have waist and chest straps to help bear the load, but take up no more space than a daypack. The Ergo may be the most space-saving, and can be worn as a frontpack, hip, or backpack carrier, converting as needed even while you wear it. Some others, like Deuter's KangaKid and Kelty's Transit models, offer the 2-in-1 convenience of a carrier and a daypack (or diaper bag), and are designed to conceal the "child cockpit" when not in use and look like a regular daypack. Most models are intended for or use with children up to 30 lbs. Although it has an internal aluminum frame (concealed) and is therefore not technically a soft backpack carrier, Kelty's TC 2.5 has an upper weight limit of 40 lbs and provides the same look and convenience of the other Transit series carriers.

Hip carrier – When sightseeing in a group by bus with a toddler, you may appreciate the simplicity of a hip carrier you can easily slip your child in and out of as you get on and off the bus. Some fabric slings may be used for hip carrying, or others, like the Combi Urban, are designed specifically for this use and fold into very small pouches when not in use, ideal for children who insist on walking—for a while, or in situations where you will only occasionally need to carry your child.

The Moby Wrap is made of cotton jersey (the fabric used for T-shirts), which makes it ideal for both parent and child when traveling in hot, humid climates.

Travel Beds and Sleeping Solutions

Play yards / playpens – Sometimes called a play yard, play pen, Pack 'n Play, or even a portacrib, these not only make a safe play space for your baby or toddler when visiting un-childproofed settings, but they can serve as a bed as well. Some come with attachable changing stations, bassinets, shade canopies, mosquito nets and other accessories as well that may also be helpful, depending on your destination. While you can fold them for travel and even check them on airplanes, many parents find them too cumbersome and heavy for travel except by automobile. Compass offers one of the most travel-friendly play yards, weighing in at only 17 lbs and folding more compactly than most others. For an even lighter weight alternative (6 lbs.), see the T2 Travel Cot in travel beds.

Infant and toddler travel "trundles" – Another option for sleeping, though not so much for playing or childproofing (once your child can climb out). They are very lightweight and fold to nearly flat. Some will fit inside a large suitcase or may be worn over the shoulder with a carrying strap. Available brands include Small Fry, Eddie Bauer, and Graco.

Co-sleepers / infant bumper beds - Compactly folding co-sleepers or "bumper" beds like the Snuggle Nest or Wee Sleep, can be used for infants sleeping between Mom and Dad in a shared bed. These are a fantastic option when staying in tight quarters like cruise ship cabins and big city hotels.

Travel beds – The Peapod works like a small pop-up tent, converting from a 14" disc in its travel bag to a 48" L and 18"H sleeping tent, with UV protective mesh sides and air-cushion mattress (see photo, page 27). It works well for babies and even preschoolers, though babies first learning to stand and walk may be frustrated by the low ceiling. The Peapod Plus opens to 52.5"L and 25"H, accommodating children up to 6 years. Most similar to a play yard is Phil & Ted's T2 Travel Cot, which opens to 47"L x 20"W x 25"H with a UV-protective top that may be left open or zipped closed. It has a self-inflating mattress, UV-protective mesh sides, and weighs only 6 lbs.

Portable bed guardrails – Indispensable when traveling with toddlers and preschoolers where grown-up beds are a given, such as hotel rooms and the homes of family and friends. Some brands include SleepTite and Regalo, though the BedBugz inflatable bed bolster packs the lightest and smallest of them all, and can be used with twin or full-size mattresses.

Products for Eating and Feeding

Travel trays - Various folding and flat trays are designed to be attached to strollers (with bumper bars), car seats, and the standard-issue trayless square high chairs you'll find in many restaurants. Created with a raised lip around the edges to keep snacks and crayons from rolling away, these trays are great aids in dining on the go, and helping to keep kids entertained during flights and even long car rides. Twingles Fold-and-Go Tray is the most compact and works with many strollers and restaurant high chairs. The flat Taby Tray is larger and works with most car seats as well as strollers. The Go Anywhere Table and Footrest is made specifically for use with car seats and boosters, with an adjustable foot rest and tilting tray with built-in cup holder. Both the Taby and Go Anywhere trays meet safety requirements for use in moving automobiles.

Portable dining boosters – Available in a wide variety of styles, including ones that can be strapped and secured to virtually any adult chair and offer 3-point safety harnesses to keep escape artists in their place. Most folding travel boosters work for babies as soon as they can sit up (around 6 months), and grow with them through toddlerhood. Those featuring snap-on trays will help keep little hands from raiding the table, and the trays can be removed once your child is ready to pass the peas (Safety 1st and Edushape offer compactly folding boosters with trays). Or starting around twelve months your child can ride high in a chair that packs down to 2" thick and inflates to offer a 4" boost, complete with soft backrest and safety straps (by The First Years, does not include a tray).

Hook-on booster chairs (ones that clamp to the table) - Make sure to get one that will accommodate the many different table thicknesses and "skirts" you will likely encounter in your travels. These have the advantage of packing down very small for your daypack or diaper bag, but consider that your baby will have easier access to the table and you may not be able to use it for as long as some other dining boosters. One Step Ahead and Me Too! both offer hook-on chairs that fit thicker tables and accommodate children up to 37 lbs and 40 lbs respectively, and work well for toddlers. However, one restaurant I visited had banned use of this type of child seat since a customer had cracked a glass tabletop when tightening his child's chair, and it should be noted that the instructions do advise against use with glass tabletops or tablecloths. Nevertheless, if space is tight at home, this seat may also be a wonderful solution to bulkier high chairs and you needn't sacrifice an extra chair (or the space one would take up) for a booster seat.

The Crumb Chum - The to-the-ankles, wipe-clean bib that will guard your child's clothing and most of the stroller from dribbles, splats, and spills (it also has a built-in pocket to catch crumbs and run-off).

Insulated and freezable cups – It's often a good idea to add some ice cubes to your child's sippy cup before heading out with a beverage, but an insulated sippy cup will help keep his drink even fresher even longer (some commonly available by Playtex). Munchkin even makes a cup that freezes to help keep drinks cool, though you will need access to a freezer during your travels to get the full benefit.

Fleece blanket - If your child tends to conduct himself at lunch as some would the symphony, consider using a light fleece blanket to line the stroller back and headrest when high chairs or boosters aren't available. The mess will cling to the fleece, which will easily wash in the sink and dry in a few hours. Also handy for diaper changes.

The Drink Deputy – Bottles and most sippy cups (without handles) can be kept within reach and off the floor with help from this inventive strapping device that attaches to car seats, strollers, and high chairs.

The Snack Trap – It keeps little fingers busy and mouths munching while keeping crackers and Cheerios from spilling across the floor. This two-handled cup with cleverly split lid is ideal for the diaper bag or daypack. Load it with Cheerios and dried cranberries to help distract your toddler as you wait in boring lines.

The Neat Sheet - A very lightweight blanket with an almost-papery texture that provides queen-size waterproof coverage for picnics on a boggy lawn or balmy beach. It also works as a tablecloth over grungy picnic tables or impromptu changing mat. Available spring and summer at most drug stores and Target stores, or try www.amazon.com.

Car adapter bottle/food warmer – Various models use your vehicle's cigarette lighter to power warmers for bottles or both food and bottles. Models by Dex, Munchkin, and The First Years, are most popular, but many parents complain these warmers take too long to heat to be practical, so advanced planning will be helpful on your part. Overheating can also result in melted bottles, so follow the instructions carefully. Sunshine Kids now offers the Warm 'n' Go bottle warmer with a stretch neoprene cover that can hang from your dash and a thermal fuse to prevent overheating. (They also claim it heats bottles 50% faster than their competitors' models.)

Flannel-backed vinyl – It's soft on both sides, waterproof in the middle, and goes through the washing machine; no wonder it's been a favorite of diaper-changing parents for years and years. Buy two yards from your local fabric store in plain white or decorated with duckies, and keep a generous yard in the car or pack in your checked suitcase for use in your hotel room or ship cabin. Cut the second yard in two halves for your diaper bag for use in airplanes or trains (if one half gets soiled, you have a backup).

Travel swings – If your baby is soothed by nothing so much as the swing, you might find the travel variety indispensable for your trip. These take up little more space than a bouncer seat and can serve both purposes, while offering multiple speed settings and recline options like your larger model at home (or use this there too). Popular models are made by Simplicity, Manhattan, and Graco.

BABY GEAR RENTALS

Strollers, swings, bouncy seats, bassinets, high chairs, full-size cribs, and play pens can all help you have a much more comfortable, and even a safer stay wherever you are bound. But of course you can only lug so much to—

and through—the airport, not to mention the miserable gas mileage you will get while crossing the country with an exersaucer strapped to the roof of your car.

If you would like to have a baby backpack carrier for hiking in Hawaii, for example, or a heavy duty buggy for touring the Old Country, it can be well worth the rental fee to avoid checking yours, risking damage, or juggling one extra item in transit. Throughout the U.S. and in many other countries, it's now possible to rent everything from exersaucers, safety gates, beach toys, and rocking chairs to baby swings and slings—even breast pumps and steam sterilizers.

Typically, these rental companies will deliver your desired equipment and gear to your accommodations, and will even set up the items for you. On your day of departure, they may need to pick up your equipment by a specific time in the morning, so be sure to check for details and arrange the appropriate time.

U.S.A.

Alaska / Anchorage and Eagle River area – Tiny Tourist
www.tinytouristalaska.com or 1-907-696-2821

Arizona / Phoenix and Scottsdale area – Anything for Baby, Inc.
www.anythingforbaby.com or 1-877-515-9783

California / Lake Tahoe – Baby's Away
www.babysaway.com or 1-800-446-9030

California / Los Angeles and Santa Monica – The Traveling Baby Co.
www.thetravelingbabyco.com or 1-800-304-4866

California / Orange County (Disneyland!) - Travel Needs for Kids
www.travelneedsforkids.com or 1-877-722-7066

California / San Francisco – Little Luggage
www.littleluggage.com or 1-877-fly-baby

California / San Francisco – Rockabye Baby
www.rockabyebabyrentals.com or 1-866-475-6825

California / San Diego – San Diego Travel Baby
www.sandiegotravelbaby.com or 1-877-738-7382

California / Santa Barbara – Santa Barbara Baby Company
www.sbbabyco.com or 1-877-240-1360

Colorado / Colorado Springs – Travelin' Tikes
www.travelin-tikes.com or 1-866-495-9789

Colorado / Denver Area and Boulder – Baby Stay
www.babystay.com or 1-877-635-9885

Colorado / Telluride and Ouray – Traveling Lite
www.travelinglite.biz or 1-888-662-8687

Florida / Orlando and Disneyworld – A Baby's Best Friend
www.abbf.com or info@abbf.com

Florida / Tampa Bay – Visiting Baby, Inc.
www.visitingbaby.com or 1-727-784-3333

Georgia / Atlanta – Baby's Away
www.babysaway.com or 1-800-282-8315

Hawaii / Big Island - Aloha Baby Rental
www.alohababyrental.net or 1-808-326-1700

Hawaii / Big Island – Dorkel's Snorkel & Baby Rental
www.dorkelsrental.com or 1-808-883-3675

Hawaii / Kauai – Ready Rentals
www.readyrentals.com or 1-800-599-8008

Hawaii / Maui – Akamai Mother's Rentals
www.akamaimothers.com or 1-808-298-1336

Hawaii / Maui – Baby Furniture Rentals
www.pamelasaloharentals.com or 1-877-299-2229

Illinois / Chicago Metro area – The Baby Rentals
www.thebabyrentals.com or 1-866-736-8572

Massachusetts / Cape Cod – Baby's Away
www.babysaway.com or 1-508-481-4696

Massachusetts / Northshore, Boston / New Hampshire - Basic Baby Rentals
www.basicbabyrentals.com or 1-978-375-4054

Michigan / Detroit and Ann Arbor – Baby Travels Equipment Rental
www.babytravels.com or 1-734-455-2526

New York / Long Island area
www.little-travelers.com or 1-631-207-1408

New York / New York City – Granny's Rental, Inc.
www.grannysrental.com or 1-212-876-4310

New York / New York City – Baby's Away
www.babysaway.com or 1-800-374-3403

North Carolina / Charlotte – Bring the Baby
www.bringthebaby.com or 1-866-301-2229

Oregon / Portland – Babies On the Go Rentals, Inc.
www.rent4baby.com or 1-888-677-2229

Rhode Island, Massachusetts, and Connecticut – Crumb Krunchers
www.crumbkrunchers.com or 1-877-2742

Tennessee / Nashville – Baby's Away
www.babysaway.com or 1-800-227-8809

Texas / Austin – Baby's Away
www.babysaway.com or 1-800-505-1734

Texas / Dallas – Bring the Baby
www.bringthebaby.com or 1-866-301-2229

Texas / Houston – Rockabye Baby
www.rockabyebabyrentals.com or 1-866-475-6825

Washington / Seattle – Crybaby Comforts
www.crybabycomforts.com or 1-425-260-4788

Washington, D.C. – Breezy Baby Travel
www.breezybaby.com or 1-301-807-2358

Canada

Alberta / Calgary & Banff – One Tiny Suitcase
www.onetinysuitcase.ca or 1-403-208-1167

Ontario / Niagara Falls (Pelham) – Borrow Til Tomorrow
www.borrowtiltomorrow.com or 1-905-526-6712

Ontario / Toronto – Wee Travel, Inc.
www.weetravel.ca or 1-416-737-1622

British Columbia / Vancouver & Toronto – Wee Travel, Inc.
www.weetravel.ca or 1-604-222-4722

Australia

Brisbane, Gold Coast & Sunshine Coast – Little Noodles
www.littlenoodles.com.au or 0417-602-989

Melbourne, Sydney & Adelaide – Little Noodles
www.littlenoodles.com.au or 0412-241-989

Mexico

Cancun – Cancun Valet
www.cancunvalet.com or 1-888-479-9095

Europe

France / Charente and Charente Maritimes – Travelling with Baby
www.travellingwithbaby.com or sam@travellingwithbaby.com

Italy - Ciao Bambino!
www.ciaobambino.com or 1-866-802-0300.

Spain / Barcelona – Baby Travelling
www.babytravelling.com or 0034-670-73-18-35

Spain / Costa del Azahar – Travelling with Baby
www.travellingwithbaby.com or ady@travellingwithbaby.com

Spain / Costa del Sol – Kidz to Go!
www.kidztogo.com or 0034-600-009-627

Spain / Southern Costa Blanca (south of Alicante) – Mother Goose Hire
www.mothergoosehire.com or 0034-966-730-431

Switzerland / Zurich – Kids Stuff Rentals
www.idarling.ch or 043-888-0021

U.K. / London and surrounding areas – Baby 2 Go
www.baby2go.com or +441 (0) 208-655-8640

U.K. / London – Chelsea Baby Hire
www.chelseababyhire.com or 0208-789-9673

U.K. – Tots 2 Go,
www.tots2go.com or 0870-333-1255

Africa

South Africa / Johannesburg, Cape Town, and Durban – Babylite
www.babylite.co.za or +27 (0)76 900 2630 or service@babylite.co.za

BABY SUPPLY DELIVERY SERVICES

Once you start packing, it isn't hard to see you could fill an entire suitcase just with the essentials for your beach vacation or adventure abroad. However, it isn't always practical to plan on spending your precious vacation time hunting down the extra things you'll need for your child — assuming you can find them once you reach your destination. If you will be renting gear for your child, the agency may also deliver essentials like diapers, wipes, formula, and baby foods along with your equipment rental, so check when you make arrangements. Otherwise, these delivery services may be able to help.

Jet Set Babies ships orders of diapers, sun care products, baby and toddler foods, formula, and more to locations throughout the U.S., in Puerto Rico, in the U.S. Virgin Islands, as well as to U.S. military bases around the world. www.jetsetbabies.com or 1-866-990-1811.

Babies Travel Lite can deliver all manner of goods in popular destinations worldwide, including baby and toddler sunglasses, swim diapers, sun block, toddler snacks, baby foods, bath and beach toys, and beverages (including boxed milk!). www.babiestravellite.com or 1-888-450-LITE.

FIFTEEN THINGS YOU MIGHT NOT THINK TO PACK

1. **Large binder clips** – Fantastic for clipping blankets to stroller canopies and infant car seats for extended shade coverage. These also help keep bags of chips and crackers closed tight.

2. **Old blanket or "Neat Sheet"** – Create a sun canopy from your tail gate (with binder clips, above) or drape over your car windows for shade when pulled over for a nursing break or rest stop. Also useful for beach outings, impromptu picnics en route, and emergency roadside repairs. Use binder clips at the corners as weights or to secure to your car or other objects as shade. You may prefer the Neat Sheet as a lightweight, waterproof alternative to blankets, as it sheds sand and shields against boggy lawns.

3. **Pillow** – Helpful on road trips for nursing, napping, and creating a level surface over bucket seats during diaper changes.

4. **Spare sun hat** – It would be interesting to know how many times the average sun hat falls off (or blows off, or gets thrown off from) a child's head. Be prepared, and try to use one with a chin strap.

5. **Small flashlight** – Not just for camping! A small (pen-sized or slightly larger) flashlight can be very helpful in searching through the glove box, diaper bag, carry-on, or suitcase without turning on additional lights that may disturb your child's slumber.

6. **Extra pair of shoes** – We've all seen it, the lone child's shoe, kicked off or slipped off, in the parking lot or along the park trail. And now that you're a parent, it could happen to you. Whether you are going away for days or a day, you may be glad you brought a back-up pair.

7. **Stationery box** – The ½" deep boxes that resume or special papers are packaged in can be indispensable in traveling with toddlers and preschool-age children. Fill with scratch paper and a few crayons and you have an art station that's ready to roam. Just open the lid and let them go—the edges of the box keep artwork from getting onto other surfaces and the crayons from rolling off the edges.

8. **Facial tissue/Kleenex** – If you are all perfectly healthy before you set foot out the door, runny noses may be the furthest thing from your minds. In case of cold or allergies, you might be grateful to have some travel-size tissue packs or a handkerchief for your daypack or diaper bag.

9. **Tampons / maxi pads** – If you are a breastfeeding mother who has not yet resumed her cycle, guess what? It could happen at any time, so be prepared.
10. **Breast pump** – Even if you are not planning to pump or have any need for bottles, it may be a comfort to express milk at some point in your trip. Restless flights, long nights spent suckling a growing babe, or traveling with a baby that sleeps more than usual (and feeds less than…) due to the hum of the car or airplane engine, may find you painfully engorged at some point.
11. **Your laundry detergent** – In case you decide to do a load of laundry after all… it may be hard to find your preferred detergent for your child's clothing (baby-friendly, low-odor, etc.), especially without purchasing an entire box or bottle of the stuff. Pack a baggie with just 1 load's worth in your suitcase's inner pocket.
12. **Velcro bands** – At home, you'll find them in your fabric store and possibly on the goodies and gadgets aisle of your supermarket. As you travel, you may find them bundling up window blind cords, attaching toys or shopping bags to your stroller, or wet clothing to the balcony rail of your vacation rental.
13. **Rubber drain cover** – The wide, flat variety could help hold a baby's bath or a small load of laundry in a leaky sink, or even convert some shower stalls into a pint-sized pool for bathing toddlers.
14. **Inflatable beach ball** – Think lightweight, soft, and safe for rolling around the hotel room on rainy days or at the airport when you're grounded in a haze. Sure, you can use it at the beach, too.
15. **Glow sticks** – Even if you travel with a nightlight, there may not be a suitable outlet (or any outlets at all in the case of a tent) where you can use the nightlight. Emergency glow sticks can be used instead, and older children may even be comforted by carrying theirs with them to the bathroom in the night. Most stay illuminated up to 12 hours, and they can usually be found at hardware stores.

PART II
TOOLS FOR HAPPY TRAVELS

- *Chapter 4* -
Preparing for Changes

NIGHTTIME SLEEPING

Snuggling a beloved blanket, reading stories, or humming a song is easily accomplished in tents, in hotel rooms, and even in row 34 of coach. But taking a bath, rocking in a chair, or plugging in a favorite nightlight may present some serious logistical challenges when it's bedtime during your trip. As a traveling parent, it will behoove you to make your routines at home as portable as possible, especially bedtime routines.

My husband and I have found it helpful to have at least one bedtime story and a poem committed to memory—they travel with us wherever we go and take up zero space in the suitcase. Better yet, we can recount them as needed, even when pacing up and down the aisles of crowded aircraft or traveling in a dark car. And in moments when your child is overtired and out of sorts, it may be more effective to softly whisper a poem or story in his ear than to pull out a stimulating book or toy. Stories and poems with simple rhyme schemes are often the easiest to memorize. If you're not sure where to begin, you might take a look at Sandra Boynton's *The Going to Bed Book* and Robert Frost's poem "Stopping by Woods on a Snowy Evening;" both have helpful rhyme schemes and are especially well suited to both bedtime and travel (and both have ending lines that can be repeated as needed, and repeated as needed).

Co-sleeping families accustomed to sharing "the family bed" may have the easiest time of all catching zzz's while traveling. When you and your children are already accustomed to sleeping side by side, you will feel right at home shutting eyes on airplanes, trains, in foreign hotels, in tents and anywhere space or beds are limited. Co-sleepers may find some challenges, however, when traveling in Europe where twin beds are quite common in smaller hotels, or on trains where most beds are bunk-style.

For families that are more accustomed to having space to sprawl and even rooms to separate early sleepers from those with later bedtimes, travel can pose some interesting challenges. Some parents have found it helpful to try one (or all) of the following:

- Observe a family bed time when sharing a single room, tent, or compartment.
- Ask your hotel if a portacrib is available or a rollaway bed for older toddlers and preschoolers. If not, consider bringing your own travel bassinet or travel bed.
- When sharing a bed with an excitable child, put the child to bed first as per your routine so she is soundly asleep before joining her on the mattress.
- Create a "safe zone" for infants and young babies at the head of the bed where the blankets will not interfere, in a gap between parents' pillows. Always be certain the child cannot slip between mattresses (as when two twin beds are pushed together) or between the mattress and the wall. Your best bet may be a "co-sleeper" such as the Snuggle Nest, which folds up for travel and provides safety bumpers for the baby in the bed between Mom and Dad.
- Get creative! Past generations often used a drawer on the floor as baby's temporary bed (but in strange places they may come with splinters or bugs, so inspect them thoroughly first). Look around, consider your resources, and be sure to use common sense.

You may also want to bring along your own source of white noise to help muffle any strange new noises, including those of crisp hotel sheets as you roll over in the night, and of course, less desirable interjections of street or hotel noise, a banging furnace or air conditioner, elevator traffic in the hallway, or perhaps a crying baby. (Wait—that one came with us.)

But what do you do when the sleeping conditions—and possibly the time zone—are wildly different from those of home, and even recordings of ocean waves or TV static can't help? First, I recommend having a good chuckle in recognition of the absurdity of your situation, e.g. it's not every couple with an infant that gets to share the wall with newlyweds (ahem), or every family with a 1-year-old who can enjoy strolling through Times Square at midnight.

So, after you laugh heartily about the parade of Vespas cracking the plaster on your ceiling with their baritone bravado, ask about changing to a quieter room—most hotel staff will recognize that all of their guests are more likely to sleep like babies if the babies among them are asleep. And use your bedspread, a beach towel, or ask for an extra blanket if needed, to help block out bright lights or block drafts.

To help overcome jetlag, try to set your internal clocks to the new time zone as quickly as possible. Don't deprive an exhausted child of a nap if she needs one, but try to keep it to a reasonable length of time for a *nap* (whatever is the norm at home if that helps). If your child wakes up raring to go in the middle of the night, you may need to simply allow her to burn off some energy, consume some extra calories to make up for a meal she's missed, or even have a bowel movement before gently returning to your bedtime routine (yes, even poop can experience jetlag).

As a last resort—though it is a controversial subject—many parents have found it helpful to give an over-the-counter remedy such as the antihistamine Children's Benadryl or homeopathic remedy Calms Forté 4 Kids to help their children rest during travel—particularly during flights. If you think you might find yourself considering this option, talk with your child's doctor ahead of time, and ensure that you know the appropriate dosage and medication you may give in case. Also, be aware that antihistamines have the opposite effect on some children, making them more active and even irritable rather than drowsy.

NAPTIME SLEEPING

Perhaps the greatest incentive of all for traveling with an infant is the incredible ease with which most will nap—and how often—while parents are on the go. Consider the soothing effect of car travel, stroller rides, and even simply being carried around in the infant carrier or sling has on most babies. However, some babies and children may nap a little too much during daytime outings. If your child sleeps many hours on the go, you may want to build in some breaks for exercise and physical activities that will be more stimulating for your child (including tummy time for infants).

As babies get older, they not only nap fewer hours of the day, but they tend to respond more to their surroundings as well. Some locations and settings (even airplanes) may simply be too exciting for some older babies and toddlers to sleep through. You may need to plan more structured breaks from sightseeing for in-room (or in-car) naps. Having more of a "home base" may also be helpful for the napping needs of an older child, as opposed to a constant on-the-go itinerary with changes in accommodations.

To help with napping while you are out and about, you might bring along a favorite small stuffed animal or blanket if there is room. Plan a walk with the stroller away from exciting scenery (e.g. through the rose garden rather than past the carousel) to help get snoozing underway. Some strollers are even equipped with speakers or portable speaker pockets to broadcast music from your portable music player (some Combi travel strollers have "acoustic canopy" speaker and music device pockets). Bring a blanket and binder clips to help keep sun or bright lights from disrupting peaceful slumbers and to block out other distractions.

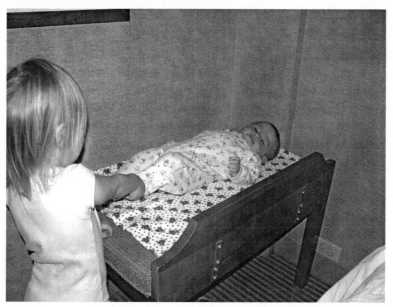

Instant bassinet: A bench found in our hotel room, turned sideways and placed in the corner.

EATING AND FEEDING ON THE FLY

Strange new foods and the unfamiliar places in which they are eaten are not always as enjoyable for babies and small children as they are to adults, though you may be pleasantly surprised when your child discovers she likes something from the new menu—a lot (all hail the pineapple). Bringing along some favorite foods and snacks to mix in with the new could make a tremendous difference during the initial adjustment, and what doesn't go well with Cheerios?

If you're your child has just begun eating solids, you may simply want to plan a trip to the market at your destination to stock up on jarred baby foods. But in more exotic or remote destinations, you may find yourself packing a heavier suitcase to accommodate jarred baby foods from home. For toddlers and older children, you might be glad to have along several of these portable foods:

- Cheerios or similar cereal
- Favorite crackers
- A few canned vegetables or fruits (don't forget your can opener)
- Instant oatmeal packets
- Applesauce in individual, sealed servings
- Fruit leather or dried fruit bars
- Dinner rolls (stay fresher and travel more easily than bread)

More of a concern, however, will likely be milk.

If you are breastfeeding your child, you will have a ready supply that requires no refrigeration, special storage, preparation rituals or paraphernalia (more travel benefits on page 116). If your child takes formula, you may find it well worth packing some bottles of ready-serve formula even though it is heavier in the suitcase and more expensive than powdered mixes. To help keep things as simple as possible, particularly for the traveling segments between destinations, you may also want to use disposable bottle liners. Or consider one of the new bottle systems that store dry formula mix and water in separate sections of the bottle until you are ready to mix and serve by twisting the lid and shaking the contents together (look for the U-Mix from Sunshine Kids).

Car adapter bottle warmers can help during drives, but often take a very long time to heat bottles effectively. By heating two smaller or partially-filled bottles instead, your first bottle may be ready faster, and the second can warm while she feeds on the first. Some bottle warmers are available now that require no electricity or batteries, but many parent reviews have revealed they do not work well, or have even melted during use. Until improvements are made, be sure to research your model carefully. Instead, you can travel with a good old-fashioned wide-mouth thermos or oversized travel coffee mug that will fit a bottle or breast milk storage bag inside and can be filled with hot water when available. Even when you find yourself on a flight with attendants who will not help you heat your child's bottle, you should at least be able to have them fill your thermos or cup with hot water.

Parents with toddlers and preschoolers that have moved on to cow's milk will have to consider this important part of their child's diet. Where and how will you get milk for your child, and where will you keep it? For most children, simply ordering a glass with a meal at a restaurant will not cut it. Having a refrigerator in your room with your own carton ready to go at all hours can be a tremendous help. We've found it helpful to travel with insulated sippy cups, like those made by Playtex, with a few ice cubes added from the hotel ice machine or restaurants—and when the ice cubes stop clinking, we know the milk has started to warm up. An insulated diaper bag or small soft travel cooler can also be helpful as you make way in transit or see the sights.

If you will be staying somewhere that refrigeration is not available, you may find it helpful to bring along boxed milk that requires no refrigeration. For extended stays, consider checking or shipping yourself a box of your preferred infant formula or boxed milk, and any other food or baby care products you may need during your stay. Some parents find that individual serving boxes of rice milk that don't require refrigeration (similar to juice boxes) are very helpful to have along for travel, and may be available at your local health food store or at Costco.

Since high chairs are rare in restaurants outside of the U.S., and even those in the U.S. often lack safety straps or adequate support, not to mention the basic sanitation required for the surfaces where the adults eat, you may want to bring along a portable dining booster for your baby or toddler. Not only will you know your child will always have a clean, comfortable, escape-free perch from which to dine, but your child will also recognize that the seat means mealtime. (Specific travel-worthy dining boosters are included in Products for Eating and Feeding, page 56.).

Nine Tips for Nursing on the Go

If you are just beginning to breastfeed, it may be hard to imagine doing so with any sort of style or grace, let alone without the help of a nursing pillow or stripping to your waist. But it does get easier with practice. In the meantime, here are some tips to help you nurse more comfortably as you travel.

1. Wear knit shirts cut just wide enough to drape over the cheek of your child as she nurses and still keep you covered to each side (your shirt needn't be ridiculously oversized, just a loose-fitting T-shirt should do). Think bottom-up as opposed to going over the top.

2. Use a sling to help position your baby and provide privacy while nursing. With practice, you may eventually be able to nurse hands-free, and quite privately, while taking in the sights at your destination!

3. Avoid aisle seats on airplanes and trains for fewer distractions to your child and greater privacy. If there are armrests, you'll be able to make use of them without getting bumped by passersby.

4. If you need breast pads, avoid the disposable variety that contain plastic and will make it difficult for your skin to breathe. The cotton variety can be sink-washed and will dry in a day in most climates.

5. Strategically place your child's stroller or diaper bag to create a privacy barrier.

6. Wear a nursing tank top or camisole underneath a shirt to keep your midriff covered and cold drafts out.

7. When dining out or attending dressy events, wear a wrap, scarf, or shawl of some sort that can drape over your child's cheek and help give privacy while nursing. (You can also use a cloth napkin.)

8. Wear a nursing bra that you can easily open and close with only one hand. This will make it much easier to fasten up with your baby still on your lap.

9. While your child is still very small, use the diaper bag or a folded jacket on your lap to help keep from hunching over, and use arm wrests where you can find them. (In airplanes and cars you may be able to use a pillow.)

Exercise and Activity

As children grow, so does their range of motion. The infant that may be content for hours in a carrier will eventually need to roll. The roller will need to practice crawling. The crawler will need to pull up. The stander will need to take steps. The walker will need to run. The runner will need to climb. The climber will need to master stealth battle moves from the Jumbo Jujitzu Dinosaur cartoons, and so on.

The older and more active your child becomes, the more your vacation will need to provide opportunities to use her new physical skills, whether that means crawling on the carpet of your hotel room or exploring playground equipment at a nearby park. Depending on your destination and the age of your child, there may be plenty of opportunities for exercise built-in to your surroundings, like expanses of sandy beach, a park with meandering paths to walk, or a hotel with stairs to practice climbing.

If your child is at a stage where she enjoys pushing a walker, consider bringing one along to let her push up and down long halls or around the campground loop (it could do you both a world of good). Doorway jumpers are also quite handy and can fit into a moderate-size suitcase. Also consider renting gear that may be helpful during your stay

Some family resorts include splash pools, playgrounds, or other active equipment specifically for small children. At some stages you may find it well worth vacationing at a resort of that nature rather than in more economical alternatives that may leave you feeling room-bound. It will also be important to weave these activities into your daily sightseeing agendas if you will be out and about. For example seeing the sights through morning, then returning in time for lunch and some good exercise before attempting a nap.

Pottying On The Go

Potty training can become even more challenging when restroom availability is unpredictable and the facilities are clearly not those of home (though a Turkish toilet may actually provide hours of entertainment for some children). Changes in time zones and diet could also affect a child's regularity.

For all of these reasons, many potty-training parents of the past felt helplessly homebound, but thanks to some very inventive new products, they are free at last. You may now slip an entire training potty into the side of your daypack—and inflate it in a few seconds (it's called the "Inflate-a-Potty"). Or simply convert the public toilet to training size with a folding seat.

If you have room enough, many parents negotiating this sensitive stage of development have found it useful to travel with their own, complete training potty from home. For unplanned roadside stops, or cold nights in the tent, this can be especially helpful. A British family visiting Palma Minorca discovered it was well worth it to have checked the potty on their flight to the island—their dedicated daughter stuck to her new routine, even on the beach.

Do keep in mind that, just as at home, some accidents may happen. To help with on-the-go "uh-ohs," the Piddle Pad fits comfortably into the car seat, stroller, or backpack carrier. For nighttime, disposable-training-type pants will do the trick for most toddlers. For the older child who has only occasional accidents, you could pack along the same waterproof sheet and bed pad you may already have at home (x2 or x3 for nighttime replacement). Or to keep things simple, consider purchasing hospital-issue disposable bed pads for your vacation. Also called "underpads" or "chux," there is a variety to choose from that fit the width of a twin-size bed, complete with wings that tuck in to help it stay put. You can find them at many medical supply stores or online at www.vitalitymedical.com / 1-800-397-5899 or www.northshorecare.com / 1-800-563-0161.

Regardless of which products you choose for your travels, don't hesitate to discuss this sensitive topic with your child ahead of time. Let him know what to expect in the way of aircraft lavatories, rest areas, or campground facilities, and introduce any new travel potties or equipment in the weeks before you leave home to ensure that he's as comfortable with these items as possible.

Still, be prepared for temporary regression. New facilities may bring on performance anxiety, and exciting days packed with sightseeing and activities can make it hard for small children (and sometimes their parents) to remember to take potty breaks in a timely manner. Be sensitive to your child's own frustrations and feelings if accidents happen, and know that any temporary setbacks will likely be overcome upon your return home.

PREPARING TODDLERS AND PRESCHOOLERS FOR TRAVEL

From the first mention of your upcoming travel plans, share your enthusiasm. Discuss the details of the adventure: Will you cover miles and miles in the car and visit exciting parks on the way? Fly in an airplane and get to look down on the clouds in the sky? Ride on a train and eat a picnic of special snacks on the way? Will you make a campfire and sleep in a tent listening to crickets? Will you visit a beach and make sand castles? Visit an aquarium and see sharks? Eat gelato and toss coins into a fountain to make a special wish?

Help your toddler or preschooler form realistic expectations for the trip. Will there be a lot of time spent in the car, airplane, or train? Discuss it ahead of time and let them help plan ways you will pass—and enjoy the time together. Do what you can to help put it in his terms, too. For example, a three-hour car ride may be difficult to imagine, but the time it takes to listen to three of his favorite music CDs may help put things into perspective (and prevent a few rounds of "Are we there yet?").

Will she need to sleep on the airplane for her regular naptime? Or will all of you spend the night on the aircraft? Again, let your child help to figure out what all will be required—toothbrushes, bedtime books, pajamas or at least comfortable clothing, or a favorite blanket. Plan together how you can all enjoy a good night's rest en route. When children feel involved in the process of travel and better know what to expect, they are much more likely to relax and enjoy the adventure.

If there will be a special event, such as a wedding or holiday meal, discuss the customs that go along with an event of that nature and how to best participate. Will there be a special time when we'll be quiet and listen to music and poems? Will we sit around the table and put cloth napkins on our laps? Will it be appropriate to offer some help—and what can we do that might be helpful? You can even practice at home, making a fun mock-version of the event.

Tips for Raising a Happy Traveler

1. Start traveling as soon as possible (before they know any better)—babies get used to what they get used to.

2. Discourage brand loyalty—this can help avert crises at Grandma's house as well as in restaurants and foreign markets.

3. Encourage a palate for universally available foods—rice, yogurt, vegetables, beans, and noodles can be had in virtually any country.

4. Emphasize "routines" over "schedules." For example, we do this and this before going to bed, regardless of the time zone.

5. Be the most enthusiastic traveler your child knows—share your excitement about where and how you will travel and your child will most likely share the joy.

6. Get a globe or put a world map on the wall and make reference to it often: when reading a story about an Emperor in China, when watching a movie about animals in the Amazon, when mentioning cousins in Indiana, and of course, when planning your next adventure.

7. Create a travel scrapbook just for your child to record his adventures, large and small. As he gets older, he can help choose the pictures and watch for special mementos along the way to add to his travel book.

BRACING FOR THE BUMPS IN THE ROAD

Travel, by its very nature, brings with it a certain amount of uncertainty. Missed connections, delays, Montezuma's Revenge, lost baggage, wrong turns, and train strikes can change the face of even the best-laid travel plans. Add to that the unplanned bouts of teething pain, upset tummies, and tantrums that are part and parcel of life as a parent, and traveling as a family can teach you lessons in patience to humble the most humble monk.

I was once asked what I thought was the single-most important item to bring when traveling with a baby. Expecting to hear about some inventive piece of new gear or perhaps a travel-size pediatric first-aid kit, the man looked stunned as I answered "your sense of humor." It prevents nervous breakdowns, makes up for lost luggage, and magically minimizes unsightly stains (grin and wear it); and while it probably won't help you find your way through the sweltering streets of Bangkok or the maze-like alleys of Venice, you are far more likely to wander through this world with a pleasant look on your face. And so is your child.

I have also found it helpful to keep in mind that many of the difficulties that arose during our travels would have happened whether we'd stayed at home or not: the troublesome new tooth, the diaper blowout, even the ear infection. If you try to plan every trip around the possibility of a rough night with your child, you might never leave your home—and you'd still have your share of rough nights.

Just remember, spit-up happens. Wouldn't you rather that it happen to *you* on the way to Waikiki?

TEN THINGS TO DO BEFORE YOU LEAVE HOME

1. Visit, or at least phone, your child's doctor. Mention your travel plans and discuss any concerns you may have including: status of vaccinations, illness while traveling, sleep disturbances, food safety and allergies, and finding medical assistance for your child at your destination. If your child hasn't seen his doctor in a while, a check-up may be reassuring ("ears are clear," etc), and it could be helpful for parents of infants and babies to have a current weigh-in.

2. Call your airline within 72 hours of your departure to reconfirm your seat assignments and, if applicable, your bassinet reservation and/or children's meals.

3. Check your child's travel kit (page 44) to see if any items are running low or need to be replaced. Move fingernail clippers, tweezers, and any other non-carry-on items into a checked bag.

4. Revisit Childproofing on the Go, page 137.

5. Take inventory of the gear that will be traveling with you. Is your car seat FAA approved for the flight? Are the stroller wheels still up to snuff? Can you find the sun shields, mosquito nets or other accessories you plan to take along?

6. Replace old sunscreens (your brand and your child's) if you're heading for a sunny destination. Sunscreens lose their effectiveness with time, and small children need the best protection available.

7. Arrange to have your mail stopped while you are away. You can do this quickly online at www.usps.com or by calling 1-800-ASK-USPS (1-800-275-8777).

8. Remove anything in your refrigerator that will not outlast your trip.

9. If needed, make arrangements with a neighbor or friend to set out your garbage can and recyclables for pick up.

10. Empty your diaper pail!

- *Chapter 5* -
Temperaments in Transit

TRAVELING WITH YOUR UNIQUE CHILD

As travel guru Rick Steves writes in his book *Europe Through the Back Door*, "Travel is intensified living—maximum thrills per minute and one of the last great sources of legal adventure." Of course, parenting a small child is no snooze either. When you combine the two, the results could either lead to a nervous breakdown or the best time off you've ever spent in your life. For the best family vacations possible, use this section to help identify and prepare for the most likely challenges that may surface during trips with your unique child.

You may have already noticed that your child thinks, behaves, and reacts to certain situations differently from his playmates, and perhaps even from how you do. Whereas one child may adapt seamlessly to changes in sleeping or eating schedules, a different child may be deeply troubled by these differences. Consider the cautious child who quietly observes at length before attempting a new activity, and then her more active counterpart who learns by simply doing—bruises, bumps, and all. These differences are not simply the consequences of good or bad behavior, nor, as parents with multiple children discover, environment or upbringing. What make children different from the get-go are their inborn temperaments.

"Temperament," as defined by *The American Heritage Dictionary*, is "The manner of thinking, behaving, or reacting characteristic of a specific person." In the late 1950s, researchers Alexander Thomas and Stella Chess identified key temperament traits that were present in individuals from birth, and influenced the way they developed and the choices they made throughout their lives. Researchers have found that often a child's dominant temperament traits can be identified as early as 4 months of age. In some children, just one temperament trait may dominate. In others, there may be multiple traits combining to create their unique worldview.

Recognizing your child's dominant temperament traits—and how you or your partner's may differ—will give you a tremendous edge in planning your trips together as a family. As you read over the descriptions of the eight key temperament traits that follow, note where your child tends toward one extreme or the other and see the tips and suggestions that follow for traveling with children of these temperament types.

ACTIVITY LEVEL

High energy - Is your child highly active, needing much more physical exercise and freedom than many of his peers? Does it seem like he's constantly on the move, even when he's playing in one area?

- or -

Low energy - Is he more relaxed and content to sit still for long periods of time, playing with toys in one area of the room, or calmly watching T.V.?

The High-Energy Child

Try to keep this child as mentally active as possible during periods when he must remain in his car seat or at the table. Bring plenty of books or books on tape, and play soothing music to help keep him calm. Coloring books and even play-dough can be helpful. We've also found the "Doodle Pro" style of magnetic drawing boards indispensable during travel and in restaurants (no mess or loose pieces). Travel trays that attach to the car seat or stroller can provide an important space for activities and entertainment (see Travel Trays, page 56). When flying, avoid pre-boarding the aircraft with this child, and instead let him remain physically active as long as possible. Book bulkhead row seats to help avoid battles over kicking a forward passenger's seat on aircraft. On trains, try for seating configurations with tables where he can color and keep busy, or where two rows of seats face each other so he can play on the floor in between. Everyday scrapes and bruises are more likely with this child at home and certainly while traveling, so keep the Band-aids and antiseptic handy even while sightseeing. Injuries could be a real concern when visiting destinations outside the U.S. where safety standards (railings, windows, crosswalks) are not what they are at home, and where pedestrians do not have the right of way. If you need to make a long-haul or overseas flight with this child, try to schedule a nighttime flight when his energy level will be lowest. Pack along some boxes of shelf-stable milk and crackers to help avoid juices and sugary foods while traveling.

The Low-Energy Child

This child not only shows a tolerance for stroller use much longer than some children, at times he may even prefer to sit and be strolled on your vacation. Try to choose a travel stroller that will accommodate a higher upper weight limit (usually 40+ lbs) and longer legs, and you will likely get your money's worth as you continue to use it for trips during the preschool years. Plan vacations packed with sit-and-do activities, like building sand castles and watching sharks and jellyfish at the aquarium. For trips by car, train, or airplane, he may be quite content to pass the time in his seat so long as he has something to do (audio books, drawing boards, or movies). On very busy and active days, respect that he will need some down time to recharge his batteries, and plan breaks accordingly.

Eager - Does he rush into new places, ready to explore, find the best toys, and make new friends? Is he happy to try a new food or wear a new jacket?

- or -

Cautious - Is he slow to warm up to new people and surroundings? Is he hesitant to talk with strangers and new acquaintances, turning away from them and in toward you? Does he prefer tried and true toys and clothes, and the same favorite books?

The Eager Child

Childproofing is a top concern when arriving on a new scene, as this child may waste no time in testing every drawer, window, door, and balcony rail before you can take off your jacket. Be ready to explore *together* so you can act on any unsafe situations and explain any new rules or procedures. Stand guard when entering the territory of unfamiliar pets as your child may get too familiar too quickly for some animals. Also be on the lookout for street dogs, strays, and wild animals so you can hopefully spot them before your child does. Each feature of the hotel room calls to him—the hair dryer, the shampoo bottles, the minibar, the phone (unplug it if you must to avoid constant battles). For relaxing vacations, it will be important to plan trips in spaces where safety concerns are minimal and activities are abundant. To your advantage, this child will most likely be delighted to join children's activity programs and drop-off nurseries, mingling with other children, discovering new toys, and engaging in activities, allowing you to join the snorkel trip or kick back by the pool without guilt.

The Cautious Child

Whenever possible, seat yourself between your child and strangers or people she is not familiar with, even if they are relatives you yourself have known since birth. Family reunions can especially overwhelm this child, where many people may expect hugs and kisses, as well as holding privileges. Remember that you are your child's advocate, and be ready and willing to politely say no to people on her behalf. Practice saying phrases like, "Now's not a good time—maybe later," and "She's a little shy, just give her some time." She may prefer to observe other children playing in the splash pool or on the playground from a safe distance before joining in, or need your company while she gets familiar with the new children and supervisors at a kids' camp type program at the resort or on your cruise ship. Understand that in all likelihood, you may be your child's playmate for the duration of your trip, so plan for activities you can both enjoy together. Your child is not just slow to warm up to new people, but also to other novelties including places and foods. Pack along some favorite snacks from home to help while she adjusts to new cuisine, or be prepared to do some of your own cooking. Single-destination vacations are favorable.

PHYSICAL REGULARITY

Very regular - Does your child keep a consistent schedule with little influence from you? Does she sleep and wake at the same times each day, nap for similar lengths of time, and even have bowel movements at predictable times?

- or -

Unpredictable - Do her physiological needs and functions vary from day to day, with different waking times and varied lengths of naps? Is it hard to anticipate when the next bowel movement will strike?

The Very Regular Child

Use her predictability to your advantage when planning your vacation days. You will have the benefit of knowing ahead of time what to expect in the way of nap times and duration, appetite, energy levels, and even bowel movements. Ideally, the itinerary will fit her existing schedule as much as possible, allowing for her regular meal and nap times, and her usual bedtime (within reason). If your child goes to bed earlier than you, consider a vacation rental with a separate space for her to sleep in while you enjoy a balcony, lanai, Jacuzzi, good book, or simply watching the T.V. If flights or drives are timed with her naps, the travel gods will likely smile upon you.

Try to avoid red-eye flights that will interrupt her sleeping schedule. When adapting to a big change in time zones, you might want to set the alarm clock for her usual wake-up time in the new time zone and jump back into the schedule as quickly as possible. Hotels and resorts where breakfasts are provided can help you all fall into a routine of filling her tummy (and yours) right away in the mornings, at the same place, at the same time. Hotel suites or vacation rentals with kitchens can also help you maintain regular mealtimes, and the separation of space in 1-bedroom units can help you enjoy your afternoons and evenings if your child needs to keep her regular nap and an earlier bedtime. Since this child often begins potty training on the early side, it may also be helpful to plan vacations where your own room and private bathroom are close at hand, from the toddler years forward.

The Unpredictable Child

This child comes with his own set of checks and balances as far as travel is concerned. What you may gain in the way of flexibility (sleeping), you may make up for in surprises (blow-outs). Although there is no guarantee he will nap on the flight, there's no reason to assume the worst if he doesn't—he'll more than likely make up for lost sleep at a later time. His unpredictable appetite means that he may not eat enough at formal mealtimes to carry him through the day's activities, so always be sure to carry some snacks with you to fend off the blood sugar blues. Accommodations with kitchens, or at least refrigerators, can help meet his varying needs for food. In restaurants, it may be wise to offer him part of your meal rather than paying for a child's meal that may sit untouched (accept the doggie bags with grace). A comfortable travel stroller will help him get the extra zzzs he needs when he needs them without slowing you down. Because his elimination process may "ebb and flow," always keep backup clothing in the carry-on or diaper bag, and consider purchasing an extra car seat cover or the Piddle Pad (see more products in Pottying On the Go, page 75). Accidents are more likely during the potty training era for this child, so plan and pack accordingly.

Fast-adapting - Does she adjust quickly to changes in routine or scenery, go with the flow when it's time to change from the crib to the toddler bed, or wear the purple pajamas instead of the pink without complaint?

- or -

Slow-adapting - Does it take a while for her to sleep or eat normally in new settings?

The Fast-Adapting Child

The stars are in your favor when you travel with this child. New scenery, new foods, and new faces are generally not a problem, and may even be met with enthusiasm. Although this trait may be a great strength when it comes to traveling, it may also bring other traits closer to the surface that shouldn't be taken for granted. Remember the expression, "I'm easy to get along with...when things go my way." Consider, for example, a highly adaptable child with low energy. She may move from one activity and destination to the next seamlessly, until suddenly her energy reserve is depleted. It seems like she melts or has a tantrum from out of the blue, and you find yourself thinking, "This isn't like her." Yet once she gets the rest or down time she needs, she is back to her usual self. Embrace this temperament trait as you travel, but be sure to honor your child's other dominant traits as well.

The Slow-Adapting Child

As a general rule, the fewer transitions necessary the better the vacation with this child, so you may lean toward vacations centered on one location, with similar sights and activities each day. Start preparing this child for the trip well in advance, creating a picture in her mind of what she can expect. Talk her through each step of your vacation beforehand, including how you will get to and through the airport, where you will be staying, and what you will do each day. Read a book about a trip on an airplane or the destination you will visit together. If she's old enough, let her help you pack for the trip, discussing in detail the things you will see and do and how you will use the items in the suitcase or carry-on. Discuss where she will sleep and in what kind of bed (bringing a familiar portacrib or bedding can be helpful). Choose seats toward the rear of aircraft where she can better observe the goings on during your flight, including the drink or meal service and passengers using the lavatory. Try to time arrivals at new destinations early in the day so that she has time to adjust to her new surroundings before dinner and bedtime. As you travel, give her as much advance warning as possible when you will be changing activities or locations, whether it's leaving the hotel swimming pool, getting back into the car, or going to a restaurant. Familiar bedtime routines will be extremely important on vacation with this child, as her supply of adaptability may well be depleted by day's end.

INTENSITY

Intense - Does he express his likes and dislikes on a grand scale? Does he use his body to help express his feelings, tensing muscles or emphasizing with his hands?

- or -

Mellow - Do you need to watch closely or ask to know if he is enjoying something or not?

The Intense Child

Watch vigilantly for your child's cues, especially if he's beginning to show signs of over-stimulation, fatigue, or discomfort. You'll want to address any of his needs or concerns before they escalate. If he acts out in a public space, remember that yelling will only throw more fuel on his fire. And if he throws a tantrum in the car, stop. Although it's important not to give in to unrealistic requests or misbehavior, it will be wise to try to uncover and address the deeper need so that everyone can proceed happily with the vacation. You may need to stay on your toes much of the time traveling with this child, but you will also be rewarded for your efforts with outstanding displays of his joy and delight when things go right.

The Mellow Child

Similar to the low-sensitivity child, you will need to check in regularly to make sure she's getting what she needs in the way of food, drinks, and temperature control—enough clothing or too much? Illness can creep up on her quietly as you likely won't hear much complaint until it surfaces full-blown, so don't overlook the possibility of an ear infection or other illness developing as you travel. Also, watch for signs of discomfort in new social settings, such as the family reunion, the kiddie pool at the resort, or the dining room on the cruise ship, and help her give voice to those feelings. You may head off some potential crises by coaxing out her concerns early on and addressing them. If you miss her cues, she may not express her feelings until much later, sometimes by acting out. Otherwise, she's an easy going traveler in most respects—enjoy!

Mood

Positive - Does your child usually look at the world through rose-colored glasses? Does she most often walk into the room with a smile?

- or -

Negative - Does she frequently anticipate trouble or disappointment, view new children or toys with suspicion, or first see others as a potential threat? Does it take a little time for her to be convinced and the clouds to clear?

The Positive Child

Most destinations and activities are perfectly fine with this child, especially since it probably wouldn't occur to him that he might not like taking a trip somewhere. He goes along happily with most activities, expecting the best of your vacation plans. But do be careful not to overlook other dominant traits that may be obscured by his overly rosy outlook until reaching a crisis state. For example, a high sensitivity child with a positive mood might be having too much fun to realize he's maxed-out his sensory threshold until he suddenly reaches the breaking point, or a low-energy child in may run himself ragged before realizing he needs to stop and rest.

The Negative Child

"Uncertainty of the unknown" can bring out her lower expectations for your trip, so help her keep her eyes on the prize by sharing pictures of the beaches or city you'll visit, showing her vacation brochures, and visiting relevant web sites ahead of time. Help assure her she'll have some control over things, but don't put her in charge of the vacation. Encourage her to try new things, but help assure her she'll have some options if she doesn't like them. For example, if she tries the kids' camp program for an afternoon but doesn't like it, she won't have to go back, or if she tries a bite of your salmon pasta and doesn't like it, she can have a hot dog. Agree you'll go to the museum and see X, Y, Z important things at the top of your list (Mona Lisa, Etruscans, …), and let her check them off your guide map as you go. Afterward, you'll break for lunch, and then do something at the top of her list. When her other dominant temperament traits are challenged, it can especially trigger negative feelings, so be sure to honor her other temperament traits and watch for signs. With a preschooler, it can be helpful to get her in the habit of using alternative phrases like:

> I don't like it! → I'd prefer something else.
>
> I don't want to! → I'd rather do something else.

Not only does it sound more polite, but it replaces the "all or nothing" kind of thought pattern with a new emphasis on finding a solution. Not only will that be valuable in life, but it's essential to having a family vacation that everyone can enjoy, big and small.

Very distractible - Is your child easily distracted from the activity at hand, jumping up from story time to investigate a toy across the room?

- or -

Very focused - Does she focus well on one activity or toy at a time, regardless of changes around her?

The Very Distractible Child

You may need to pack a little extra patience when traveling with this child, as a crack in the ground on the path to the beach may be every bit as interesting to him as the beach itself. You never know when something will catch his fancy, or what it will be next. This child may have trouble eating enough at meal times while you are out at restaurants, in a ship's dining room, or on an airplane or a train. Help him stay focused on his food—and seated at the table—by bringing a familiar dining booster from home and seating him as far from the busiest distractions as possible, like away from the kitchen, the entrance, or windows, if possible. You may even want to feed him something in your room first to be sure he gets enough to eat and prevent the blood sugar blues. Be very careful in airports, and especially at train stations where something may catch his attention before you realize he's off and exploring. Use your stroller to keep your child safely strapped in while you check-in at the airport or use a public restroom. Child safety harnesses (a.k.a. "leashes") could be a very wise idea for toddlers and early preschoolers that are prone to bolting or wandering wherever there's just too much exciting new stuff to see, observe, and explore (especially if yours is also a highly active child). Be prepared that your child may not sleep a wink on the airplane or train. On the bright side, with your positive and enthusiastic prompting, this child will usually move from one sight or activity to the next without much hesitation, allowing you to enjoy many experiences in a shorter vacation.

The Very Focused Child

Taking in too many differing sights and activities in a day can be frustrating for this child, when just as she becomes fully engaged with one place or one toy, she has to let go and turn her attention to something new. Give her plenty of notice when, in ten minutes… and in five minutes… and in two minutes… you'll all be switching gears, even when that may simply mean getting out of bed for the day in a new time zone. It may be helpful to bring along a special travel toy, activity book, or puzzle that she can return to throughout your trip as a reprieve from many changes around her. To your advantage, she may be entertained at length by the same water fountain, or set of stair steps, or bucket of beach toys.

SENSITIVITY

Highly sensitive - Is he easily upset by loud noises, bright lights, and stimulating environments? Does he wake up easily from unexpected noises?

- or -

Low sensitivity - Could he happily go about his business in the middle of a tornado? Do you need to remind him to adjust his volume in some social settings, or not to play with other children's toys without asking?

The Highly Sensitive Child

Take care with how you express yourself when the trip doesn't go as planned (flight or train delays, traffic jams, lost luggage); in addition to experiencing her own frustrations, this child picks up on other people's frustrations as well. A picky eater may be helped by having her favorite foods from home and/or requesting a special meal if available. If she is sensitive to noise, prepare for take-off and landing by saying "We'll hear the engines start in a minute, they'll sound like a loud hum…can you hear them?" or something similar. And accept that Disneyland-type experiences may simply be overwhelming for this child — three rides may be enough for her, regardless of how long you planned to visit. Be careful not to plan too tight of itineraries as what feels like a full, fun day to you may get to be too much pressure to arrive too many places on time, and too many different experiences to process in her own special way.

The Low-Sensitivity Child

This child has few inhibitions, and usually few complaints, which makes him an easy travel companion in many respects. However, you may want to avoid red-eye and overnight long-haul flights and train rides where he might not sense or appreciate that other passengers are trying to sleep before he is ready to. When visiting holy places, be sure to explain to toddlers and preschoolers ahead of time what makes the place extra special and what you will and won't do while visiting it. Remember to check in with your child frequently to make sure he is comfortable as he might not notice his discomfort until it becomes a real problem, like carsickness, low blood sugar, or dehydration. Also, be aware that low-sensitivity can sometimes amplify other traits. For example, an eager child with low sensitivity may talk the ear off a stranger during your train ride—which can be great, so long as the stranger doesn't mind. And an active child with low sensitivity may literally climb the walls, which won't be a problem if you vacation somewhere with a playground and plenty of suitable structures for him to climb!

MORE TOOLS FOR TEMPERAMENT

In the words of Sir Francis Bacon, "Knowledge is power," and knowledge about your child's temperament can be a powerful tool for parenting— while on vacation and at home. If you'd like to learn more about temperament, here are some helpful resources for parents and caregivers.

Online Assessment and Information

The Preventive Ounce is a nonprofit organization and research project created to better help parents understand their children's temperaments. Visit their Web site to create a custom temperament forecast for your infant, toddler, or preschooler and use it to help navigate upcoming issues for your unique child in the months ahead. www.preventiveoz.org

Books

Raising Your Spirited Child: A Guide for Parents Whose Child is More Intense, Perceptive, Persistent, and Energetic, by Mary Sheedy Kurcinka, 2006, Harper Paperbacks (revised edition).

The Temperament Perspective: Working with Children's Behavioral Styles, by Jan Kristal (Foreword by Stella Chess), 2005, Paul H. Brookes Publishing Co., Inc.

Temperament Tools: Working with Your Child's Inborn Traits, by Helen Neville and Diane Clark Johnson, 1998, Parenting Press, Inc. (foreword by James Cameron, Ph.D.).

Understanding Temperament: Strategies for Creating Family Harmony, by Lyndall Shick, 1998, Parenting Press, Inc.

PART III
SPECIAL CONSIDERATIONS

- *Chapter 6* -
The Baby Abroad

YOUR CHILD'S FIRST U.S. PASSPORT

W hen passports are required of U.S. citizens, they are required of *all* of them, even newborns and infants. Be prepared to present passports for each family member, any required visas, and other required travel documents whenever you cross international borders with your child, including when you travel between the U.S. and the Caribbean, Bermuda, Panama, Mexico, and Canada.

As with any first-time passport application, your child will have to apply for his passport in person. A few things differ when applying for passports for minors under the age of 14, however. In addition to proof of citizenship, you must also:

- Provide proof of relationship to the applying parents or guardians
- Provide parental identification, and appear together, both parents in person, or submit a notarized statement of consent from the absent parent (form DS-3053, available online at www.travel.state.gov).

To save time, you can print your child's passport application from the U.S. Department of State Web site at www.travel.state.gov/passport and complete it at home. Sure, you might feel a little silly stating the color of eyes that may still be changing—or the color of hair that has yet to sprout. Just do the best you can and remember that you'll get a second chance in another 5 years when your child's first passport expires. Following are the step-by-step instructions on getting your child's first passport.

Steps to Getting Your Child's First Passport:

1. **Fill out an application form** – You can download a passport application form (DS-11) online from www.travel.state.gov/passport or pick one up from any passport agency to fill out in advance. Do NOT sign it until you are standing before the Passport Acceptance Agent and are told to do so.

2. **Submit proof of U.S. citizenship for your child** – Most commonly, this is a certified U.S. birth certificate with a raised registrar's seal.

3. **Present evidence of child's relationship to parents or guardians** – A certified U.S. birth certificate that names both parents will suffice. Also acceptable: an adoption decree with adopting parents' names, certification of birth abroad with parents' names, or a court order establishing custody or guardianship.

4. **Provide identification for parents** – Your own valid U.S. or foreign passport, driver's license, military or government I.D., or alien resident card from BCIS.

5. **Appear and sign in person—BOTH parents** – Yes, BOTH parents must be present at the time of application, or one parent may appear and sign if there is a notarized statement of consent authorizing passport issuance signed by the second parent (form DS-3053, also downloadable at www.travel.state.gov/passport). If there is no other parent to apply, you must submit proof of "sole authority to apply," such as a certified birth certificate or court order listing only one parent as guardian, or death certificate of the non-applying parent.

6. **Provide two passport photos** – Photos must be identical to each other, measure 2" x 2" in size, and have been taken in the past 6 months, showing "current appearance"! More details on photos and how you can take your own follow in the next section.

7. **Provide a social security number** – you will need to provide your child's social security number.

8. **Pay the fees** – Passport fees include an application fee and an execution fee. For children under age 16, the current fee is $52, and the execution fee is $30, for a grand total of $82 (fees may change).

9. **Wait for the passport** – With increased demand for U.S. passports, 10 weeks is not an unusual amount of time to wait for processing. If you are in a hurry, you may pay an additional $60 to expedite processing, and pay for faster shipping methods each way (overnight or priority).

Getting a Passport Photo for Your Child

Getting acceptable passport photos for someone who can't even sit up—let alone support his own head—can be a bit challenging. Be warned that some passport paparazzi simply refuse to photograph infants, and even toddlers, but a few have come up with creative methods to get the shot. Call prospective passport photographers first to make sure they will accommodate your needs (and timing), or better yet, take your own photos at home.

If you have a basic digital camera, you can easily save yourself the sitting fee, time, and potential chaos of having a stranger snap the shot. You can use your computer or the equipment at your local drug store to crop the picture as needed and print your copies. Here are the guidelines and some tips for taking your child's passport photo yourself.

Guidelines for Taking Your Child's Passport Photo:

- Your child should appear against a plain white background—a simple bed sheet, blanket, or white wall will suffice.

- Your child's face should appear in full view, looking directly at the camera (think "nose level"). If your child is still an infant, enlist a helper to prop him up against one hand, or simply photograph him lying down and looking straight up at the camera. Just be sure your photo is not taken at a strange angle and doesn't obscure part of his face.

- The final photos should be 2" x 2", with your child's face (from chin to top of head, including any hair) appearing at least 1" and not more than 1 3/8".

TRAVELS WITH ONE PARENT, GRANDPARENTS, OR OTHER ADULT ESCORTS

If you will be traveling with your child across international borders without her other parent—whether by airplane, automobile, train or cruise ship— you must have a notarized letter of consent from the other parent which includes the names of all children traveling, name of adult(s) accompanying children, dates of travel, method of travel (e.g. cruise line, airline) countries to be visited, and the consenting parents' contact information. The same situation applies when a child will be traveling abroad with his grandparents or other adults that are not his parents, and a similar letter will need to be written and signed by both parents, and notarized.

Following is a sample letter of consent you may customize for your trip. Also included in the sample letter is a clause giving permission to the "trip custodian" to authorize any necessary routine or emergency medical treatment during the trip—which is especially recommended when a child will be traveling without either parent.

If you are legally the sole guardian of the traveling child, you may instead provide the legal documentation that names you as such, be it a court order of sole custodianship, a death certificate, a birth certificate that names only you as parent to the child, or an adoption decree.

Sample Letter of Consent for One Parent Traveler:

Date: [DATE OF WRITING]

I/we [YOUR NAME] give consent for my/our minor child(ren) [CHILD OR CHILDREN'S FULL NAMES] to travel to [NAMES OF ALL COUNTRIES TO BE VISITED] with [FULL NAME(S) OF ADULT TRAVEL COMPANION(S)] from [DATE OF DEPARTURE] to [DATE OF RETURN] aboard:

[LIST ALL AIRLINES AND FLIGHT NUMBERS, CRUISE LINES, TRAIN NUMBERS, OR STATE "BY AUTOMOBILE"].

In addition, I/we give permission to [NAMED ADULT TRAVEL COMPANION(S)] to authorize any necessary routine or emergency medical treatment for our child(ren) during this trip.

If needed, I/we may be contacted at:
[YOUR PHONE NUMBER(S)]
[YOUR ADDRESS]

[YOUR PRINTED NAME(S)]
[YOUR SIGNED NAME(S)]

Notary's printed name:
Notary's signature and seal:

Passports for Canadian Children

For citizens of Canada, applying for your child's first passport is a similar process, but a few key differences apply.

- **Children under 3 years of age** – Passports issued to children in this age range are valid for no more than 3 years. Children who receive their first passports before their first birthdays are also allowed a one-time free replacement passport, valid for the duration of the original passport's 3 year period, to help ensure the photo is a "true likeness" of the child. Current fee: $22 Canadian.

- **Children 3 to 15 years of age** – Passports issued to children in this age range are valid for 5 years. Current fee: $37 Canadian.

- **Passport photos** – Dimensions of Canadian passport photos should be 2" wide by 2 ¾" long. Canadians residing in the U.S. may submit U.S.-size passport photos, however.

- **You need not apply in person** – You may send your child's application by mail, but you must have the Declaration of Guarantor section of the form completed by an eligible guarantor who has known you for at least 2 years. The guarantor must also sign a statement on the back of one of your child's passport photos to certify that it is a true likeness of the child.

Printable forms and instructions are online at www.pptc.gc.ca/forms, or you can call 1-800-567-6868 from within Canada or 1-819—997-8338 from the U.S. and other countries. For Canadian children residing in Canada, use form PPTC 046, or use PPTC 142 for Canadian citizens residing in the U.S. Canadian children traveling across borders with one parent or other caregivers should also carry with them a notarized letter of consent, similar to the sample shown on page 100.

Parents and Children with Different Names

Parents should be prepared to provide proof of their relationship to their child in spite of the difference in names appearing on passports, e.g. a mother that has chosen to keep her maiden name, which is different from her child's surname. Most commonly, a notarized copy of a birth certificate that lists both parents can be used to provide this information. When traveling abroad, even hyphenated last names may cause confusion at some borders, so any extra documentation that may help explain your naming convention and expedite your crossing could be of help.

Convenient Conversions

Renting car seats, buying diapers, reading the weather forecast… there will likely be times on your trip that you'll need to know weights and measures in the local system. Before you leave, at least be sure to jot down your child's current weight and height in metric in case you need it.

Temperatures in Celsius and Fahrenheit (Rounded Off)

0°C	32°F
7° C	45°F
15°C	60°F
24°C	75°F
30°C	85°F
35°C	95°F
40°C	104°F

Normal body temperature: 37°C or 98.6°F

Children's Weights in Pounds and Kilograms:

7 lbs = 3 kgs

10 lbs = 4 ½ kgs

13 lbs = 6 kgs

17 ½ lbs = 8 kgs

22 lbs = 10 kgs

33 lbs = 15 kgs

44 lbs = 20 kgs

55 lbs = 25 kgs

67 lbs = 30 kgs

80 lbs = 36 kgs

Children's Heights in Centimeters:

18.5" = 47 cm

22" = 56 cm

25" = 63.5 cm

28" – 71 cm

30" = 76.2 cm

32" = 81 cm

35" = 89 cm

38" = 96.5 cm

41" = 104 cm

45" = 114 cm

48" = 122 cm

At Least They'll Speak "English"

When choosing a destination abroad, your little family may find it somewhat comforting to choose one that frees you from carrying a traveler's phrase book in your already crowded diaper bag. But that would be too easy, and hardly worthy of the stamp in your passport. So as your little Ambassador of Goodwill launches you into conversations with the Queen's locals or other members of the ex-Commonwealth, you may find it helpful to commit to memory a little of the baby-speak. If it begins to sound a bit silly to you, just remember that *they* are the ones speaking English.

American	*English*
Stroller	Pushchair
Travel stroller	Buggy
Baby buggy	Perambulator (or pram)
Pacifier	Dummy
Diapers	Nappies
Crib	Cot
Portacrib	Travel cot
Airplane bassinet	Sky cot
Infant car seat	Baby Capsule (Australia)

Preparing for Cultural Differences

Your guidebook warns you to cover your shoulders when visiting the sacred places, to remove your shoes when entering a home, and to never place your chopsticks on your bowl in "prayer" position. But there are some cultural differences that only the traveler with a baby may appreciate.

Hands Off My Baby!

Throughout much of the world, and in Asian cultures especially, it is considered quite normal and even polite to touch a stranger's baby when expressing admiration and affection for the child. Stroking cheeks, tickling feet, and squeezing hands (that almost immediately go back into the mouth) may happen at any turn.

We were shocked as everyone from flight attendants, security guards, taxi drivers, and street sweepers (while holding the trash collection bag in her other hand) had their hands on our baby before we could blink. But we soon came to appreciate the times when strangers only briefly pinched her cheeks or held her hands before allowing us to go on our way.

A quick clap of the hands and extension of the arms is code for, "Give me the baby." Although holding a stranger's baby is considered a perfectly normal expectation to many people in the East, it can be extremely alarming to the average American parent, who would never dream of passing her child off to a stranger—especially in a foreign land. If your child is secured in a frontpack carrier or stroller, you have one immediate layer of defense, which makes it much easier to smile and continue on your way.

In restaurants and on airplanes, you may have a more difficult time politely escaping the requests of your child's admirers. But if you aren't comfortable letting strangers hold your child, don't. Just remember, your obligation is first and foremost to your child, not random strangers you meet on your journey. If you still feel awkward, or cornered, just say your child is shy, or explain that it's naptime and you don't want to excite the little one.

Attracting Older Women

In places like Korea, India, and Italy, where grandmothers play a key role in the upbringing of children, older women may especially show an interest in your child—every time you turn around. Get ready. Grandma knows why your baby is crying. Grandma knows what your baby needs. And rest assured, Grandma can help. She will tell you what you need to know (even if you can't understand a word she's saying).

Try not to take offense if you are offered suggestions or unsolicited advice. Remember that you are a guest in someone else's country, and you wouldn't be there if you didn't have some interest in experiencing the culture. Smile. Nod. Say, "Thank you, Grandma," as you high-tail it on to your next destination.

One American mother living in Italy quickly came to accept that any time she left her house with the baby, she'd better bring a sweater — even on a hot summer's day. Every twenty paces along the city street, another grandma would stop her to admire the baby and quickly convey the shock and horror that the baby was too cold and she needed to put on its sweater right away. Twenty paces later, another grandma would insist that the baby was too hot and the sweater must come off at once. Twenty more paces, and the child would die of exposure if the sweater wasn't put on at once.

Trips to the market became exhausting for mother and child alike, but she quickly discovered it was much easier to bring the sweater along than to have a grandma follow her all the way home, to make sure she got more clothing for the baby.

The "Tourist Attraction"

In some cultures, children are so revered that you may find your family surrounded by a small crowd of locals at times, especially if yours is the first child of its kind that they've seen in real life (with light hair and light eyes, in particular). It can, at times, border on frustrating as you try to make your way to the dock on time, compete for a taxi cab, or breastfeed your baby without a flock of strangers snapping photos with cellular phones. Or as you enter a much-anticipated holy site in respectful barefooted silence, only to find an enthusiastic group of worshippers facing not the Golden Buddha before you, but the golden child in your arms. Hands are no longer pressed together in prayer, but are clapping along to sing-song rhymes as they compete for the biggest smiles from your child. If it should happen to you, embrace the moment. It may well become one of your fondest memories of travel with your child.

Breastfeeding and Other Cultures

Although breastfeeding is "back in fashion" in much of North America, as in much of Western society, there are still pockets where you'll find people unaccustomed to seeing babies nurse, especially in public and social situations—which is where you'll often find yourself as a traveler.

Some mothers have found they are actually more comfortable nursing their children abroad than they are doing so at home in North America. Of course, this can depend on which part of the continent you call home. Berkeley, California, held the first Guinness World Record for simultaneous breastfeeding, and with good reason; breastfeeding is so commonplace in the San Francisco Bay Area that a new mother may actually feel more conspicuous bottle-feeding in public than she would be nursing a child.

Many Latin and Asian cultures in particular hold fast to the notion that breastfeeding is only done out of necessity by those who cannot afford to bottle-feed their children. I have seen mothers become stunned when they realize that I, an American woman who can afford to travel the world, have chosen to breastfeed my babies. But clearly, awareness of the benefits to both mother and child is growing worldwide. Recently, the Guinness World Record for the most women simultaneously breastfeeding their children was broken in, of all places, Manila, the Philippines! When it comes down to it, I think you'll find that regardless of race, class, or nationality, most people would much prefer to see a happy, breastfed baby than listen to a crying, hungry one.

What is most important is that you are as comfortable nursing as you can be, regardless of where you roam. If you find your comfort level is affected by the comfort levels of the people around you, there may be times when *you* would be more comfortable nursing in private. Likewise, there may be times when your child may also feed much better in a quiet setting where there are few distractions. If you need to, don't hesitate to ask waiters, museum guards, or tour guides where you might find a quiet spot to sit down with your baby.

SIGHTSEEING WITH PRIVATE GUIDES AND ESCORTS

As experienced do-it-ourselves adventurers, my husband and I explored many a foreign city entirely by public transportation and by foot—in our pre-parent lives. We were "low-to-the ground" and loving it, catching glimpses of local life and seeing cities block-by-block-by-block (whether the blocks held any particular interest or not).

At some destinations abroad, this may still be the best way to explore with your child as well, pushing the stroller along, wearing the backpack carrier, or letting your child stretch his own legs, all the while discovering any hidden city parks or points of interest along the way. In others, it may be well worth joining a small group on an organized tour for a half or full day, especially where:

- The heat or air pollution may be oppressive, and especially hard on your child
- Public transportation is not reliable or is nonexistent
- The sites you wish to visit are far from one another, or from your accommodations
- A language barrier may make it difficult to get the most from your visit
- Your family's safety may otherwise be at risk.

While visiting Bangkok with our daughter, one of the best moves we made was to take a half-day escorted tour of the temples with an English-speaking guide. With just six of us along for the ride (plus our daughter) in an air-conditioned minivan, we had no trouble hearing our guide or getting answers to our questions. And after spending his entire life in the city, our guide taught us far more about the city and culture than our guidebooks offered us. At the same time, we befriended a handful of folks from the farthest English-speaking corners of the globe. Before we left Thailand, we'd opted to join a couple of similar groups in other regions, and we still have a hard time imagining how we could have seen, done, and learned half as much on our own—especially while attending to the needs of our daughter.

These day trips and half-day trips can be more affordable than you might expect, especially when you consider the alternative cost of a car rental, insurance, gas, entrance fees and any fees for an audio or a human guide. However, your "baby" (if riding along for free) will probably be expected to ride in your lap—with no space allotted for a car seat. Depending on the size of the vehicle (a typical city bus, mini bus or motor coach doesn't typically offer seatbelts anyway), the destinations and route, and your comfort level with the entire picture of the specific outing, you may wish to reconsider—or inquire if you can buy an extra ticket for your child's seat. If you are visiting a destination where taxis and private vehicles do not typically have seatbelts for rear passengers (India, Thailand, etc.), traveling in a larger vehicle like a minibus may actually be your safest option on the road.

If you decide to join a group, it is always a good idea to contact the tour operator before booking and fill them in about your situation (an infant in a sling travels easily through ruins or past priceless frescoes, a walking 2-year-old is another situation), and ask them plenty of questions about theirs, like:

- Are there restrooms available at each stop—and time to use them?
- Are children welcome at all the tour stops?
- How much time is spent driving (it may be more than you think)?

Your hotel can probably put you in touch with some local travel agencies offering excursions, or visit the city or region's Web site to see if they have recommended local excursions and guides. You can also visit www.grayline.com to get an idea of what tours are available at your destination.

Another option may be to hire your own private car and driver—an especially great option when you have two children or more, or would simply like more flexibility. For example, in Cancun you can hire a van that seats up to 12 people for one flat day rate (10 hours) with a driver and cooler included, and choose your own start time and destination (Tulum, Chichen Itza, etc.). You can make as many stops for swimming, refreshments, photos, and diaper changes as you like along the way. Or pay $35 per hour for open service to do your local sightseeing and shopping (www.cancunvalet.com or 011-52-998-848-3634).

To line up private sightseeing excursions for your family in some of the world's most popular destinations—and in some of its most remote, visit www.octopustravel.com. Popular excursions and prices are posted for destinations on all continents.

- *Chapter 7* -
Health "Ensurance"

PRE-TRIP TIPS FOR HEALTHY TRAVELS

The best way to deal with illness or injury during your vacation is to avoid it in the first place. As Ben Franklin liked to say, "An ounce of prevention is worth a pound of cure," and that's certainly the case when traveling—especially with a child. Here are ten things to do before your trip to help ensure your crew stays as healthy as possible during your travels.

1. **Visit the Center for Disease Control's Web site** at www.CDC.gov to read up on any health issues, risks, or advice pertaining to your destination.
2. **Drink plenty of water** the days leading up to your trip, as well as during your trip. It will help keep your body functioning at optimal levels and make you less vulnerable to illness.
3. **Make sure everyone's vaccinations are up-to-date**, including the adults. Schedules are available for both at www.CDC.gov.

4. **Consider getting flu shots** if they are available. (See more in following section.)
5. **Have your child visit the pediatrician** for a check-up before your trip. It's a good opportunity to update any vaccinations, check the ears one last time (especially if they are prone to infection), and weigh-in so the proper dosage of medicine may be given if needed during the trip.
6. **Make sure mom and dad have supportive, practical shoes** that are well broken-in before the trip begins. Travelers tend to spend a lot of time on their feet as it is, and traveling parents often have the added weight of their children on their feet as well. Nothing slows down a traveler like blisters or, worse, a twisted ankle.
7. **Stash travel packs of antibacterial "Redi-Wipes" or "Wet Ones"** (premoistened hand wipes) in the sides of purses, diaper bags, day packs, etc. and use often to fend off mischievous microbes that may thwart your travel plans. As you pack for your trip, be sure to include them in your carryon.
8. **Check the status of your child's travel kit** (page 44).
9. **Make sure everyone will have appropriate clothing that fits** to handle the full range of weather conditions you may encounter, including surprises. Lack of warm clothing or adequate sun protection, for example, can create extra stress for the body and make you vulnerable.
10. **Keep a healthy attitude!** As Deepak Chopra writes in *Ageless Body, Timeless Mind*, "Our cells are constantly eavesdropping on our thoughts and being changed by them. A bout of depression can wreak havoc with the immune system; falling in love can boost it." So if you haven't already, fall in love with your trip and the idea of traveling with your child!

HAVING FUN IN (SPITE OF) THE SUN

It's no secret that little ones have more sensitive skin than adults, and that includes a sensitivity to the sun's harmful rays—and the products created to help absorb them. Most of this sensitivity is due to the baby's developing skin still being relatively thin, and even naturally darker-skinned babies can sunburn far more easily than older children. For these reasons, it's best to avoid sun exposure as much as possible for all children less than one year of age.

Fortunately, there are many ways to minimize baby's sun exposure without passing his entire first summer indoors with the shades drawn. Although an adult's first precaution is often to "lube up" with a powerful sunscreen, such products should only be considered back up to other methods of sun protection where babies and young children are concerned. Be aware that the American Academy of Pediatrics does not recommend the use of sunscreens—even those formulated for babies and small children—on babies younger than six months.

Even older babies can be sensitive to the active ingredients in sunscreen, so be sure to use only a product made for children, and to first test on a small area of your child's skin. As with an adult's sunscreen, be sure it provides protection from both UVA and UVB rays, and reapply at least as often as the label advises, even if the lotion is "waterproof." (Avoid using sunscreens that contain the insect repellent DEET. See next section on Managing Mosquitoes, beginning on page 113 for more information.) If a child under the age of one develops a sunburn, you should contact your pediatrician right away.

Here are some tips to help minimize sun exposure on your vacation. For more ideas, see Great Products for Healthy Travels, page 118.

1. **Bring portable shade** – Pop-up sun tents and sun canopy extensions or UV shields for strollers can all help your child stay cool and protected, and fold compactly for travel.

2. **Wear UV-protective clothing** – Available now in everything from swimwear to casual corporate attire, it blocks far more harmful UV rays than clothing alone. Many garments are also designed for maximum coverage with clever ventilation and/or moisture-wicking capabilities.

3. **Rent the umbrella** – Beaches often leave babies exposed without escape from the sun. If sun umbrellas are available for rent, waste no time in renting one (they may run out as the crowd thickens). If

deciding between a public beach or paying admission to a private one, the extra facilities—including shade umbrellas—at the private beach may be well worth it, and may enable you to enjoy more time at the beach as well.

MANAGING MOSQUITOES

In the past, mosquito bites were regarded as little more than a nuisance outside of malaria-risk zones (malaria prevention addressed on page 128). But now there is growing concern for other mosquito-transmitted diseases, such as West Nile Virus as far north as Canada—especially among parents of young children and infants. But before you grab the can of mosquito repellent this summer, be aware that traditional insect repellents contain the active ingredient DEET, which studies have indicated may be especially harmful to children.

The American Academy of Pediatrics (AAP) advises against using DEET-containing products on babies under 2 months of age, and the Canadian Pediatric Society advises against using DEET on babies under 6 months of age. Both organizations agree that young children should receive no more than one application per day, and in a low concentration not to exceed 10% (most products for children are 4.5%). The AAP also discourages parents from using products that combine repellents with a sunscreen as DEET is not water-soluble and the amount of DEET on a child increases each time the sunscreen must be reapplied.

Fortunately, there are many DEET-free ways to deter mosquitoes. The most obvious way to avoid a brush with the blood-suckers is to simply stay away from them, or at least avoid areas where they thrive, especially during their peak hours. Mosquitoes are most active around dawn and dusk, so plan your outings accordingly.

You can also employ physical barriers such as mosquito nets, many of which are now made specifically to fit around strollers, cribs, infant carriers, and beds. Tots in Mind makes a two-piece net system created to works on strollers as well as full-size cribs and play yards (get help finding mosquito nets at TravelswithBaby.com). Long-sleeved shirts, pants, and hats are also helpful, but keep in mind that mosquitoes can bite through loosely woven fabrics. (The tighter the weave, the better the sleeve.)

You may have also heard of various bath and plant-based oils that can be used to help repel insects. Soybean oil, for example, has indeed been found to effectively repel mosquitoes from humans, and it was recently added to Canada's list of registered insect repellents. This oil may provide protection from mosquitoes from one to 3 ½ hours, depending on the product (more info follows).

Lavender oil and bath oils like Avon's Skin-so-Soft may also be used, but their effectiveness is limited to less than an hour, and lavender oil itself is considered effective for only 30 minutes or less. (Citronella-containing products are not recommended for children under the age of 2.) As well, tests of wristbands and electronic sound deterrents have been found to be ineffective in repelling mosquitoes.

And Now, For Some Good News...

According to a study published in *The New England Journal of Medicine* comparing DEET and non-DEET products, "Only the soybean-oil-based repellent was able to provide protection for a period similar to that of the lowest-concentration DEET product we tested" ("Comparative Efficacy of Insect Repellents Against Mosquito Bites," N Engl J Med, Vol. 347, No. 1; July 4, 2002). As the parent of an infant or small child, you will be interested to know that the "lowest-concentration DEET product" they refer to was a product formulated for children: OFF! Skintastic for Kids (SC Johnson). The soybean oil-based product they tested was also formulated for children: Bite Blocker for Kids (HOMS). Since then, HOMS has created an even longer-lasting formulation that is also safe for use on babies and children — meaning the new, DEET-free Bite Blocker product may actually outlast many DEET-containing products for children. We first tried Bite Blocker on our family's trip to Thailand, and with much success. And after using it on my own babies, I can confidently recommend it to other parents.

10 DEET-Free Ways to Help Prevent Mosquito Bites

Before giving up on the family camping trip or the eco-tour, consider these simple, DEET-free ways many travelers have found to help prevent mosquito bites.

1. Avoid using scented shampoos or lotions on Baby—or yourself, as sweet fragrances attract mosquitoes.
2. Dress yourself and your baby in lighter, plain-colored attire as bright colors attract mosquitoes—and yellow jackets as well. (Also keep this in mind as you choose toys and gear to bring along.)
3. Use mosquito nets designed to fit around strollers and infant carriers.
4. Avoid mosquito-prone areas at dusk and dawn as much as possible.
5. Find out which time of year mosquitoes are least problematic at your destination and try to visit at that time.
6. When camping, try to choose a site as far away from still or slow-moving bodies of water as possible.
7. In severe mosquito zones, look for air-conditioned lodgings where mosquitoes are least likely to penetrate your sleeping quarters.
8. Apply Avon Skin-So-Soft mixed with rubbing alcohol to exposed skin.
9. Have the entire family take cool showers or baths after a hot afternoon since mosquitoes can be drawn to skin's heat, scent, and perspiration.
10. Use a soybean oil-based repellant such as Bite Blocker on exposed skin.

Guidelines for Using DEET-Containing Products on Children

If you feel the risk of mosquito-borne disease at your destination warrants the use DEET on your child, take care to not apply it to their hands, nor over scrapes or irritated skin, nor underneath clothing. Also be sure to keep sprays from getting into children's eyes, and wash off with soap after the risk of mosquito bites is passed. Here are some general guidelines to play it safe when using DEET with small children.

- Never use DEET-containing products on a child under 2 months old.

- Only use DEET-containing products as a last resort, when other measures will not sufficiently protect children against the risk of mosquito-borne disease.
- Do not apply DEET to children under 2 years more than once per 24 hours.
- Only use a product that is created specifically for children.

BREASTFEEDING FOR HEALTHY TRAVELS

If you are breastfeeding, there are plenty of reasons why you may want to continue doing so through your upcoming travels. Most obvious is the convenience of having nourishment on-demand, with nothing to pack, wash, refrigerate or warm-up along the way. But there are other advantages to breastfeeding while traveling as well, particularly where your child's health is concerned.

Boosted immunity – According to the United States Breastfeeding Committee, breastfed children "are less likely to suffer from infectious illnesses and their symptoms (e.g., diarrhea, ear infections, respiratory tract infections, and meningitis)." As you travel the world—or your neighborhood, your body creates antibodies to counteract the illness-causing germs that you encounter (ahh-choo!). These antibodies can be passed along to your child through your breast milk to help boost her immunity to the same bugs she has likely encountered. In their widely acclaimed resource *The Breastfeeding Book*, Martha and William Sears report that a drop of breast milk contains around one million white blood cells, which can help a baby resist infection. That's powerful medicine—without medicine.

Sterile source of nourishment – Having to sterilize bottles and find suitable water for drinking and mixing formula can complicate travel with infants and small children and increase the risk of illness. But with breast milk on tap, you can nourish and hydrate your child anytime and anywhere in your journey—and without worry of water safety issues concerning other travelers.

Ease of water absorption for child – Because breast milk is absorbed so perfectly in an infant's digestive system, there is no need to supplement with water in addition to breastfeeding, even when traveling in extreme heat or suffering from diarrhea.

Supply and demand – You needn't worry over how much to have prepared for the flight or day of sightseeing, how many bottles or nipples or sippy cups you'll need to have clean and ready, or how to handle the surprise growth spurt during your vacation. Your traveling child has perfect nutrition, regardless of flight or train delays, or heightened airport security regulations.

Breastfeeding Resources for Traveling Mothers

These organizations can provide you with breastfeeding information and support before or during your trip.

La Leche League International

The Web site includes information on breastfeeding and culture in some select regions around the world, with local contact information for many chapters around the world. http://www.lalecheleague.org or 1-800-LALECHE.

International Lactation Consultant Association (ILCA)

Find an International Board Certified Lactation Consultant in destinations across the U.S. and around the world. www.ilca.org or 1-919-861-5577.

Mini waterless vaporizer – Sooths stuffy noses and dry throats with aromatic oils warmed in a small "plug" used in a standard electrical outlet, similar to plug-in style air fresheners. PediaCare and Sudacare both make non-medicated versions for children with refill pads available.

Hyland's Calms Forté 4 Kids – A homeopathic remedy claimed to: temporarily relieve the symptoms of restlessness, sleeplessness, night terrors, growing pains, causeless crying, occasional sleeplessness due to travel and lack of focus in children. Dry, quick-dissolve tablets can be brought into the cabin. Package has dosage for children 2 years and older; discuss appropriateness and dosage for younger children and babies with your pediatrician. Available in most health food stores.

BiteBlocker insect repellent – A soybean-oil-based insect repellent made by HOMS that is safe for use on small children. Available in spray and lotion formulas.

EarPlanes – Soft ear "filters" (similar to ear plugs) that help regulate air pressure in the Eustachian tubes and prevent discomfort, particularly while flying. The child size is for ages 1 to 10 years, but you may want to wait until your child is old enough to know better than to eat them.

The indispensable sun hat – Your best bets will brim over on all sides and have some form of strap to help keep the hat on in a breeze or when the child inspects it. An extended back flap will help guard the gap that sometimes forms between shirt and hair (good designs at www.flaphappy.com). Keep an extra in the day bag in case the primary blows overboard or otherwise disappears.

Wide-brimmed hat for parent carrying a baby – We call it "the sombrero effect." Don't forget to shade thyself—and you may sometimes help shade your child in the process.

Pop-up shade tents – Great for creating a shady retreat on sunny beaches and in campsites where shade is scarce and sun is plentiful. Many models include sand pockets on the sides to help keep them in place, plus windows that can tie up for increased ventilation, or tie down for increased UV protection when desired.

Rear and side car window shades - They not only shield your child from the sun, but also help keep the car's internal temperature down. Available in roll-up styles, with suction cups, and static clings—including a photochromic (light sensing) shade for improved visibility from One Step Ahead. The First Years makes a fabric shade for the rear window of sedans that can be especially helpful for backseat passengers.

SPF clothing and swimwear – Hi-tech fabrics can now offer little ones UPF 50+ protection (up to 98% of the sun's rays). A wide variety of hats and clothing are available for infants through preschoolers, including ultra lightweight jogging-style suits complete with built-in vents and sun protection hoods, and sporty-looking swim attire styled after wetsuits. Another plus: Many of these fabrics clean up easily and dry overnight (if not sooner). Check out those made by One Step Ahead (www.onestepahead.com), Solartex (www.solartex.com), and Coolibar (www.coolibar.com).

Light, white, cotton clothing (long sleeves and pants) – It's hard to beat the basics. Cotton breathes well and feels good against the skin. In its lightest colors, it also helps to keep temperatures down and mosquitoes at bay.

Infant, toddler, and children's sunglasses – A small selection is available, though the most popular continue to be Baby Banz and Kidz Banz sunglasses with soft straps that go behind the head to help keep them in place. For the picky baby, SoftShades offer the comfort of wrap-around foam.

The Tropic Screen – It's a fully enclosed, lightweight pop-up mosquito/insect protection tent. Available in both single and double sizes based on adult-size sleeping cots.

- *Chapter 8* -
Going Farther Afield

Food and Water Safety

Hepatitis, Giardia, and Salmonella are not words that often headline travel brochures, but they are among just a few of the harmful microbes a tourist may experience first-hand if he doesn't exercise some caution when eating and drinking far from home.

As the CDC and countless travelers advise, "Boil it, cook it, peel it or forget it!" especially when it comes to foods for your children. Babies and children, given their inexperienced digestive systems and immature immune systems, are far more susceptible to food- and water-borne illnesses than their parents. But the temptation of icy fruit drinks and treats can be a real and regular temptation that you may have to confront, particularly when offered directly to your child by well meaning strangers. Trying to assuage a picky eater may make it even more tempting to okay the ring of pineapple or mango lassi that peaks her interest. For small children, this can be a dire mistake.

To find out if your destination is considered to have a high risk for food- or water-borne diseases, visit the CDC's Web site at www.CDC.gov/travel. You can also see the drinking water safety rating for countries worldwide at the Safe Water for International Travelers Web site: www.safewateronline.com.

Guidelines for Safe Dining and Drinking

If you are traveling to an area where food and water safety is a real concern, be prepared to:

Avoid foods from street vendors – as friendly and generous as they may be, they often have little or no refrigeration available for the foods they prepare, and likely do not have a place to wash their hands with clean water and soap.

Dine in restaurants frequented by many western travelers – they are more accustomed to satisfying western stomachs and standards, and if they don't, you would probably have heard about it. Restaurants in larger chain hotels are generally a safe bet, and ask for recommendations from other travelers, and/or hotel staff, and check online ahead of time for traveler recommendations on sites like www.tripadvisor.com.

Prepare some of your own meals – Even if you are staying in a room without a kitchen, your family can still enjoy some of the local produce brought home and washed carefully. If you will be staying somewhere with cooking facilities, you may have better luck satisfying your child's tastes and save money by cooking your own meals—not to mention, you can make sure your foods are thoroughly washed and cooked. A trip to a local market and experimenting with local foods can also be a fun way to experience your destination.

Bring along plenty of snacks – Nonperishable snacks in the daypack can be critical in staving off hunger between the sights when other options, like street vendors and small restaurants, may pose a risk. Dried fruit, energy bars, granola bars, packaged cheese and cracker "kits", sealed packages of applesauce, and crackers are quite portable and can be brought from home. (And there's nothing like peanut butter on crackers to help with the midnight munchies of a jetlagged traveler.) You can also pick up sealed and safe packaged foods in local markets.

Drink sealed, bottled water and beverages – A general rule of thumb is to not accept any bottled water you haven't broken the seal of yourself, and the same is true for other beverages when visiting questionable establishments (where your soda may be watered down, but the profits are not). If the bottled water isn't a brand you recognize, check the label for "IBWA" (International Bottled Water Association) or "NSF" (National Sanitation Foundation) certification. Fresh-squeezed and prepared juices should be thought of as the triple threat: as delicious as they may be, they can harbor hazardous germs from either the fruit, the water, or the ice (not to mention the hands preparing them), so it is generally best to avoid them and stick to packaged and bottled juices.

Pass on the ice – Even if you've made sure your drinks are safe, the ice could still be a big gamble. Few establishments actually make ice from bottled water, and those that do will likely include a mention on the menu. Freezing water does not kill the harmful microbes that may be in it.

Bring prepared formula – If you are using formula for your child, it may be safest and easiest to pack a cardboard box (or extra suitcase) of pre-mixed formula that is ready to serve and requires no water. If refrigeration isn't available for the leftover portions, or you will be gone too long for this to be practical, you may need to make due with bottled water, in which case you may be glad if you packed a few starter bottles of water from home (again, a checked cardboard box may be helpful) until you can purchase more from a trustworthy source at your destination. Distilled water is preferable to "spring water" or "mineral water" as it won't interfere with the balance of minerals already present in the formula.

Bring it to a boil – If you need to boil water for safe consumption, the rule of thumb is to let it boil for one full minute, or for three minutes at high elevations (over 6,562 feet or 2,000 meters). Boiling drinking water for extended periods of time is not recommended as it can increase the concentration of lead in the water. (Note: The kinds of water filters commonly used by backpackers do not filter out many worrisome microbes, including Giardia, so travelers who use these are still advised to boil or purify their water after filtering.)

Purify in a pinch – If all else fails, be prepared to purify some water yourself with purification tablets available at most outdoor stores and pharmacies. Bring your own water bottle(s) from home and head out each day with your own safe supply (a 1-liter water bottle will simplify things since it is usually 1 tablet to 1 liter of water). Since purification does little to improve the flavor of drinking water, you may also want to pack along a little powdered Gatorade or Kool-Aid to mix in for good measure—you will all need to drink plenty of water, so make it as enticing as possible!

Wash and sterilize with care – Although the tap water in U.S. cities is now considered safe enough for washing infants' bottles, it would be prudent to raise your standards when you travel. Especially if the water from the tap is not considered drinkable where you stay, do not use it untreated for washing bottles and nipples, nor sippy cups, reusable water bottles, and the like (air-drying does not necessarily kill the critters). The same care should be taken with any teething toys, pacifiers, or other items that go into your child's mouth.

Wash the hand that feeds you – All of these precautions will do little good if, in the end, you don't wash your hands and those of your children before eating. Keep antibacterial "Redi-Wipes" or "Wet Ones" in your daypack and use them often—especially for children whose hands frequently find their way into their mouths (mealtime or not).

Small Children Swimming Abroad

Nobody likes the thought of it, but the truth is some amount of sewage may be present in the water we swim in at beaches, in lakes, in streams, and even in swimming pools—even in our own hometowns. Human and animal feces can carry with it any number of diseases, many of which can survive for long periods of time in salt water and in chlorinated pools and spas. And since babies and small children are the most likely candidates to swallow some of the water they are swimming in, parents should exercise extreme caution when deciding where to let their children swim, especially when visiting destinations where standards for sanitation and sewage treatment are not as high as those at home.

Waterborne illnesses are especially common:

- Where the diseases already thrive (illness begets illness)
- Where the waste water is not treated or strictly regulated
- Where spas or hot tub temperatures help the chlorine evaporate quickly
- Where swimming pools receive inadequate or insufficient maintenance
- Where babies and very young children play in the water, diapered or not.

Although a host of skin, ear, and upper respiratory illnesses can be contracted through swimming, diarrheal illnesses are by far the most common ailments contracted by swimming, and it should be noted that an infected person who has been suffering from diarrhea can spread the disease in water even without having an accident. (If you are sick, kindly stay out of the water!)

You can check for waterborne illness advisories at the destination you'll be visiting at the CDC's Web site: www.cdc.gov/travel or www.safewateronline.com. Depending on where you travel, your safest bet may be to avoid taking your child swimming.

Wherever you vacation, remember that babies and small children, even in swim diapers, contribute to the communal pool of germs when their stool comes in contact with the water. So if your child does go swimming or wading, please do your part as a parent to keep your child diapered in the water and change those swim diapers frequently.

VACCINATIONS AND TRAVEL SHOTS

Modified Immunizations for Babies and Small Children

It's especially important that your child's immunizations be up-to-date when traveling because, while many of these diseases may now be rare or nonexistent in the U.S., they are still common in other parts of the world. Since the recommended immunization schedule for infants and children in the U.S. does not account for international travel at very young ages, your child's physician may advise an accelerated schedule for certain immunizations. Be sure to discuss your travel plans and timeline with your child's physician, and address any upcoming immunizations that may need to be adjusted for your timeline for travel. The U.S. recommended childhood immunization schedule is available at www.aap.org and www.cdc.gov (where you'll also find further discussion on this topic). You will also need to find out if additional travel shots are advisable for you or your child for your destination.

Travel Shots for Babies and Small Children

When traveling abroad, be sure to check with the Center for Disease control (www.cdc.gov or 1-877-FYI-TRIP) for any health advisories concerning the area you'll be visiting, including additional travel shots that may be recommended or required for you or your child. Any decisions about vaccinations for your child should be made with the help of a qualified healthcare provider who will consider the specifics of your trip, your child's age, and medical history. Plan a talk with your child's physician and/or a professional at a travel health clinic.

As mentioned earlier, your child's routine immunizations cover most major illnesses of concern to travelers, but some modification of the schedule may be needed for babies and young children traveling abroad. You should consider updating your own immunizations before traveling as well. The recommended adult immunization schedule is also available on the CDC Web site. Since most vaccinations require four to six weeks to become fully effective, do not delay any vaccinations needed for your trip.

Flu and Flu Shots

If you will be traveling during flu season, discuss your plans with your pediatrician and find out when the flu vaccination may be available for your child. Children under the age of 5 receive the inactivated influenza vaccine that is given as a shot; children age 5 and older may be given the nasal mist

125

flu vaccine. Since the flu virus itself is a moving target, the vaccination must be updated annually to remain effective against the latest strain.

If you would like your child to receive a flu shot, do so as soon as possible to avoid untimely infection and the possibility of a vaccination shortage. As fellow travelers and the primary caregivers for your child, it may be wise for you and your partner to get vaccinated, too. And remember, the official "flu season" can vary by destination.

Flu seasons around the world

Northern Hemisphere: November – February

Southern Hemisphere: April – September

The Tropics: All year long…

Common Travel Shots

Hepatitis A – Destinations worldwide

Children do not commonly receive their first Hepatitis A vaccination until 2 years of age. If your child will be eating table foods where food and water safety is a concern, consult with your pediatrician to find out whether an earlier vaccination or immune globulin (IG) shot is advisable. Throughout much of the world, the disease is quite common, so it is a good idea to keep the whole family current with this vaccination.

Yellow Fever Vaccine – Africa and South America

Because Yellow Fever, a disease transmitted by mosquitoes, is very common in some parts of Africa and South America, proof of yellow fever vaccination is required for entry into some countries (visit www.cdc.gov to see if your destination is among them). However, the CDC reports that infants are at a high risk for developing encephalitis from the vaccine (which contains live virus). The vaccine is not given to children under 6 months of age. The CDC advises that the vaccination be postponed until the child is at least 9-12 months old if possible, and to avoid travel to yellow fever regions before a child is 9 months of age. Yellow fever vaccinations can only be given at designated clinics; locations by state are available at www.cdc.gov or by calling 1-877-FYI-TRIP. Be sure you receive your certificate of proof of this vaccination, and keep it with your travel documents to avoid any hassles.

Typhoid – Destinations worldwide

Typhoid fever is transmitted from person to person, usually through contaminated food and water. Therefore, practicing food and beverage safety smarts should be your first line of defense against this disease. Children 2 years and older may also receive a vaccination to help prevent Typhoid.

Vaccinations for Breastfeeding Mothers

According to the Centers for Disease Control and Prevention, many travel vaccinations and routine immunizations have been shown to pose no danger to a breastfed child when given to the nursing mother. In some cases, vaccinations are not recommended for breastfeeding women because a live virus used in the vaccine may pose a risk to the child or because not enough data has been collected with regards to breastfeeding and a particular vaccination (as noted below).

If you are breastfeeding and need to be vaccinated for your trip, you may want to discuss the vaccinations with your doctor (and which, if any, are covered by your insurance). And be sure to mention you are breastfeeding when visiting a travel health clinic to receive your vaccinations. See the CDC Web site for more details on this topic at www.cdc.gov/breastfeeding.

Vaccinations considered safe for nursing mothers:

- Immune globulins (IG)
- Diptheria-Tetanus
- Hepatitis B
- Influenza (inactivated)

- Measles
- Meningococcal meningitis
- Mumps
- Polio (inactivated)
- Rubella
- Varicella

Vaccinations with precautions for nursing mothers:

- Hepatitis A (Immune globulin recommended instead)
- Influenza (flu) (Inactivated virus "flu shot" encouraged instead of live virus)
- Japanese encephalitis
- Pneumococcal
- Rabies (Data not available, but it is commonly given to nursing mothers without observed effects in infants)
- Smallpox
- Tuberculosis
- Typhoid (Data not available, but may be used when risk of exposure is high)
- Yellow fever (Theoretical risk of transferring to breastfed infant, but unavoidable if traveling to endemic areas)

MALARIA PREVENTION FOR YOUNG CHILDREN

If you don't already feel lucky for having the ability to choose when and where—and whether you take your children to visit other countries, consider this: According to the World Health Organization, malaria kills an African child every 30 seconds. It spreads as easily as mosquitoes bite people in the night, and the CDC declares malaria to be "one of the most serious, life-threatening diseases affecting pediatric international travelers." Traveling to a malaria-affected region with small children should be considered with the utmost seriousness.

Malaria is presently considered a risk in parts of Asia, Africa, Central and South America, Eastern Europe, the South Pacific, and certain Caribbean Islands. If you must take your infant or child to a malaria-affected area, consult with your pediatrician immediately to figure out your child's best course of prevention. While there is no vaccine for malaria, a handful of anti-malarial drugs are available and are recommended for travelers who will be visiting affected regions—though many people are wary of the possible side effects. A few anti-malarial drugs can be given to infants and small children (Doxycycline is not suitable for children under 8 years, Atovaquone/proguanil is not suitable for children under 25 lbs, and some anti-malarial medications should not be taken by breastfeeding women). Your pediatrician will determine which drug is appropriate for your child and the strain(s) of malaria present at your destination.

If you can't be certain your accommodations will be air-conditioned and your family will be adequately shielded from mosquitoes at night, pack your own mosquito bed nets for nighttime use. Bed nets treated with permethrin are most effective as the insecticide both repels and kills mosquitoes (consider carefully how you will safely use these nets around your child's sleeping zone). Treated mosquito nets are available through numerous Web sites, or you can buy your own permethrin to treat netting, clothing, etc. Remember that most mesh netting used in play yard side panels and other baby gear has holes large enough to be penetrated by aggressive mosquitoes, so use a mosquito net over these. Mosquito nets fitted to standard-size cribs and play yards are available, as well as strollers and infant car seats. The Tropic Screen is a pop-up screen tent that is fully enclosed and offers protection from mosquitoes and other insects (cockroaches, etc.) while sleeping, available in single and double sizes to fit sleeping adults. The Peapod travel bed is a smaller, fully enclosed, self-standing tent for babies and toddlers, but it should be used with additional mosquito netting over it when visiting malaria-affected regions.

Mosquito repellents containing DEET are strongly recommended for most travelers visiting malaria-risk areas, but it should be used on children only sparingly and in lower concentrations. Be sure to read the details about DEET and tips for Managing Mosquitoes beginning on page 113. If at all possible, try to plan your trip during your destination's driest months of the year, when there should be a reduced population of mosquitoes.

- *Chapter 9* -
In Case of Illness…

MEDICAL HELP WHERE YOU NEED IT

The bad news is, sometimes babies and children get sick. The good news is, it's a universal phenomenon and virtually anywhere you go in the world, you can find the help and resources you need for dealing with it. Following are some recommendations for how you can best prepare to nip illness in the bud should it strike during travel.

Create an iHealth Record – An iHealth Record stores all of your health information—or that of your child—in one convenient, secure place that may be accessed by a medical professional if and when needed. This can be especially helpful when traveling, should someone in your family need unexpected medical care; your insurance information, vaccinations, allergies, prescriptions, and even emergency contact information can be instantly accessed. The iHealth Record is offered through the Medem network, and may be available through your physician's Web site. More information at www.iHealthRecord.org.

Ask about online consultations – Your child's physician (and your own) may offer online consultations, which can be a great help if you have unexpected health concerns or questions far from home. Check with the doctor's office to see if this is an option.

Ask about an advice nurse – Your doctor's office and/or your medical insurance provider may offer an advice line staffed by registered nurses. Many medical insurance companies offer this service to subscribers, though it is not always widely publicized. Contact your insurance provider and your doctor's office to find out if this is available to you.

Find a local doctor online – You can use the American Academy of Pediatrics' Web site to search by location for doctors, pediatricians, or pediatric dentists in the U.S. and Canada, all of whom are are members of the American Academy of Pediatrics. www.aap.org/referral

Join IAMAT – If your family will be traveling to a region where English-speaking or Western-trained doctors may be difficult to find, the International Association for Medical Assistance to Travellers (IAMAT) can help you find a doctor if needed, and at pre-set prices. Membership is free, but a donation to the organization is encouraged. More information at www.iamat.org.

Ask the front desk – Many hotels often have local doctors they can recommend, or addresses of nearby clinics and hospitals in case their guests need medical care.

A Traveler's Guide to Ear Infections

Just the thought of a possible ear infection during travel is enough to keep some parents from ever leaving home. It is hard to see a child in pain, it is hard to soothe a child in pain, it is hard to sleep with a child in pain, and it is sometimes impossible to tell on your own what the pain is even from. "Is it an ear infection?" sends countless parents to the pediatrician's office each year, many getting assured that it's probably just teething (not that teething is any easier to manage).

Yet FamilyDoctor.org reports that more than three out of four children will have at least one ear infection before the age of three. So what do you do if you suspect that one of those children is yours—and you're nowhere near your pediatrician's office? First, stay calm. Monitor your child's symptoms. If she is not old enough to tell you, "I have acute pain in my middle ear," or something to that effect, consider the following:

It's less likely to be an ear infection if your child...

- Has not recently had a cold. Ear infections generally begin when "germs" from the illness travel up the eustachian tube.
- Has no fever or a low fever of less than 101° F (could be teething).
- Meets the above criteria and becomes more like herself after a dose of acetaminophen or ibuprofen.

It's more likely to be an ear infection if your child...

- Has been fighting a cold that has produced yellow or greenish mucus.
- Has a fever of 101° F or more.
- Cries or fusses more in a reclined position than when sitting up.
- Has pus or bloody discharge coming from the ear (pus without fever could indicate swimmer's ear).

If your child's symptoms point toward an ear infection, and no discharge or pus has been seen, you can begin treating the pain immediately with Similasan Earache Relief drops, which are available over the counter at most pharmacies (good to have in your suitcase if your child is prone to ear infections). You may also give the correct dosage of either ibuprofen or acetaminophen (Dr. Sears advises that you can safely use both medications together if one alone is not enough), and apply a warm compress to her ears (or warm washcloth, or water bottle filled with warm water, whatever you've got on hand).

Continue to monitor and alleviate your child's symptoms, as you are able. If they persist, you can proceed to find a local doctor in the morning. And it may be helpful, possibly even reassuring, to understand a little more about ear infections and their treatment. Here are some of traveling parents' biggest fears about ear infections:

What if we can't see a doctor—or get antibiotics right away?

Many parents' first thought about an ear infection is that antibiotics must be acquired and begun immediately. Ear infections may be the result of either bacteria or a virus reaching the inner ear—and since antibiotics cannot treat viruses, they simply will have no effect on some ear infections, though they are often prescribed regardless. Recent studies have also shown that 80% of ear infections will clear up on their own in less than a week without antibiotics. In fact, the American Academy of Family Physicians and the American Academy of Pediatrics now recommend a treatment approach that emphasizes observation and pain relief before using antibiotics. However, on occasion, complications can occur, and if antibiotics can help your child begin to feel better and recover more quickly (which they most likely will if it's a bacterial infection), that is worth a lot—especially when traveling! So the bottom line is, don't panic if you can't get to a doctor immediately when you suspect an ear infection, but by all means do what you can to help your child feel better until you can get there.

Does the drainage from the ear mean the eardrum has ruptured?

Pus or bloody drainage from the ear can be alarming and, in the case of an ear infection, usually means the eardrum has ruptured. This is not as devastating as it sounds, however, and it usually results in an immediate feeling of relief for the child. The ruptured eardrum is usually treated with antibiotic eardrops prescribed by your child's physician.

Should we delay the flight?

If your child is indeed diagnosed with an ear infection, it could be a good idea to delay flying until the infection has passed—if possible. Extra fluids built up in the ears can make it even more difficult for the pressure to equalize in a child's already narrow Eustachian tubes. Discuss the type of ear infection and stage that it's at with the doctor and tell her when your flight is currently scheduled. If possible, bring some pain reliever (e.g.

infant's or children's Tylenol) and Similasan Earache Relief drops onboard when you do fly, just in case there is any lingering discomfort.

COMMON TRAVEL AILMENTS AND AIDS

Babies and children can be even more susceptible to common ailments than adults while traveling. Their inexperienced immune systems and indiscriminant hand-to-mouth contact combines with the usual stresses we may all encounter while traveling—less sleep, strange foods, greater exposure to the elements, etc.—to make our tiny travelers more vulnerable. Following are some common ailments to creep up on kids during travel, along with practical info and tips for dealing with them when away from home.

Dehydration

Approximately 50% of an adult's body weight is water, but a baby's weight is more than 75% water. For this reason babies and young children can become dehydrated far more quickly than adults, so it is especially important to keep the fluids flowing to them and through them as you travel. Heat, sun, high altitudes, and wind exposure, can all increase the risk of dehydration, as can illness accompanied by vomiting and diarrhea. Breastfeeding mothers must be extra careful to stay hydrated enough for themselves and their babies who depend on their milk. If you think your child may be at risk for dehydration, watch out for the following warning signs.

Common signs of dehydration in infants and young children:
- Fewer than six wet diapers in a day
- No tears when baby or child cries
- Dark urine
- Sunken eyes
- Wrinkled-looking skin

If increasing your child's fluid intake doesn't seem to be helping, or illness is causing dehydration to worsen, be sure to contact a doctor right away. If you will be traveling to a remote location, discuss treatment options with your child's doctor before you leave. If children's pre-mixed oral electrolyte solutions like Pedialyte or Ricelyte will not be easily available at your destination (including on cruise ships in exotic regions), it may be wise to pack along some just in case you need it. Your child's doctor can advise you on the proper portion and strength for your child before you go. Note: Gatorade and adult sports drinks are not recommended for babies or young children.

Diarrhea

Diarrhea is one of the most common ailments a child may suffer from during travel, primarily because their inexperienced immune systems are more likely to succumb to food- and waterborne illnesses encountered through eating or merely from their frequent and indiscriminant hand-to-mouth contact (or even toys or pacifiers touching the floor). Watch closely for symptoms of dehydration (described above) as it is the greatest risk associated with diarrhea in babies and small children. The CDC advises immediate medical attention for infants and small children with the following symptoms.

Seek immediate medical help when diarrhea is accompanied by:
- Signs of moderate to severe dehydration
- Blood in the stool
- A fever greater than 101.5 F
- Persistent vomiting

Milder cases of diarrhea or unpleasantly loose stools may be improved by eating these popular toddler foods we affectionately call "hinder binders," or you might remember them best as, "The Firm Five":

The Firm Five

- Cheerios
- Bananas
- Applesauce
- Cheese
- Yogurt

Constipation

Constipation can affect children for many reasons while traveling, including a refusal to eat new and unfamiliar foods that may be necessary to maintain a balanced diet or, for potty-trained or –training children, a fear of using new facilities. If you suspect diet is the cause of the constipation, try to reduce the constipating foods in the diet, including The Firm Five listed above, and replace them with more high-fiber options. If fruits and vegetables are refused, remember these alternatives can also work wonders. Note: high fiber foods should always be consumed with plenty of fluids.

High-fiber foods for picky eaters

- Beans (baked beans, kidney, pinto, etc.)
- Sweet potatoes
- Peas
- Popcorn
- Graham crackers
- Whole wheat bread

Cough and Congestion

It's not always practical to travel with a humidifier (if ever). If the air is particularly dry where you're staying, run a hot steamy shower to help humidify the air. Vapor plugs that simply plug into standard electrical outlets (like the air fresheners) can also be used to release aromatic oils of menthol, eucalyptus, etc., into the air to ease congestion. Brands include SudaCare and Pediacare. Vicks BabyRub can also be massaged on the chest and neck to help clear congestion and sooth dry passages for babies 3 months and older.

- *Chapter 10* -
Safety Concerns

CHILDPROOFING ON THE GO

Rarely are traveler's accommodations designed or furnished with small children in mind. In our stays at various hotels, we have brazenly rearranged what furniture wasn't bolted down, barricaded minibars with our luggage, and modified window coverings with pony tail holders—much to the amazement of hotel housekeepers—all in the name of child safety.

One of our most memorable hotel moments was when we entered a thoroughly modern hotel room to find someone had brought us a portacrib as requested, though he had set it up directly beneath an enormous light sconce that would have served well on a whaling ship. If it didn't catch our daughter as she stood up in the crib, it surely would have harpooned one of us after laying her down beneath it.

Childproofing on the go isn't easy, especially once your child becomes highly mobile but has not yet developed a sense of danger. Not helping the situation, most childproofing gear you may use at home doesn't travel well or translate to temporary use (what does is included at the end of this chapter). As you arrive at your new digs, it may be prudent to place mobile babies in a portacrib, or leave toddlers strapped into their strollers as you survey the new surroundings and eliminate immediate risks. As your child grows, the childproofing concerns will continue to change and evolve, so it may be helpful to revisit this list before each of your journeys.

Checking-In Safety Checklist:

Door locks – Can you latch the main door to ensure your child won't go sightseeing without you? Does the bathroom or any other room have locks within your child's reach?

Low / large windows – Are the windows low enough for the child to run into, or climb out of, or access by climbing on other furniture in the room? Do they open wide enough that toys—or a child—might fall through (remember, screens will not stop children from falling)? Can they be locked shut so your child cannot open it? Is there a "protective" rail or grillwork outside the window that might tempt the child?

Patio doors – Can your child unlatch or operate the door unassisted? Is the glass so wide it is a walk-through risk? Is the glass so thin or old it might break if bumped by a toy or gallivanting child?

Balconies or decks – Are the railings close enough to keep curious children and babies from slipping under or through? Even more modern hotel buildings may still have railings spaced too widely for small children and babies (remember they're much narrower turned sideways), so be sure to inspect for yourself before your child comes exploring. Are there steps to the deck or down from the balcony? Any outdoor furniture that could give your child "a lift" too close to danger?

Curtains, blinds, and window treatments – Give draperies a friendly tug before your child does to ensure they're securely anchored. Get loose operating cords, delicate drapes, and unsafe window treatments up and out of the way, bundled with a rubber band if needed.

Heating / AC – Is the heating or AC unit accessible to your child? Could it be dangerously hot or pose a risk from the operating fan? Are the controls within his reach?

Electrical appliances, outlets, and cords – Watch out for coffeemakers, alarm clocks, and hairdryers that may be pulled off of surfaces by curious toddlers, either by their cords or the objects themselves. Lamp, T.V., and Internet cables and cords may also need attention. Outlets may appear where not expected, such as at the base of lamps on desks or bedside tables.

Kitchens or kitchenettes – Check cupboards and drawers for knives, coffee makers with glass carafes, and other hazards that may be within reach, including matches if the stove is gas. Dish washing detergent and / or cleaning supplies may be kept in an accessible cupboard. Be aware that ovens, refrigerators, or dishwashers may be more easily opened than yours at home.

Bathrooms – Soaps, shampoos, and lotions may need to be moved from within reach. In vacation rentals and personal homes, check for cleaning supplies, medicines, matches, and other hazardous products that may be stored in the bathroom. Be sure to store your own toiletries and travel kits out of reach of your child (those with built-in hooks or loops that can be hung from robe hooks, or from shower or closet rods can be helpful).

Minibars – Can your child open the minibar by herself? Are there items inside that could be of danger (glass bottles, peanuts or other allergens in snacks, etc.) or could set you back more than you had planned for this vacation? You may need to set a suitcase in front of it or rearrange furniture.

CITY SMARTS FOR THE NEW PARENT

After traveling across the country, across the Atlantic, and across the Pacific with my family, I've become more convinced than ever that people are essentially good. You may be pleasantly surprised, and at times overwhelmed, by the kindness and generosity strangers may show you as you travel with your baby or small child. (I hope so.)

But don't take it for granted. The truth is the world has its fair share of pickpockets and others who regularly prey on out-of-towners, and the preoccupied parent whose arms seem always burdened with gadgetry or gear if not a child can be an easy target. And remember, pickpockets come in all shapes and sizes, and fashion statements. Parents, on the other hand, stand out in any crowd.

How to look like a target for pickpockets:

- **Wear a backpack** – Yes, that handy contraption that helps parents keep their hands free. Not only do they scream, "I'm a tourist! Hit me!" but their zippers can easily be transgressed without your even knowing it, especially in crowds.

- **Wear impractical shoes** – Flip-flops, high heels, huaraches and the like can make you extra awkward as you negotiate street curbs and subway steps with your stroller or child in hand. One little push can send you fumbling while a better-shod stranger makes off with your wallet or purse.

- **Carry a child in your arms** – Terrible as it sounds, most unsavory characters know that a person holding their life's most precious possession in their hands will be able to do little else with them — even if they feel a hand in their pocket.

- **Push a stroller** – Would you abandon your stroller on a busy street corner to chase down a purse-snatcher? Would you let go of your stroller on an escalator to push away a pickpocket? There are people in this world who have thought through these answers and look forward to spending your cash.

- **Take lots of pictures** – That fancy camera you bought for Junior's birth is itself an attractive target, but so are other items of interest as you gaze through the view finder, focusing on your child's every facial expression, trying to capture that perfect photograph for the next Christmas card.

As my husband and I exited the busy metro in Barcelona, pressing on through the morning commuters to the promised "elevator—si!" only to get pushed onto an escalator instead, we acted confidently as ever that we knew what we were doing and where we were going—in spite of the daypack that surely gave us away, but we couldn't seem to do without. Tim balanced the loaded stroller on the steps in front of him as I stood behind him, thus guarding the daypack.

During our ascent, a few people passed beside us, including a blond woman in a business suit who, with all manner of importance, inserted herself in between us as if she had no idea that we were together. In a matter of seconds her fingers had found the heavy-duty Velcro securing Tim's front pocket, the one in which he happened to be carrying his wallet. As she struggled with the Velcro, I had to wonder what was keeping her arm so busy while riding an escalator. A moment later, I saw a wide box of cigarettes in the same hand—but she wasn't smoking.

Before I could fully appreciate the fact that an attempted robbery was in progress on the steps in front of me, we were at the top of the escalator and off she went with an empty carton of cigarettes among a dozen downtown professionals. I have never heard my husband speak so harshly of a beautiful stranger, but oh, how he praises the many virtues of heavy-duty Velcro.

GREAT PRODUCTS FOR ON THE GO SAFETY

Portable safety gates – These pressure-mounted gates can be installed in minutes without any hardware or alteration to existing door frames. KidCo has a "Gateway to Go" that folds compactly enough to fit in the suitcase (but not in the carry-on). Evenflo offers an Extra-wide Soft Travel Gate that

141

expands up to 5 feet wide and rolls up for travel at 27" high. Neither is designed for use at the top of stairs, however.

Door finger guards – They keep children from locking themselves in bathrooms and other rooms, while also preventing doors from shutting on little fingers. A dense foam "clamp" slips onto the door itself up where little hands can't reach it, and slips off easily for when you are ready to shut the door (or check out). These can also be helpful when sharing connecting rooms in a hotel or cruise ship. Brands available include Safety 1st and The Door Mouse.

Sliding cabinet locks – These handy gadgets work with all manner of cabinet knobs and pulls that are positioned side by side (generally up to 6" apart). Adjustable for a custom fit.

Rubber bands – Helpful when bundling long blind cords or electrical cords, or temporarily shortening draperies. Be sure to keep out of your child's reach.

Garden training wire – This coated wire (usually green) works wonders wending its way through and around cabinet drawer pulls and knobs of all shapes and sizes, regardless of the distance between them. Helpful in blocking access to Grandma's china, among other things.

Child safety harness – It helps prevent children from wandering or bolting in crowds and at dangerous locales. Many brands are available, including the Kid Keeper and Sure Steps Safety Harness. Some, like the Baby Buddy Deluxe safety harness, can also be used to help keep climbers in shopping carts and high chairs. For hands-free convenience, choose one that has a locking ring or use a carabiner clip to attach to your belt—especially helpful when you'll have a younger child in a stroller and one at your side.

Inflatable bath tub inserts – Like a little inflatable raft for your baby or toddler, but with the water on the inside for bathing. Not only do these help provide bruise-free bathing for babies on the go, but they also fill a critical niche for most cruisers who don't have the benefit of a bathtub in their cabin (most only have a shower stall). And in warm weather, yours may even serve as an impromptu splash pool for your child. Some brands include Kel-

Gar's Safe Tub, The Secure Transitions Tub by One Step Ahead, and the Safety Duck Tub by Munchkin (complete with squeaking beak).

Angel Alert Distance Monitor – This two-part warning system helps prevent children from wandering away. An alarm sounds on the adult's receiver when the child has strayed too far.

Mommy I'm Here Child Locator – It looks like a little teddy bear and attaches to shoe laces, belt, or overall strap. The parent carries a corresponding transmitter in his pocket or on his keychain, and activates it if needed, sounding a high decibel beep to help locate the child. Works at a range of up to 150 feet apart.

TEN TRAVEL SAFEGUARDS

No one likes to think about the unpleasantries that can befall a traveler, let alone a traveling family. But being prepared for all manner of complications will help you travel with confidence and swiftly manage any complications.

1. **Share trip details with friend or family** – It's important that the folks at home be able to contact you if needed, but it is also a wise idea to check in with someone as you travel so that they know right away if you aren't in the right place at the right time, and can act quickly in case your family needs help or assistance.
2. **Make copies of important documents** – Passports, airline tickets, birth certificates, driver's licenses, itineraries, and the like—where would you be on your trip without them? It's a good idea to keep copies of your important travel documents in your suitcase as you travel, along with the phone numbers for your credit and ATM cards in case they become lost or stolen.
3. **Keep it under wraps** – Where tourists wander, pickpockets follow. When traveling with your child, you will find yourself in even more compromising positions, keeping your attention on getting your child safely through a crowd, taking pictures, struggling with gear, changing diapers in public restrooms, and so on. This is no time to

take chances with your cash, credit cards, or other important travel documents. Get a good travel wallet that you like and use it.

4. **Take and tuck a business card** – If your hotel has business cards at the front desk or in your room, pick one up—or two if possible. Tuck one in your child's pocket each day, and keep a second in your travel wallet. In the unfortunate event that your child wanders or gets separated from you, it could help you get reunited much more quickly. Or if you are out sightseeing and have trouble finding your way back, by car, bus, taxi, or train, having the hotel address handy could help, not to mention having the name and address as translated in the local language when you're abroad.

5. **Always consider your exit strategy** – When venturing out to some sights, it may be easiest for your family to take a taxi. But will it be as easy to take a taxi back? And how might you return otherwise? Make sure you bring along phone numbers for local taxi companies just in case there aren't any in sight. But more importantly, be wary of situations where unscrupulous drivers may charge you an astronomical return fare knowing you (and your precious little family) have no other options. In some situations, it may actually be safest to take public transportation, or hire a local guide to escort you and your family, or join an escorted group tour for visits to outlying destinations.

6. **Register your trip** – If you are a U.S. citizen and will be traveling abroad, you may want to register your trip with the U.S. Department of State. It's a free service that helps ensure the Department of State can assist you quickly in case of an emergency at your destination, including a natural disaster, terrorism, or civil unrest. More information at https://travelregistration.state.gov.

7. **Flock together** – Rarely do travelers expect to lose track of each other at the market, the train station, the amusement park, or even the beach. But boy, oh howdy, it happens. By resisting the urge to split up, you could save yourselves much anxiety and many vacation hours lost to looking for one another.

8. **Insure your trip** – You can purchase trip insurance to protect against a wide range of unforeseeable problems and related expenses, including trip cancellation, interruption, and delay; emergency medical treatment or evacuation; lost, stolen, or damaged baggage; financial default of an airline, cruise line, or tour operator; hurricanes; and terrorism. Travel Guard International

offers a wide range of travel insurance options and includes free coverage for one child age 16 years or younger with each covered adult (www.travelguard.com or 1-800-826-4919). Your credit card company may automatically include some level of travel insurance if you use it to purchase travel (including car rental insurance), so be sure to ask for details.

9. **Take extra precautions for your child** – If your child is prone to bolting or wandering, remember it only takes a moment to lose sight of each other in crowded settings or step into harm's way— especially in unfamiliar territory. Keep your child close to you at all times, and make good use of your child carrier or stroller while you're out and about. When this isn't possible, consider using a safety harness that attaches to you and / or an alert system like the Mommy I'm Here Child Locator or Angel Alert Distance Monitor (more info in Great Products for On the Go Safety, page 141). Also, complete a child safety kit or card complete with an updated photo of your child to carry with you during your trip. At www.yoursafechild.com, you can order child safety kits, shoe labels, and self-laminating child ID cards the size of a credit card— handy for your wallet. The Polly Klaas Foundation offers free child safety kits and includes a booklet for parents on "How to teach abduction prevention without scaring your child (or yourself)," which can be ordered online at www.pollyklaas.org or by calling 1-800-587-4357.

10. **Bring the ugly diaper bag** – Many diaper bags are tastefully designed to "blend in" with grown up attire, and on your trip to the Culture Capital, especially, you may prefer a sleek diaper tote to the one covered in Winnie the Pooh. To the untrained eye, however, one may look a lot more like a purse or even a laptop case. If you travel with it anyway, keep in mind how enticing it may appear set on the park bench, slung over the back of your stroller, or left on the seat of your rental car. There are times you may prefer to leave it gaping open wide with a clear view of the treasures that it holds.

PART IV
TRAVELS BY AUTOMOBILE

- *Chapter 11* -
Before You Go by Car

CAR SEAT LAWS ACROSS STATE LINES

J ust a few years ago, children 2 years and older were only required to wear an adult seatbelt in Montana. In West Virginia, children 3 years and older were also considered legal in adult seatbelts. Now, children in each of these states not only must ride in appropriate car safety seats until age 4, but they are also required to use safety boosters until they are 6 years old in Montana, and 8 years old in West Virginia. Times are changing. And each year, the laws concerning car seat and safety booster seat use continue to change across the U.S. (For car seat requirements abroad, be sure to read Driving with children in foreign countries, page 153.)

All states and the District of Columbia have now enacted laws requiring children younger than 4 years of age and / or weighing less than 40 lbs to ride in an approved child safety seat—except for the state of Kentucky, where the law states that children under 40″ in height are required to ride in an approved car seat, regardless of age or weight.

So how do you keep up with the new legislation in states where you don't even live? By following these recommendations based on advice from the U.S. National Highway Traffic Safety Administration (NHTSA), you can rest easy knowing you're legal anywhere in the United States and its territories and, most important, are providing the safest seating possible for your child.

How to Play It Safe in Every State:

- Children under 1 year old ride in a rear-facing safety seat, regardless of their weight.
- Children at least 1 year old, weighing 20 to 40 lbs, ride in a forward-facing safety seat (rear-facing may still be safest, see details in next section).
- Children who have exceeded the height or weight limit for their forward-facing safety seat, are nine years old or younger, and are less than 4'9" tall should ride in a safety booster seat.
- All children under the age of 12 ride in the back seat.

If your child has outgrown his car seat and your state does not yet require booster seats, you may need to purchase one for your trip. Families with older children should also be aware that, while many states require that children use booster seats up to age 6, some states are increasing the age requirement to 7 years, 8 years, and even 9 years (Wyoming and Tennessee). Plus, some states are also enacting safety laws that require child passengers to sit in the back seat.

Currently, booster seats are required until *at least* 6 years in the 39 states listed here. To check the latest booster seat laws by state, visit www.boosterseat.gov.

States Requiring Booster Seats Until 6 Years or Older

Alabama	Iowa	Nevada	Rhode Island
Arkansas	Illinois	New Hampshire	South Carolina
California	Indiana	New Jersey	Tennessee
Colorado	Kansas	New Mexico	Vermont
Connecticut	Louisiana	New York	Virginia
Dist. of Columbia	Maine	North Carolina	Washington
Delaware	Maryland	North Dakota	West Virginia
Georgia	Missouri	Oklahoma	Wisconsin
Hawaii	Montana	Oregon	Wyoming
Idaho	Nebraska	Pennsylvania	

Installing Car Seats with Confidence

The first time you installed a car seat, you may have spent hours wrestling the seatbelt or fishing for LATCH attachments, checking the angle, jiggling the seat, tugging on the tether, only to swear at long last that the seat would stay put until you sold the car (whether your child still used it or not).

If you plan to travel far and wide, you will need to become fluent in "Carseatese." You will want to be able to remove and install your child's car seat in any manner of rental car, relative's car, shuttle van or taxi—quickly and with confidence. The good news is that, like most things, practice and a few good pointers make it all possible. As you prepare for travels with your car seat, remember these installation basics:

Installing Your Car Seat

1. **Route the vehicle safety belt or LATCH belt** through the appropriate path and buckle.
2. **Apply your weight** to help press the car seat into the vehicle seat, with your knee if possible, and tighten the belt.
3. **Make sure car seat doesn't move** more than 1 inch in any direction.

Installing Your Child

1. **Rear-facing seat straps** should be at or below the shoulders.
2. **Forward-facing seat straps** should be at or just above the shoulders.
3. **Chest clip** should be at armpit level.
4. **Straps should be snug** so that only one finger fits between it and child's collar bone.

Seatbelt Specifics

If you have grown accustomed to the simplicity of LATCH at home (standard in vehicles model year 2003 and newer), it may be daunting to face the prospect of myriad seatbelt configurations awaiting you and your car seat as you travel. Shoulder belt? Lap belt? Locking clip? Here's what you need to know when seat-belting your car seat into unfamiliar vehicles.

Types of Seatbelts You May Encounter...

1. **Manually adjusting lap-only belt** – Similar to seatbelts found on airplanes, you can pull the free end of the seatbelt to shorten it, and the latch plate locks to hold the seatbelt in place once adjusted.
2. **Automatic locking retractor (ALR)** – This belt pulls out from the retractor, then locks in place at the specified length. It cannot be lengthened from this point until it has been completely retracted again.
3. **Emergency locking retractor (ELR)** – This seatbelt moves freely in and out of the retractor and only locks in place when the vehicle comes to a sudden stop. These belts are not recommended for use with car seats unless a vehicle manufacturer's belt-shortening clip is provided. ELRs were discontinued after 1995.
4. **Switchable ELR/ALR combination retractor** – Most of these belts will move freely for normal, adult use, like an ELR. But they can switch to ALR mode by pulling the belt all of the way out of the retractor (after you have buckled the seatbelt through the car seat), then allowing the belt to retract to fit the car seat. There may be a label with instructions on switching modes affixed to the seatbelt.
5. **Continuous loop lap/shoulder belt** – One belt passes through the latch plate of this belt, forming both the lap and shoulder segments. If the latch plate locks in place once buckled, holding the car seat in place with the lap belt portion, no locking clip is needed. If the latch plate slides freely along the belt, you will need to use your locking clip.
6. **Automatic seatbelts** – These should never be used with car seats. If the lap belt portion is not automated, and you can unhook the automatic shoulder belt, that may be wisest—but check to see if the lap belt is an ELR, in which case a manufacturer's belt shortening clip should be used. Most automatic seatbelts are in the front seats and can be avoided by simply using the back seat.

The Lowdown on Locking Clips

Vehicles manufactured after September 1, 1995 (model year 1996 and beyond) for the U.S. market have all been required to feature safety belts that can secure safety seats without the need for locking clips or additional hardware. If you might be riding in vehicles from earlier years, you may need to use a locking clip. Locking clips are the H-shaped metal clips that still come packaged with most child safety seats, and are usually stored under the base. The clip is used to fasten together the lap and shoulder portions of a shoulder seatbelt where the strap slides freely through the latch plate. The clip should be used just above the latch plate to prevent the seatbelt from sliding through it. See your car seat manual for specifics on using a locking clip with your model.

Seven Ways to Smooth Your Travels with the Car Seat

1. Improve your manual dexterity - First, take another look at your car seat manual, where you'll find instructions for use with all the various seatbelt configurations and safety features you might encounter on your trip. If you've misplaced your manual, you may be able to find the instructions online (TravelswithBaby.com also has links to manufacturer Web sites with instructions and manuals online). Most new car seats include a place to store the manual in them or allow you to tuck them in under the car seat cover so you will always have it with you—a great help when you find yourself scratching your head in the back of a rental car or taxi. Fold over the corners of the most relevant pages for installation for easy reference.

2. Get clipped - If it isn't already in use in your car, check to make sure a seatbelt locking clip is stored under your seat. If you don't have a locking clip, it is a good idea to travel with one just in case you come across a seatbelt that slides freely through the buckle (see your manual for details on when and how to use with your model of car seat). You can pick one up for around $2 or $3 at most stores selling car seats and baby gear.

3. Move it - While experts generally agree the center of the back seat is the safest place for your child's car seat, that may not always be practical (or possible if you have two children in car seats). Differently shaped back seats may force you to use a side seat or remove head rests to get a secure fit. You may also need extra space in the backseat for diaper changes. Practice installation in a friend's car if you can, and in the various possible seating positions.

4. Recline 'er - Back seats of cars can vary widely in shape, slope, and size, so make sure your infant is reclined a full 45 degrees to prevent her head from drooping forward, even if this means inserting a rolled up baby blanket or shortened foam swimming noodle at the crack in the car seat. If her head still droops forward, chances are, the seat is not reclined enough and an adjustment should be made.

5. Be so inclined - Let toddlers and older babies that can support their heads well and have gained good control of their neck muscles ride rear-facing with less recline, in the range of 15 to 30 degrees from vertical. This helps them see out the window, look around the car more easily, and generally ride more happily. This may also help you fit that rear-facing convertible car seat into the back of a cramped rental car.

6. Consult the experts - If you'd like a second opinion on your installation or help working out any kinks, a quick trip to www.seatcheck.org or a toll-free call to 1-866-SEAT-CHECK will help you find the nationally certified safety seat inspectors located in and around your zip code.

7. Look before you buy - The next time you are in the market for any kind of car seat or safety booster, be sure to take a look at the NHTSA's latest Ease of Use Ratings available online at www.NHTSA.dot.gov. The annual report provides usability ratings for nearly one hundred child restraint systems, including ratings for installation instructions and execution.

DRIVING WITH CHILDREN IN FOREIGN COUNTRIES

Driving abroad can be exciting enough without a diaper-clad copilot. After climbing confidently behind the wheel, you may find yourself confronted by road signs that appear to be related to driving, or possibly to parking, or—at third glance you realize they are actually illustrating the picking up of dog poop (Spain). Elsewhere, you may quickly discover that red traffic lights actually mean a rolling stop to local residents, who for some strange reason are getting out of their car to help move yours on its way (Italy). Or you might discover that the painted street lanes are merely for decoration in the few places you encounter them (India). Or after finally relaxing during the windy drive down the "wrong" side of country roads, a flock of sheep suddenly appear on the highway before you (New Zealand). Driving in other countries can give you plenty to think about besides following a map or minding your speed—which may be gauged by numbers that make no more sense to you than the gear shift pattern of the car that you have rented. Not to mention that, yes, you need to shift gears again—with your left hand, and for a moment you can't remember which side of the road you should be driving on.

If I had only one bit of advice to give on driving abroad with small children in the car, it would be: "Don't." Yet once you add children to your equation, you're more likely than ever to consider renting a car when you travel. Be prepared. Unless you have grown up in the country or have already spent a great deal of time driving there, the experience may well take years off your life. Chances are it will be far more pleasant to take the train, public transportation, a bus, or a taxi. Whenever possible, I say let someone else do the driving while you enjoy the scenery and attend to the needs of your child.

Nevertheless, if your trip abroad will require driving at some point, you will want to learn all you can about driving in the country before you get behind the wheel. A simple Google search for "driving in…" and the country you're planning to visit may connect you with plenty of information on the subject. You can also visit the country's tourism site(s) and search for driving information (find it at the Tourism Offices Worldwide directory www.towd.com), or contact that country's embassy in your own country to see if they can provide you with driving rules and regulations. To find contact information for the embassies in Washington, D.C., visit www.embassy.org.

Car Seats and Other Countries

International standards for child safety and car seat use vary widely, so find out what you can before you go. Generally, following the NHTSA's guidelines mentioned earlier will be fine most places around the world, and will far exceed local safety standards for child passengers in some regions, but may not meet the stringent requirements of some countries.

In parts of Southeast Asia, like Thailand and Vietnam, it can cost the average factory worker more than 100 hours' worth of wages to purchase a car seat. As you might expect, you won't see many people using them, and renting one may be virtually impossible. Your best bet in these regions will be to rent a car from a large, international agency (Avis, Hertz, etc.) and to verify ahead of time that your rental car will have suitable seatbelts or LATCH in the backseat for your car seat. Taxis, shuttle vans, and other cars for hire often do not have suitable seatbelts. Plan to bring your own car seat to use on vacation.

There are some destinations, however, where child passenger safety laws exceed current U.S. standards—or your car seat may not meet the local standards. Some key examples to be aware of:

- **In the U.K.,** all children under 12 years old or less than 4 feet 4 inches tall must have an appropriate car seat or booster seat when traveling in an automobile (with the exception of taxis or for-hire shuttles that do not provide a car seat).
- **In Germany,** all children under 12 years are also required to be in an appropriate car seat or booster, and you can be fined 30 Euros just for allowing a child under 12 years old to ride in the front seat of a car.
- **In Sweden,** children ride rear-facing in their car seats until they are three years old—and many safety experts feel that's why Sweden boasts the lowest traffic fatality rate for children in the world. In fact, The American Academy of Pediatrics and many other sources advise that small children use their rear-facing car seats up until the maximum height or weight limit allowed for the car seat (convertible car seats accommodate rear-facing riders up to 30-35 lbs and around 36" tall—some limits are even higher).
- **In Australia,** you will need to rent a car seat there that meets Australia's safety standards—some of the most stringent in the world—that works with the special tether anchors found in Australian automobiles. Car seats manufactured for the USA and U.K. markets are not accepted. Car seats that are will be stamped with the Australia Standards mark "AS."
- **In New Zealand,** some U.S. and European safety certified car seats are accepted IF they also bear the New Zealand Standard "S" mark to show it is certified for use in the country.
- **In Canada**, all forward-facing car seats are required to be installed with an upper tether in addition to the seatbelt or LATCH.

To find out more about child passenger safety practices at your destination, visit www.childcarsafety.org.uk, where you can find car seat rules and regulations for countries around the world. To rent a car seat that meets local standards and specifications, see Baby Gear Rentals on page 58 or page 170 for car rental agencies that may provide these.

Driving Culture

It is also a good idea to spend some time observing the driving "culture" and traffic patterns in the area before you join in. While the printed literature may tell you that you're required to have a security vest in your vehicle at all times (Austria), it may not mention anything about motorcycles having the right of way on sidewalks (Taiwan). Now add to that a potentially crying baby or shouting child, low blood sugar, and a complete lack of legal (for all you can tell) parking spaces, and you will quickly see why public transportation is preferred by parents in many cities.

Okay, I do realize that plenty of parents have enjoyed perfectly wonderful driving vacations with their children in foreign countries, touring the French countryside in a rented campervan, exploring Costa Rica by Jeep, and so on. And so can you. Just be as prepared as possible for the adventure.

International Driver's Licenses and Permits

In addition to your valid driver's license from home, you should bring along an International Driver's Permit (IDP). This additional form of I.D. is recognized in more than 150 countries and translates your information into eleven different languages (including English). The simplest, fastest way to obtain your IDP will most likely be to visit the American Automobile Association's Web site, www.aaa.com, and print the online form to complete at home. You will also need two passport-size photos with your signature on the back of each and a photocopy of your valid U.S. driver's license. If you bring this to your local AAA office (member or not), they can issue your IDP immediately. The current fee is $10, payable by check or money order.

International Road Signs

At www.aaa.com, you will also find a helpful collection of international regulatory, warning, and prohibitory road signs that you might encounter when traveling abroad. You needn't be a member to take a look (or take advantage of any of their other AAA Travel Agency features), and it can certainly help prepare you for the abundance of less-than-intuitive signage that awaits you out in the world. If you have trouble finding it through your local AAA site online, try:
http://www.aaaorid.com/travel/travel_int_signs.asp.

Maps and Directions

Any language barriers could make it especially challenging to ask for—and follow directions in an unknown land. So before you leave home, get all the maps and directions you can to help plan your drive. In addition to any destination guide books or maps you may purchase for your trip, it may also be helpful to map points of interest specific to your trip—like the car rental pick-up and drop-off offices, and the hotels or campgrounds where you'll be staying. With Web sites like Maporama (www.maporama.com) and Mapquest (www.mapquest.com), you can map pretty much any address or point of interest in the world, and zoom in for a detailed block-by-block view, or zoom out for a regional view. Point-to-point online driving instructions are still mostly limited to routes in the U.S., Canada, and Europe (as is the case with Mapquest), but Maporama can also show you the way in a wide range of countries around the world.

- *Chapter 12* -
On the Road

PACING YOUR JOURNEY

Making good time doesn't always make for a good time, especially with children. Instead of pulling over for a quick refueling or a quick diaper change on an as-needed basis, try to lump as many things together as you can in a single stop, including some sort of physical activity and a change of scenery from that of the car's interior. Plan ahead to take scheduled, meaningful breaks, and address the major issues before they become a crisis.

The mother of an active toddler explained to me that she used to find the long drive to her in-laws unbearable—until she began planning the trip with strategically timed breaks at certain fast food restaurants along the way. To qualify, each restaurant features indoor (climate-controlled) playgrounds. Their son gets an adequate break from his car seat, burns off some energy in a suitable (and safe) environment, often meets other playmates, and has more stops to look forward to throughout the long day of driving to Grandma and Grandpa's house. What's more, Mom and Dad don't have to worry about finding food he will like, and they can relax knowing there will be a restroom.

If "the McDrive" isn't for you, look for State Parks and points of interest along your route that may combine a rest area with a nature trail, beach access, or picnic area. Even interstate rest areas often include lawns, picnic tables, and short paths of some kind (pack a ball to toss or roll, plenty of snacks, and drinks). If you will be traveling in inclement weather, it may work best to take a break at a shopping mall where your family can stretch its legs indoors, find sustenance, and perhaps a play area (if only a toy store). By taking time for activities during your drive, you will also improve your odds of having a more restful night when you arrive at your destination.

DEALING WITH DIAPERS, DINING, AND SUCH

The Quick Car Change

One of the most daunting details for many new parents is how to change all those messy diapers on the go. Sure, SOME restrooms are equipped with changing tables, but can you expect them to be at all (or any) roadside rest areas as you travel? State parks? Historic sites? Restaurants and delis? Unfortunately these conveniences are still few and far between. I once purchased a milkshake at a national fast food franchise just for the privilege of using its diaper changing station in the restroom—only to discover there wasn't a changing station, nor was there room by the sink or anywhere else to change a diaper, aside from the dirty floor. I was obliged to return to the parking lot and change my daughter on the passenger seat of our car as burger-munching patrons watched from the restaurant windows in disapproval. Oddly enough, I have had more luck finding baby changing stations in Starbuck's cafés than in the national fast food franchises that target families.

As far as vehicles are concerned, minivans, SUVs, and station wagons are the most accommodating for roadside changes as you can simply open the rear gate and utilize the level surface there—assuming it isn't loaded with gear. But if you're on the go in a sedan, try this formula:

Equipment Needed for the Quick Car Change:
- One firm bed pillow (also handy for breastfeeding)
- Flannel-backed vinyl (you can trim for a custom fit)

- Clean diapers
- Diaper wipes
- Plastic bag for disposal, slide lock or other
- Antibacterial wipes or a liquid hand sanitizer

Step 1: Wedge the bed pillow against the passenger seat or backseat so that it creates as level a surface as possible (and overlaps the emergency break, if applicable).

Step 2: Lay flannel-backed vinyl over the pillow to create a waterproof, but soft barrier. You can purchase it by the yard at a fabric store or in crib size at most baby stores.

Step 3: Be sure to place the fresh diaper beneath the baby before removing the dirty diaper—just in case.

Step 4: If there isn't a trash receptacle handy, use your plastic bag to store the dirty diaper until you find one. (A slide lock bag is especially helpful in sealing away odors.)

Step 5: Since most diaper wipes do not contain germ-killing agents (namely alcohol), Antibacterial "Redi-Wipes" or "Wet Ones" are an easy way to ensure clean hands on the go. You can also use liquid hand sanitizer (e.g. Purell), though it can be nice to have the disposable cloth for wiping off assorted "stickies and ickies" on hands and other surfaces.

Travel-size antibacterial wipes and baby wipes fit easily into the glove box (or console in larger vehicles), plus a couple of diapers. With your glove box loaded, you have your diaper changing essentials ready to go at a moment's notice, all within easy reach when you use the passenger seat.

You may have also seen some "car changing mats" or "stations" that provide a built-in wedge on one side to help even out the slope of the car seats and may even have some pockets for organization. One of these could save you some space in the car, but they're not nearly as comfy for grown-up naptime as a good old-fashioned pillow.

Eating and Feeding on the Road

Even if you are solely breastfeeding at the time of your trip, it could be very helpful to have a couple of bottles of your milk ready to go in case baby's hunger pangs are not timed with a safe place to pull over. The same is true for bottles of formula or "moo juice" for older children. If your little one is picky about temperature, you might consider a bottle warmer that plugs into your car's lighter—just be sure yours will fit the brand of bottles you use. Food warmers are also available, and some warm jars of baby food as well as baby bottles.

Drinks and snacks can be conveniently stowed in a small ice chest or insulated pack that will fit on the floor of your car's back seat (in most cases, it will be accessible to the passenger riding in the front seat) or between the front seats in minivans or SUVs with space. A waterproof chest is especially helpful if you'll be relying on hotel ice to keep things cool—there aren't any zippers to leak water as the ice melts, as there might be in some soft-pack coolers.

Restaurants may be convenient and give shelter from inclement weather, but they don't often do much for the imagination or help burn off energy (the "McDrive" may be an exception). A happier alternative can be a good old-fashioned picnic, which can save you money while providing a healthy dose of fresh air—not to mention room to throw a Frisbee or fly a kite while the sandwiches are made.

Cloth Diapering on the Go—Are You Crazy?

To our newest generation of moms, even those who opt to use cloth diapers at home, taking cloth diapers for a weekend outing may sound ridiculous and completely unnecessary. But as parents who traveled with babies just a generation or two ago know, it is plausible. And for parents interested in keeping up cloth, a weekend of cloth diapering on the road needn't be any more trouble than a weekend of cloth diapering at home.

First of all, if you aren't already using flushable diaper liners, I strongly recommend adding them to your diapering routine (made by Imse Vimse, Kooshies, and Diaperaps). They greatly simplify poop patrol (the solids stick to the sheet, not the diaper), and help shield your child's skin from a wet diaper—especially helpful while traveling. In fact, they can also be helpful while traveling with disposable diapers as well.

Using the dry-pail method, which is most popular now and how commonly done with diaper services, we found that a large plastic pail we had originally purchased filled with kitty litter (since emptied) made the perfect diaper pail for weekend trips by car. The lid divides so that two-thirds can be flipped up to add soiled diapers, and then it snaps closed airtight. It even had a nice carrying handle for transporting it to and from the car.

If you are using disposable wipes while traveling, simply keep an extra plastic slide-lock bag handy for stashing the used wipes until you next encounter a trashcan. For the bigger jobs, consider using flushable toddler wipes that can go into the potty with your flushable diaper liners.

CARSICKNESS SURVIVAL GUIDE

Carsickness can sneak up on any member of the family, but children—trapped in the back seats and oftentimes seated lower than the car windows—can be especially prone to the condition. Before you hit the highway, be sure you're as prepared as possible in case the condition arises, and do what you can to avoid it all together.

Tips to Avoid Carsickness:

- **Decrease the recline** of rear-facing car seats for babies once they can support their heads well. The American Academy of Pediatrics suggests a 33 to 15 degree recline for older babies and toddlers riding in rear-facing seats.

- **Avoid the blood sugar blues** by keeping meals balanced and as timely as possible. Back-up snacks should be low in sugar (beware of fruit juice) to avoid sugar spikes and the woes that follow.
- **Stay hydrated.**
- **Keep fresh air circulating** through the car either through open windows or vent settings.
- **Avoid entertainment through toys or books that are held down** on your child's lap. Instead, help encourage your child to look up and out the windows by playing games like "Red car! Blue car!" and singing songs, or listening to books on tape. You can find a number of children's audio books at www.audible.com.
- **Use motion sickness wristbands.** Many adults and children alike swear by special medicine-free wristbands that use acupressure to relieve motion sickness. Some are available now sized specially for children.

Tips to Help Manage Carsickness:

- **Pack along ginger snaps and cold soda** (e.g. ginger ale or 7up) for those prone to carsickness who are old enough to enjoy them.
- **Keep some sizable slide-lock bags handy** (or airsickness bags should you have them on hand…) in case an episode arrives before the next turnout.
- **Invest in a second car seat cover** if your child gets carsick often or easily so you'll have a fresh one ready to go in times of need (the whole family may thank you). Extra covers are usually available through the manufacturer or baby gear retailers (or see TravelswithBaby.com for help finding yours).
- **Install an under-the-car-seat seat protector.** Most create a waterproof barrier and allow for easy clean up of the various spills and thrills associated with driving with children, including carsickness.
- **Keep a plastic trash bag (or a few) in the glove box to** contain soiled items and their odors until they can be cleaned (large slide-loc storage bags may work, too).
- **Have sanitizing wet wipes ready to go** (like antibacterial "Redi-Wipes" or "Wet Ones") to help clean surfaces, seat straps, hands, and more.

- Pack along a bottle of Folex brand upholstery cleaner, which requires no rinsing, is non-toxic, and odor-free.
- Discuss carsickness with your child's doctor if it is a frequent problem, and ask about any suitable medications that may be of help on your next driving vacation.

PACKING FOR A COMFORTABLE TRIP

When planning a trip by car, it is tempting to "just bring everything." But as you load your car, you may quickly discover that's not possible—nor is it practical if you hope to access some items during your journey without unloading the entire vehicle. On the other hand, less is not necessarily more when you pack for a trip with children. As you strive to simplify your packing list, here are some pointers to keep in mind:

If your child is still in diapers, it will be very helpful to have seat or floor space reserved where diapers can be changed.

If your child is potty training, it may prove invaluable to have a training potty in the car for unexpected stops.

If your child is a sensitive sleeper, accustomed to sleeping in her own space, it might be well worth the space needed to accommodate her portacrib or bassinet (newer models detach from their bases and can even fold flat in most cases). These will also provide safe, clean spaces for your child to sprawl and play while you do any childproofing or other setting up at your destination. Travel beds are another space-saving option for traveling infants through preschoolers.

Pack a 3-gallon water receptacle with a tap. It's easy to use for refilling personal water bottles and cups on the go, and is convenient at your destination—plus, you won't have empty water bottles of the disposable type cluttering the car.

Keep a flashlight handy for double-checking maps and finding snacks without waking up your child. It can also be helpful when searching through an overstuffed trunk at night and staying in hotel rooms or at other unfamiliar lodgings.

Bring extra receiving blankets and keep them accessible for roadside stops and picnics. Roll up the end of one blanket in the window of your car for a little shade and privacy. Spread it out on the lawn at a grassy park to give your baby a place to stretch and sprawl.

Bring a small ice chest that will fit on the floor of your automobile's back seat. It's a convenient place to store water and drinks, bottles, teething toys, and snacks, and in most cars it will be accessible to the person in the passenger seat.

Bring a firm bed pillow along for the ride. It helps even out bucket seats for a diaper change, provides support while breast- or bottle-feeding, and provides extra insulation from heat for your back-seat cooler.

Pack a small suitcase for each family member instead of sharing larger luggage. This will help you find things more quickly (e.g. that unexpected change of clothes) and stay better organized throughout the trip.

EVERY PARENT SHOULD HAVE IN THE CAR...

- Fix-a-flat emergency tire repair (in a can)
- Spare tire & jack
- Jumper cables
- Replacement wiper blades
- Replacement headlight bulb
- Umbrella
- Quarters for unanticipated parking meters or turnpikes

- First-Aid kit, complete with infant and child medications
- Flares or emergency lights/reflectors
- Emergency blanket ("space blanket" recommended)
- Emergency water reserve
- Emergency snack reserve
- Emergency cash reserve (perhaps stored in your wallet)
- Pen and paper for emergency note-taking or note-leaving

TAXIS, KIDS, AND CAR SEATS

While taxis can be a major convenience for travelers near and far, the traveler with a baby or small child in tow may find them especially helpful—except, perhaps, for the need of a car seat. You may find yourself wondering if you really need to bring along the car seat for your next urban adventure if the only times you'll be in a car are on quick jaunts around the city by taxi. If you've spent any time in large cities you may have already noticed parents popping in and out of taxis with their children on their laps. To answer a very frequent question, it is done and, outside of perhaps Scandinavia, it is in most cases legal. Whether or not it is safe, or preferable, is another matter.

You may be wondering how this can be legal in a time when children are required to ride in car seats and safety boosters until 6 years, 8 years, or even 9 years in some states. I took this up with a police officer on a street corner in San Francisco one afternoon. In between writing up parking tickets (thankfully not for me), he begrudgingly cited the clause pertaining to for-hire vehicles and car seats in the state of California. As in most states, cities, and countries around the world, drivers of taxis and other for-hire vehicles (shuttles, minibuses, town cars) are not legally responsible for providing child safety seats. In turn, this means that parents and caregivers hiring the driver are not legally responsible for having their child in a car seat because one does not exist in the driver's vehicle. Privately-owned passenger vehicles, however, are subject to different laws (which can vary by state).

But while you may not be thrilled at the prospect of bringing along your car seat during your day's outings to Central Park, the Statue of

Liberty, and the Metropolitan Museum of Art, you will hopefully think twice before leaping into cars driven by complete strangers with your child on your lap. Here are some alternatives that may work instead:

Get a travel-friendly car seat for infants and toddlers.
For infants, rear-facing carrier car seats that can be used without their bases are simple to install and remove using basic seatbelts (read your manual for details) and can be paired with a basic stroller frame during sightseeing. Some manufacturers, like Britax and Combi, are creating infant carrier car seats with higher upper weight and height limits so they can be used even longer than earlier models (e.g. up to 30" in height vs. 26"). Theses models also weigh less than their predecessors, too, which helps when you're toting along a heavier baby. The new Graco SafeSeat infant carrier can even be used with children up to 30 lbs. and 32" tall—if your wrists can manage the load.

Another possibility is the Sit'n'Stroll, a car seat made for specifically for travelers that installs quickly with shoulder or lap seatbelts buckling around it (or LATCH straps). It can be used both rear-facing and forward-facing, from birth up to 40 lbs. As you lift it out of the taxi or shuttle, you can pop out the retractable wheels and convert it to a stroller. See more about the Sit'n'Stroll in Car Seats, Accessories, and Alternatives, page 48. (You can also see photos and more details about the Sit'n'Stroll at TravelswithBaby.com.)

The Tote 'n Go DX is an alternative to car seats altogether. Although it is not considered a replacement for everyday use, it can be used forward-facing with older toddlers and preschoolers from 25 lbs up to 40 lbs. This "Travel Safety Vest" provides a 5-point safety harness with an impact-absorbing stress plate and works with either shoulder or lap-only seatbelts. Folding to 16" x 10" x 3" it fits easily into your suitcase, daypack, or stroller basket when not in use. Unlike the other car seats mentioned, the Tote 'n Go is not approved for use in aircraft.

Similarly, Eddie Bauer has introduced a "Portable Car Seat," that can be used forward-facing for children weighing 22 lbs to 40 lbs who are 34" to 43" tall. It weighs less than 4 lbs, and folds flat to fit in a tote bag or backpack. It should be noted, however, that while it is called a "car seat," it does not have a rigid shell and is not tested to meet the federal safety requirements of child car seats, but rather the standards for travel vests (like the Tote 'n Go DX, hence it is also not approved for use in aircraft). Still,

167

with a 5-point safety harness, it is a safer alternative to no car seat at all, or using an adult seatbelt.

For older children, use a folding or backless booster, or a travel harness. Once your child has outgrown the car seat (in age and weight limit), you may want to consider a folding booster seat, like the one manufactured by Compass, or a backless booster since it may be your easiest option to transport. But since booster seats are not to be used in aircraft and can only be used with shoulder seatbelts (no lap-only seatbelts), you may prefer to travel with a travel vest or harness instead. Most travel harnesses can be used with lap-only seatbelts as well as with shoulder belts, which is a comfort when you can't be sure what vehicles you'll be riding in. These vests also fit easily into a daypack or beneath your stroller in between uses. As an example, the RideSafer vest from Safe Traffic Systems, Inc., provides a 5-point harness (which booster seats do not) and meets Federal Motor Vehicle Safety Standards (FMVSS 213).

Use alternative transportation.
In major cities, you may be able to use public transportation during most of your visit, and in many locations this will be preferable to sitting in traffic and far more affordable than relying on taxis. If you are planning on taking a taxi just between an airport and your hotel, you may be able to book a shuttle service, taxi, or town car ahead of time that can provide a car seat for your child (call local services to inquire about car seats and make reservations). Many major airports also have train service from the airport to the city center (or other destinations), so if you can manage your group and your luggage without an airport cart, you may be able to skip the taxi ride or at least shorten it significantly (possibly avoiding interstate or highway driving). Buses and minibuses can also be a safer option when available, especially when visiting destinations where seatbelts are few and far between, particularly in taxis.

- *Chapter 13* -
Renting a Vehicle for the Drive

CHOOSING A RENTAL CAR AND AGENCY

B ranches of the major international rental agencies, like Budget, Hertz, and Avis, have sprouted up everywhere from Austria to Zimbabwe. Their omnipresence makes these megabrands seem especially convenient if you need a one-way rental for your trip (from Austria to Zimbabwe, however, is not recommended). They are also the most likely agencies to be able to offer you the options you seek, such as an extra-roomy vehicle or a child's safety seat. And naturally, they might also charge you the most for these conveniences.

To help determine which agency will really provide the best value for your trip, contact the companies directly with all of the specifics of your driving itinerary, and be sure to find out what "a standard midsize" or any other model of car means at their office—car models and brands can vary widely from office to office, even within the same corporation. Hopefully this will reassure you that you are getting the best value possible.

If you are planning to rent in a small town, be especially sure to call ahead and make contact. You might be surprised to learn that just because there is an office of said agency in a certain village on the Spanish border, it isn't open on the day of the week, or on the certain holiday you've never heard of, when you need to pick up the car. Or that, even though the agency's location is listed as being at a train station in Pennsylvania, you must call a local number when you arrive and wait 40 minutes for the manager's nephew to pick you up in his pizza delivery car and drive you to the office on the other side of town.

Renting from major airport locations and offices in large cities is usually a fairly straightforward procedure, but again, be sure you know the hours of operation for the days you'll be renting and returning. If you are deciding between two or more agencies located at an airport, make sure you know if either or both require a shuttle to an off-site location. If you have a choice, the cost savings may not be worth the time spent waiting with your child (possibly in rain, snow, wind, or cigarette smoke) for the next shuttle to arrive, or riding in a crowded minibus stacked precariously with other people's luggage.

Also, be sure your rental car will have enough room for your family and its gear. The economy or "subcompact" models are generally described as holding 4 people, 1 large suitcase, and 1 small suitcase, and though you may only be 3 people, chances are your luggage and gear will exceed these standards. Also, be forewarned that if your child uses a rear-facing car seat, some rental cars—especially in Europe—may not have backseats large enough to accommodate your car seat. Unfortunately, as rental car sizes go up so do rental car prices. Try to do your homework ahead of time to make sure your getting the best deal on the car you'll need, so you don't get stuck with an overpriced last-minute substitution.

RENTING CAR SEATS

If you are arriving at your destination by train or by plane with a lap child, or if the driving is just a small portion of your adventure, it may be a great convenience to rent a car seat along with the car. Most car rental agencies now offer to rent child safety seats for somewhere between $7 and $10 per day, or sometimes for a flat fee of around $35 for your trip. But be aware they may not be guaranteed at all locations. I once hashed out all the details of a one-way rental between small towns with a car seat included, and in finalizing my reservation, I was then told to call back (at no specific time or date) to confirm whether or not the car seat would be available at my pickup location. Since that "minor detail" had everything to do with whether or not the car rental would work for us, and our planned itinerary, I elected to cancel and make other arrangements, as you might too.

Generally, if you are renting from an office in a major airport or city, this shouldn't be a problem. The agency should ask you for details about your child's age, weight, and height, to ensure the proper car seat or booster seat will be provided (and if they don't, you tell them). When you arrive at the rental office, your car seat may already be installed for you, or it may be handed to you along with the car keys. So be prepared to install it yourself, or at least perform a thorough inspection to make sure it has been installed properly for you.

You may also be able to rent a vehicle with an integrated (built-in) car seat, though you should call the rental agency directly to confirm availability and make your reservation. Integrated car seats are available in some newer Chrysler, GM, and Volvo cars, but are generally only forward-facing (for children at least 1 year and weighing 20 lbs or more) and offer little or no recline, with minimal side support, all of which makes them less than ideal for napping during travel. Those that can also be used as belt-positioning boosters for older children, however, may prove a great convenience to some families.

If you'd like to rent a car seat or safety booster with your car, here are some of your best bets for rental agencies to try:

Alamo	www.alamo.com	1-800-462-5266
Avis	www.avis.com	1-800-331-1212
Budget	www.budget.com	1-800-527-0700
Hertz	www.hertz.com	1-800-654-3131
Thrifty	www.thrifty.com	1-800-847-4389

The Case For and Against RVs

Having a complete kitchen, restroom, and beds at every stop of the way can be a major convenience for a parent with babies and children along for the ride. If inclement weather strikes, you are well sheltered and well equipped to pass the time with lights, a stereo, and possibly a TV. And if you are driving to only one amazing destination where you may park and settle in for days, enjoying the views from your home away from home, while cooking up your favorite homemade recipes in your own kitchen, even using a microwave oven to reheat your refrigerated leftovers, an RV may indeed be a great way to go (if you don't mind cooking and washing dishes every day of your vacation).

But for all the conveniences an RV affords while stopped along the way, it will not help you escape certain realities of the road trip. For one, your family may still be spending hours on the road, belted into seats, the car seat included (perhaps even more hours as you watch traffic pass you on the hills and at highway turn-outs). You may still get lost, you may still get stuck in traffic, you may still need to stop for gas—and lots of it.

What's more, traveling with your "house on your back" presents certain burdens you may never face when driving your passenger car. Let's not kid ourselves, RVs are BIG and, for many people, they can be stressful to drive (even as a back seat driver)—especially through mountains or cities or even parking lots. And for all of the space RVs require on the road (almost the entire width of the lane), they offer little play space inside for children. Even that convenient toilet will have to relieve itself at some point, and it's not potty trained. And unless you plan to spend your nights at roadside rest areas, you will still have an additional expense of paying for a place to park it (an extra $10-$50 per night, or more in some cases).

Speaking of expenses, you will want to carefully consider the total cost of your RV rental before committing. When I considered an RV rental for one week in the mid season, with pick up and return from the same location in Los Angeles, my total quote came out to $1334. It would have been an additional $35 per person, but we opted to bring our own linens and blankets. The costs broke down as follows:

Sample Standard Mid-Season RV Rental for 2-5 Passengers

- $945   7 Nights (includes comprehensive insurance)
- $203   700 Miles (additional miles: 29 cents/mile)
- $70   Supplemental Liability
- -$70   Promotional Discount
- $85   Kitchen Kit (Plates, bowls, cookware, utensils, can opener, broom, etc.)
- $102   State Tax

Total Charge $1335

Additional damage deposit (refundable after trip) $300

Additional RV Vacation Expenses

- Mileage fees (if you pay by the mile or go beyond your flat-rate package, in this case 29 cents/mile)
- Campground fees ($10-$50 per night)
- Reservation fees ($5 and up, in addition to campground fees)
- Generator fees (about $3/hour of use where applicable, and/or cost of gasoline)
- Campground hook-up fees if applicable (electric, water, sewage, estimate $20-$30/day for full hook-up)
- Dump fees when not using hook-ups (around $5 for sewage)
- Fuel fees for driving (expect between 6 and 13 mpg of unleaded gasoline)
- Propane (usually needed for refrigerator, heater, water heater, stove and range)
- Groceries for trip
- Budget for any additional restaurants, entertainment, and attractions

- Pet deposit, if applicable ($50-$150, usually non-refundable)
- One-way rental fee, if applicable ($200 and up)
- Return airfare or train tickets from one-way rental, if applicable

As I pondered how much our week's vacation could total, all costs considered, I quickly realized there were a lot of other ways we could spend that same money—and time. For one thing, just putting the same $1300 toward a luxury tent, new sleeping bags, and other outdoor gear could have us camping in Fat City—and at the end of the vacation, we'd still own all of the equipment. Or we could take advantage of any number of 3-day vacation packages that could include airfare and hotel for the three of us with little to no time spent driving. Even renting a cabin, a beach house, or condo might prove far more cost-effective—and comfortable for your family, so do consider your options carefully.

Still, there may be situations where an RV rental is ideal. Particularly if you want to visit a remote setting where other lodgings and facilities are not available and tent camping is problematic (security issues, hostile fauna, inhospitable climate, etc.). If you will be traveling with extended family, and perhaps an elderly relative or a pregnant traveler, an RV rental can be a marvelous way to go. Or if you simply need additional accommodations while visiting someone's home, an RV can be the guest cottage escape you need, with all the comforts of home. In other situations, renting a conversion or campervan may provide much of what you're looking for while saving you some money—and quite possibly time.

If you are still considering an RV rental, be sure to read the next section on car seat usage in RVs. A list of RV rental agencies follows on page 176.

The RV / Car Seat Conundrum

When I spoke with one of the largest RV rental agencies in the U.S., I was assured that, while they do not rent car seats, lots of people who rent their RVs use them with their own car seats. I asked for more details and was told that I might need to rent a larger RV than I'd planned on in order to accommodate a car seat (belted positions in the smaller RV were reportedly restricted by a table). As we discussed more details, I learned that not one of the seats in any of their RVs provided a forward-facing belted seat that could fit a car seat other than the driver's and front passenger's seats.

As I explained that car seats are supposed to be installed either forward- or rear-facing, I was once again assured that plenty of parents rent their RVs and use car seats—generally installed on the sideways-facing sofas found in most models. At this point, the agent suggested that (since I was such a stickler) I could just install our car seat on the front passenger's seat, and we grown-ups could take turns riding in the back. When I asked if their RVs have front passenger airbags, he confessed he didn't know.

Two other major U.S. RV rental agencies also assured me that plenty of parents use their RVs with car seats—usually facing sideways on sofa areas. One of these RV rental agencies also assured me that it is not illegal to use a car seat sideways in their RVs on road trips in the U.S.—and that their insurance provider would not cover them if it wasn't legal (cover *them* vs. cover *the renter who installed the car seat*? I had to wonder). While there is a vast gray area surrounding the legalities of this issue, it seems that by and large rented RVs, as fore-hire vehicles, are exempt from the same child safety seat requirements of standard passenger vehicles. Of course, it's legal to carry your child in your arms in the back seat of most city cabs as well, or on your lap in an airplane, but it doesn't mean your child will be protected in the event of a collision.

In Canada, there is already some legislation addressing this very issue. For example, the Alberta Traffic Safety Act specifically requires child safety seats to be used in RVs just as they are in other motor vehicles, and states: "CR (child restraint) can only be installed on forward-facing vehicle seats. Rear- or side-facing vehicle seats in RVs cannot be used for a CR."

To that point, Cruise America's rental FAQ on their Web site currently states: "Child safety seats should be used where applicable. The installation and use of these seats should follow the recommendation of the child seat manufacturer." I'm still looking for a child safety seat manufacturer that recommends installing their forward- or rear-facing car seats sideways.

Most likely your car seat manual will feature a warning like this found in the Britax Roundabout convertible car seat manual: "Forward-facing vehicle seats MUST be used with this child restraint. Side-facing or rear-facing seats in vans, station wagons or trucks MUST NOT be used." The Graco SnugRide manual reads, "The VEHICLE seat must face forward" (their caps) above diagrams of rear- and side-facing seats shown with lines through them. And the Combi Yorktown Booster Car Seat manual states, "DO NOT use this Booster Car Seat on the following types of vehicle seats: Seats which face sides of vehicle. Seats which face rear of vehicle."

The bottom line? Before hitting the highways, freeways, and scenic bi-ways with your family in a rented RV, be sure the model you are renting will properly accommodate your car seat(s). If possible, stop by the rental agency ahead of time to take a look at the model you have in mind and see if your car seat will indeed work. Also, consider renting a conversion van or a campervan as an alternative—in addition to some other advantages, most feature rear passenger seats that face forward while driving. Information on renting campervans follows this list of agencies.

RV Rental Agencies

Adventure Touring, U.S., www.adventuretouring.com / 1-866-672-3572. RV rentals in Los Angeles, San Francisco, Las Vegas, New York, Boston, Chicago, Miami/Fort Lauderdale, and Denver.

All Star Coaches, U.S., www.allstarcoaches.com / 1-866-838-4465. Luxury RV rentals in California, Florida, Ohio, and Pennsylvania.

Auto Europe, Europe, www.autoeurope.com /1-888-223-5555. Campervan and RV rentals in Australia, France, Germany, New Zealand, and Spain.

El Monte, U.S., www.elmonte.com / 1-888-337-2214. RV rentals across the United States.

Calcamper, Spain, www.calcamper.com, Small RVs for rent from Barcelona.

Cruise America, U.S. and Canada, www.cruiseamerica.com / 1-800-671-8042. RV rentals throughout the U.S. and Canada.

Motorhome Rent, France, www.motorhomerent.fr. Small RV rentals throughout France.

Motorhomes Worldwide, International, www.motorhomesworldwide.com. Helps you locate RV and campervan rentals in far-flung destinations around the world, including Cuba, Namibia, Thailand, Argentina, South Africa, and dozens of other countries.

RENTING A CONVERSION VAN OR CAMPERVAN

If you shuddered as you read the gas mileage range for RVs (yes, that was an average 6 to 13 mpg), you should be pleased to know Volkswagon's Westfalia campervan gets between 18 and 21 miles per gallon—good news if you're crossing the continent! Most conversion vans and campervans, even at 12 to 16 mpg, will save you on gasoline expenses over an RV rental while providing many—nearly all of the conveniences you will find in an RV (some even have flat-screen TVs, mood lighting, and more). Yes, you can even get a flushing toilet if you like, in addition to a refrigerator with freezer, cook-top range, etc., and even the kitchen sink. However, you will most likely need to do without an oven and use the campground or resort showers, though there are a handful of conversion vans out there with ovens, microwaves, and showers (expect prices to go up, gas mileage to go down).

As a comparison with the standard RV rental outlined earlier in this chapter, on page 173, I priced out a Westfalia campervan for the same dates in the mid season. This model has four belted seating positions that face forward during the drive, and two double beds during the night. Again, we opted to provide our own bedding, and also dishes, cups, and silverware this time to save the $35 per person to rent these as a "camping kit" (some other items were included this time as a "kitchen kit" as listed below). Here is how the costs broke down:

Sample Mid-Season Westfalia Campervan Rental for 4 People

- $690   7 nights
- $105   Insurance (no charge if your auto insurance covers rental cars)
- Included at no extra charge:

    700 Miles (extra miles 25 cents ea.)

    Kitchen Kit (cookware, utensils, propane, first-aid kit)

State Tax

Total Charge $795

Additional security/damage deposit (fully refundable after trip) $1,000

Optional extras for this rental include a porta-potty at $25 per trip, an electrical heater $15, child safety car seat $15, or a lawn chair $5. This and most other campervans may be used with electrical and water hook-ups where they are provided.

Additional campervan expenses may be similar to those outlined for RV vacations, except for the reduced gas mileage, gasoline-powered generator, and in most cases the sewage hook-up fees or dumps (unless your conversion van has a bathroom with hook-up).

One final note: A campervan or conversion van is not only likely to be less expensive and less stressful to drive than an RV, it will also be vastly easier to park along the way (campsites included). Consider that the next time you need to pull over to change a diaper, check your map, or park near the wharf. Here are some campervan rental companies you might consider.

Campervan Rental Companies

California / San Francisco Bay Area – California Campers VW Westfalia campervan rentals. www.californiacampers.com / 1-650-216-0000.

California / SoCal Area – Vintage Surfari Wagons Restored vintage 1970s VW buses for rent (and surfboards, if you like). www.vwsurfari.com / 1-714-585-7565.

Hawaii / Big Island – G.B. Adventures VW Westfalia campervan rentals. www.gb-adventures.com / 1-877-864-8361.

Hawaii / Big Island and Maui – Imua Camper Company VW campervan rentals. www.imua-tour.com / 1-808-896-3158.

Hawaii / Maui – Aloha Campers VW Westfalia campervan rentals. www.alohacampers.com / 1-808-268-9810.

New Jersey / Philadelphia and Atlantic City – Northeast Camper Rentals
VW Westfalia campervan rentals. www.northeastcampers.com / 1-856-207-5560.

Utah / Salt Lake City – Western Road Trips Newer model VW Eurovan Westfalia Weekender rentals www.westernroadtrips.com / 1-801-953-6068.

Vermont / Burlington – Vermont Campers VW Westfalia campervan rentals. www.vermontcampers.com / 1-802-310-6973.

Washington / Bellingham – Northwest Campers Refurbished Volkswagon Westfalia campervans. www.northwestcampers.com / 1-360-733-1982.

International – Auto Europe Campervan and RV rentals in Australia, France, Germany, New Zealand, and Spain. www.autoeurope.com / 1-888-223-5555.

Scotland / Edinburgh – Scooby Campers Restored 1960s VW campervans and microbuses for rent. www.scoobycampers.com / 0131-467-1312.

PART V
TRAVELS BY AIRPLANE

- Chapter 14 -
Before You Book Your Flight

TICKET PRICING AND OPTIONS

D epending on the age of your child at the time of your flight, the airline, and the type of flight, you may be able to purchase a specially discounted ticket or have her fly for free on your lap. So before you purchase tickets, be sure you understand which options are available and the advantages of each. A good way to find your family's best total fare is to use a search online using a booking engine that takes your child's age into account and whether or not she will fly as a lap child (as described below), and applies any available discounts to your search results.

Booking Engines with Automatic Infant and Child Pricing:

- www.cheaptickets.com
- www.expedia.com
- www.orbitz.com

Some sites, like Hotwire.com and Travelocity.com, currently factor in available discounts for children 2 and older, but not for children under 2 years.

Lap Child

Children under 2 years old. If your child will be flying before her second birthday, she has the option of flying as a "lap child," defined by the airlines as a child under the age of 2 who rides on an adult's lap and has no assigned seat to herself. A lap child generally flies free on domestic flights, meaning flights within the U.S. or flights that begin and end within the same other country, and virtually always for 10% of the adult fare on international flights. A lap child is not generally given a luggage allowance other than a diaper bag that may be carried onboard, but her collapsible stroller and car seat may be checked at the gate as well. A handful of airlines, however, will also allow you to check an extra small suitcase for your child (as noted in the airlines table). If you decide to travel with your child on your lap, be sure to read about Lap Child Safety, beginning on page 220. Also, if your child will turn 2 years old *during* your trip, you will most likely be required to purchase a seat for her return flight. Call the airline to negotiate a split fare rather than paying for a pricier one-way ticket.

Infant's Seat

For children under 2 years old. To help ensure greater safety and comfort for all passengers onboard, especially the small fries who would otherwise likely ride on a parent's lap, most airlines now offer a specially discounted fare for infants who occupy their own seats. Infant seats are for children younger than 2 years of age, and are most often offered at 50% of the adult fare. If you purchase an infant seat for your child, you will need to bring your FAA-approved car seat (CRS) onboard, or reserve a child safety seat with your airline if they offer these (see airlines table). Note: Alitalia and Eurofly are exceptions in that they do not allow children under 2 to fly in their own seats (even when purchased).

Child's Seat

For children 2 years to 11 years old, where available. Since children over the age of 2 years must have purchased seats of their own, it is helpful to know which airlines offer child discounts, and at what rates (see airlines table). Unfortunately, many U.S. airlines have had to eliminate this discount, and other may soon follow suit. Some airlines also vary their pricing for children's seats by season, country of origin, or destination, so it may behoove you to check for these special offers on airline Web sites. Alaska Airlines, for example, doesn't offer a standard discount for child passengers, but periodically allows children to fly free to select destinations (www.alaskaair.com).

Please note that even when an airline offers a standard child's discount, the discount may not apply to special-offer ticket prices where there is already a dramatic discount given for the adult fare. Again, it is helpful to use a search site that will automatically calculate any available discounts for your family and show you a side by side comparison of available airlines and fares.

CHOOSING THE AIRLINE

Not all airlines are created equal in the eyes of traveling parents. Which airline you fly can greatly impact your experience when traveling with babies and small children, from the prices you pay for your child's seat to the services received before and during your flight. When you have a choice, choose well. Consider how some of these differences between carriers could impact your travel plans.

Some airlines do, some don't:
- Offer infant fares (discounted seats) for children under 2 years old
- Offer children's discounts for flyers between 2 and 11 years old
- Give lap children a baggage allowance
- Provide diaper-changing tables in lavatories (can also vary by aircraft)
- Warm bottles and baby food for passengers
- Offer preboarding for families (and pregnant women)
- Provide infant formula and/or baby food
- Provide toddler or children's meals on request
- Provide toys, games, or coloring books for children
- Provide special in-flight programming for children (music, DirectTV, etc.)

To see how popular airlines differ at a glance, you can compare the family-friendly amenities they offer in the airlines table).

Flying the Foreign Skies

When traveling abroad, I have found that the best perks generally come from foreign carriers. One of my favorite perks is that you may feel your travels have already begun before you even part the runway. The flight crew and fellow passengers are more likely to speak in other languages and even the meals and programs shown in flight often reflect your destination. In my pre-parent life, I quickly learned the differences between flying a major U.S. airline to Europe and flying a major European carrier. Whereas one airline served champagne to all passengers after take-off (yes, even in coach) and provided nonstop food service that included premium wines, fresh bread, and more, with complimentary cognac offered after dinner, etc., the other warned us three times before reaching cruising altitude that passengers were not permitted to drink their own alcoholic beverages onboard, and that American domestic beers would be available at $5 each. For meals, they served us cold sandwiches, and not with a smile.

As a parent traveling with small children, I have also seen stark differences between carriers for longer flights. For example, one U.S. airline charged us for meals and gave away our originally reserved window seats, then tried to reseat us across the aisle from one another in spite of our having a lap child (we were lucky—our honeymooning neighbor couldn't even see her spouse in his new seating assignment, and they'd made their original reservations several months in advance). Flying foreign airlines in both Europe and Asia, we've been greeted with care packages including everything from baby food and teething biscuits to toys and diapers, and offered a bottle of formula mixed and warmed in time for our take-off. One Asian airline even offered us use of a bassinet if we wanted it—during a mere one-hour flight.

Singapore Airlines has dedicated "Infant Assist Attendants" that will also help you through all phases of your flight, including warming bottles and baby food, and holding your baby for you when you need to visit the lavatory. If you have occasion to fly Gulf Air, you may look forward to the assistance of a college certified "Sky Nanny" who will meet you at the gate, help you board the aircraft with your child, arrange separate meal times for your child so you can eat in peace, and even help entertain and look after your child for you while you rest during long-haul flights.

So be sure to consider your options carefully when you travel abroad with your child. A good way to get started is by using an online booking engine like those you'll find at www.orbitz.com or www.kayak.com, where you can easily see all of the possible carriers to your destination, and the fares per passenger, including infant and child discounts where available. When you take into consideration the various perks and discounts available, sometimes you can get *more* than what you pay for. The following Airlines Table will help you see how many major airlines measure up for families.

Notes on a Few "Exceptional" Airlines

With rare exception, you can count on the same basic truths to apply to travel with infants and small children across the airlines and around the world. Here are a few of the exceptions I found.

Exceptions for infant seats – Alitalia, EuroFly, and Ryanair will *not* allow infants (children under 2 years) to fly in purchased seats. Children younger than 2 years may only fly on an adult's lap with these airlines.

Exceptions for lap child fares – For international flights, a lap child fare is *almost* always calculated as 10% of the adult fare. Ryanair, however, will charge a flat fee from 6 Euros to 12 Euros for a lap child, and Jet Blue will charge $12 for a lap child for a round trip international flight.

TABLE 1: A NEW PARENT'S GUIDE TO AIRLINES[1]

Airline	Infant Fares (0-2 years)	Child Fares (2 years +)	Lap child luggage allowance	Warm Bottles & Food	Bassinets on long-haul flights	Changing Facility	Other Perks (reconfirm within 24 hrs)
Aeroflot www.aeroflot.ru 1-888-340-6400	Free lap or 50% seat on domestic, 10% lap or 33% seat internat'l	50% domestic, 75% internat'l	Up to 22 lbs. (10 kg.)	Yes	Yes	Varies	Infant and children's meals, diaper kit for long flights
Aer Lingus www.aerlingus.com 1-800-223-6537	10% lap 90% seat	90%	1 diaper bag	Yes	Yes	No	
Air Canada www.aircanada.com 1-888-247-2262	Free lap on domestic and to U.S. 50% seat	100%	70 lbs checked, +stroller, bassinet, car seat	Yes	Yes	Varies	Infant and children's meals, kids' fun packs
Air France www.airfrance.com 1-800-237-2747	Free lap on domestic 10% lap internat'l	50% domestic 33% internat'l	22 lbs + lightweight stroller	Yes	Yes	Yes	Baby food and biscuits, toiletry kit

[1] Please bear in mind that some details may be subject to change, so always confirm critical information with the airline at time of booking.

Airline	Infant Fares (0-2 years)	Child Fares (2 years +)	Lap child luggage allowance	Warm Bottles & Food	Bassinets on long-haul flights	Changing Facility	Other Perks (reconfirm within 24 hrs)
Air New Zealand www.airnewzealand.com 1-800-262-1234	Free lap domestic 10% lap internat'l 75% seat	75%	Same as adult, + car seat and stroller	Yes	Yes	Long-haul	Long-haul flights: infant and child meals, formula, diapers
Alaska Airlines www.alaskaair.com 1-800-252-7522	Free lap 50% seat	100%	None, but car seat and collapsible stroller can be checked	Yes	No	No	
Alitalia www.alitaliausa.com 1-800-223-5730	10% lap, seats for 2+ only	Varies by route	2 checked pcs, + carry-on	Ask	Yes	Varies	Children's meals, diapers, games
Aloha Airlines www.alohaairlines.com 1-800-367-5250	Free lap, 100% seat	100%	Car seat and stroller	No	No	No	
American Airlines www.aa.com 1-800-433-7300	Free lap domestic 50% other	50%	Diaper bag, Umbrella stroller	Yes	No	Yes	

Airline	Infant Fares (0-2 years)	Child Fares (2 years +)	Lap child luggage allowance	Warm Bottles & Food	Bassinets on long-haul flights	Changing Facility	Other Perks (reconfirm within 24 hrs)
Austrian Airlines www.aua.com 1-800-843-0002	10% lap 67% seat	67%	Stroller	Yes	Yes	Varies	Baby food, bottles, diapers, children's meals
British Airways www.ba.com 1-800-247-9297	10% lap 50% seat	50%	1 carry-on, + 70 lbs checked + collapsible stroller	Yes	Yes	Varies	Adoption fares, infant safety seats
British Midlands www.flybmi.com +44-0-1332-64-8181	10% lap 100% or child fare for seat	100% most flights Flexible internat'l C class fares are 67%	22 lbs. checked + collapsible stroller	Yes	Yes	Yes on overseas	Early check-in, children's meals, diapers, teddy bear, Nintendo
Cathay Pacific www.cathaypacific.com 1-800-233-2742	10% lap	75%	70 lbs, but only 45" total measurements, + collapsible stroller	Yes	Yes	Yes	Baby food, children's meals, kid's fun packs
Czech Airlines www.czechairlines.cz 1-800-223-2365	10% lap Up to 50% seat	Up to 50%	One small suitcase + collapsible stroller	Yes	Yes	Varies	Infant meals, coloring books, games

189

Airline	Infant Fares (0-2 years)	Child Fares (2 years +)	Lap child luggage allowance	Warm Bottles & Food	Bassinets on long-haul flights	Changing Facility	Other Perks (reconfirm within 24 hrs)
Delta www.delta.com 1-800-221-1212	Free lap domestic 10% lap internat'l Varies for seat	Varies by flight (often other carriers)	Only with 10% or 50% paid ticket, + collapsible stroller, +booster/safety seat, + bassinet	Varies	Yes	Varies	Ask. Baby food offered on some long-haul flights. Other perks when flight operated by a foreign airline
Easy Jet www.easyjet.com 0871-244-2366 (fee)	Free lap 100% seat	100%	Included in paid adult's carry-on	Yes	No	Varies	
EuroFly www.euroflyusa.com 1-800-459-0581	10% on lap Seats for 2 years+ only	75%	1 carry-on bag up to 5 lbs, + checked stroller and car seat	Yes	Yes	Yes	
Eva Air www.evaair.com 1-800-695-1188	10 % on lap Seat varies	75%	1 checked bag of 45" total combined dimensions or 22 lbs., + stroller	Yes	Yes	Yes	Baby meals, diapers, children's TV
Frontier Airlines www.frontierairlines.com 1-800-432-1359	Free lap 50% seat	100%	One diaper-type bag for baby	No	No	No	

Airline	Infant Fares (0-2 years)	Child Fares (2 years +)	Lap child luggage allowance	Warm Bottles & Food	Bassinets on long-haul flights	Changing Facility	Other Perks (reconfirm within 24 hrs)
Hawaiian Airlines www.hawaiianair.com 1-800-367-5320	Free lap domestic 10% internat'l 67% seat	100% domestic 67% internat'l	No, and checked car seat or stroller counts toward 2 pc. limit for adult	Varies	No	Varies	
JetBlue www.jetblue.com 1-800-538-2583	Free lap domestic $12 lap internat'l 100% seat	100%	Diaper bag, stroller, and car seat	No	No	Yes	DirectTV at all seats with family friendly channels
Korean Air www.koreanair.com 1-800-438-5000	Free lap domestic 10% internat'l	75%	One checked bag up to 28 lbs., + either collapsible stroller or car seat	Yes	Yes	Yes	Baby meals and infant formula if booked in advance, child's menu
Lufthansa www.lufthansa.com 1-800-645-3880	10% lap	75%	18 lbs carry-on OR 70 lbs checked, + umbrella stroller, + bassinet	Yes	Yes	Yes	Baby food
Northwest www.nwa.com 1-800-225-2525	100% seat on domestic, 50% seat most internat'l	100%	No, but 1 diaper bag as carry-on	Ask	Yes	Varies	Adoption fares, snacks for sale only

Airline	Infant Fares (0-2 years)	Child Fares (2 years +)	Lap child luggage allowance	Warm Bottles & Food	Bassinets on long-haul flights	Changing Facility	Other Perks (reconfirm within 24 hrs)
Qantas www.qantas.com 1-800-227-4500	10% lap internat'l, 100% seat	100%	Internat'l flights only: 1 checked bag 45" total	Yes	Yes	Yes	Infant, toddler, and child meals, diapers for international, kids kits
RyanAir www.ryanair.com +353-1-249-7791	Flat fee of 6 to 12 Euros for lap child Seats for 2 yrs + only	Varies, online promo fares are best	No	Ask	No	Yes	
SAS www.flysas.com 1-800-221-2350	10% lap, 75% seat	75%	22 lbs checked + collapsible stroller	Yes	Yes	Yes	Baby food, toys, video games
Southwest www.iflswa.com 1-800-435-9792	Varies, by phone only, currently capped at $129 max each way	Minimal discounts by phone only, promo fares online are best	No	No	Ask	Yes	
Thai Airways www.thaiair.com 1-800-426-5204	10% lap domestic and internat'l, seat is 50%-67%	50% domestic 75% internat'l	One checked bag not exceed 45 inches total, + collapsible stroller or infant carrier	Yes	Yes	Yes	Diapers, baby food on request, "gifts" for children

Airline	Infant Fares (0-2 years)	Child Fares (2 years +)	Lap child luggage allowance	Warm Bottles & Food	Bassinets on long-haul flights	Changing Facility	Other Perks (reconfirm within 24 hrs)
United Airlines www.united.com 1-800-241-6522	Free lap in U.S. and to Canada, 10% lap internat'l 50% seat	100%	None, but car seat and collapsible stroller can be checked	Maybe	Yes	Varies	Domestic meals for purchase, baby food on request for international flights
U.S. Airways www.usairways.com 1-800-428-4322	Free lap in U.S. 10% lap internat'l, 100% seat	100%	No	Maybe	Yes	Yes	
Virgin Atlantic www.virgin-atlantic.com 1-800-862-8621	10% lap most flights, 75% seat	75% adult ticket price	Yes, 1 checked suitcase 22 lbs and 45" max overall, + 1 carry-on	Yes	Yes, to 12 months, and child safety seats on request for 6 months to 36 months with seat	Yes	Child safety seats, in-seat TV with children's programming, children's meals

CHOOSING THE FLIGHT

When you have a choice between flights, it can be difficult to decide which times and options may be best for your family. Yet the particular flight you choose can play a key role in how smoothly your trip begins and ends, especially when considering naptime flights, nighttime flights, or stopover flights, and taking into consideration the timing of your travels to and from airports. As your child progresses through various ages and stages, your flight preferences may also change. Here are some points to consider as you decide between flights:

Naptime Flights

Blessed are they whose children may sleep during a long-haul flight. Infants who nap more frequently and often for longer periods than their older counterparts will, in general, have an easier time napping during flights. Nursing or enjoying a warm bottle at take-off can especially help to set the mood for a snooze. As well, some older children just respond well to the hum of the engines and the familiar comfort of their car seats. However, some toddlers and older children may be too stimulated by the newness of the situation, the bright lights, numerous passengers, engine noise, and announcements blasting forth from the speakers to actually nap during the flight. If your child becomes overtired from his overdue nap, this could prove to be an exhausting flight for you all, and it may be wiser to try and time your flight for another time of the day, and make the most of the flight time for other purposes like reading books, playing games, or eating snacks. You may also try and time his nap with a long drive to or from the airport, if those are options.

Nighttime (or Red-Eye) Flights

Overnight flights can be ideal when flying the long-haul with a child. Unlike daytime flights, "red-eyes" cater to a resting crowd with a period where cabin lights are dimmed and announcements are minimal. Sometimes these flights are less crowded, too, which can mean shorter waits for the lavatory and food or beverage service, and possibly more room onboard for your family to sprawl (but don't count on it). Depending on the length of your flight, you may board in time for dinner, which can help set the mood for evening rituals and bed time for your child, or you may not leave until the middle of the night, when everyone is thoroughly exhausted and will hopefully go right to sleep. The risk is that, if your child has trouble sleeping for some reason, you will all miss your nighttime sleep. And if your child voices his complaints or frustration with the situation, your neighbors onboard may also miss their nighttime sleep, possibly adding feelings of awkwardness or guilt to the challenges you already face. To help ensure as smooth an overnight flight as possible, make sure your child gets plenty of exercise and stimulation in the hours leading up to the flight, and help him visualize how the flight will go, including the time the family spends sleeping. Anything that can make it seem more like bedtime—putting on pajamas, reading bedtime stories, etc., can also help.

Stopover Flights

Sometimes flights with a stopover en route can save you some money—but not always. Generally passengers prefer nonstop flights, as they shave at least a couple of hours off the total travel time and reduce the risk of parting ways with their checked baggage. Parents of infants and small children also like direct flights because there is only one descent to challenge the ears.

There is your stomach to consider, too: If you're deciding between one long flight from your city of departure to a destination overseas, or flying cross-country first before connecting with an overseas flight, meal service most likely will not be included in a domestic flight segment (unless it's provided at a fee). The direct overseas flight, however, will provide you with meals and possibly provide a children's meal or baby food if the airline offers it and you've requested it in advance.

And just as there are definite advantages to flying directly without a stopover, there can also be advantages to taking a break when flying with small children. First of all, children get a change of scenery and a chance to stretch their legs—something you may be very grateful for if your child is energetic or will not be sleeping during the flight. When switching airplanes, you can also trade-in your neighbors (in case things didn't go smoothly in round 1). And you may have a chance to find food or refreshments at the airport, which can be helpful if your flights don't include meal service, and you'd rather not pack along every meal for everyone. At the same time, you'll have twice as many ascents and descents, so think twice about this option if your child is troubled by the noises and sensations of take-off or has problems with ear pressure during descents.

WHAT TO KNOW WHEN FLYING WITH A LAP CHILD

Electronic Tickets and Lap Children

If you are flying internationally with a lap child, be aware that even if you purchase electronic (paperless) international tickets for the seated passengers in your party, as is often the case when buying tickets directly from an airline's web site, your lap child will still be required to have her own paper ticket to cross the border. In most cases, you will need to contact the airline by phone to purchase your lap child's ticket and arrange to have it mailed to you after purchasing your e-tickets. While on the phone with the airline, be sure to request your preferred seats and reserve a bassinet and/or child's meal if available, and ask any questions you may have about the availability of changing tables onboard, gate-checking gear, and luggage allowances for your lap child.

Airline-Provided Bassinets

For overseas and other long-haul flights, many airlines offer special bassinets for babies that attach to the bulkhead wall (depending on the airline, these may also go by the name "infant cots," "sky cots," or "baby beds"). Some larger aircraft, like those operated by AirFrance, even offer bassinets that attach beneath the overhead bins throughout the aircraft. This complimentary convenience allows parents to fly with babies at the lap-child rate, and also have a bed for their child—provided he is still small enough to fit in the bassinet and is not yet capable of climbing out of it. This benefit may prove invaluable as you negotiate your dinner tray or simply need to give your arms a rest.

Sizes of bassinets vary, so ask the airline for specifics for your flight. Since the number of bassinets per flight is limited and they are often only available for passengers seated in the bulkhead rows, be sure to make your reservations as early as possible to ensure you get the appropriate seats and a bassinet reserved for your family. Most airlines recommend reconfirming your seating and bassinet reservations within 72 to 24 hours of BOTH outbound and return flights. If your airline is in the practice of offering unconfirmed seats to passengers as they check in (as many are), you may lose your seating assignment, and therefore the privilege of having a bassinet, so always be sure to call ahead and reconfirm your seats.

Believe it or not, there is still one more way you could loose your rights to a bassinet you've already reserved for your flight. When all of the above is said and done, the bassinets are still provided on a first-come, first-served basis, and there are only a limited number of bassinets available on each airplane. So check in as early as possible to make sure one of them will be yours. Occasionally there are more babies onboard than bassinets.

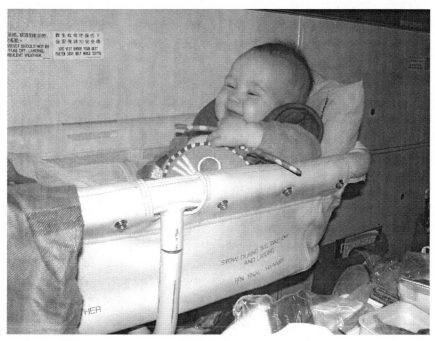

A bulkhead-mounted bassinet can be a great convenience—especially during meals.

SELECTING YOUR SEATS

Which seats are ideal for your family depends on a number of variables, namely the age of your child, his temperament, the duration of the flight, the size of the aircraft, and how many of you will be flying together. In some cases, you can request your preferred seats in advance; in others, it may be a first-come first-served free-for-all in which it may help to have your strategy formed well in advance.

Before You Book Bulkhead Seating...

I am often surprised how many people recommend outright that you should always book bulkhead seats for flights with a baby or small child. Bulkhead seats can definitely have their advantages, especially if you want to use an airline bassinet during your flight. Bulkhead rows also have extra leg room, making it easier to slip in and out to the lavatory for diaper changes or trips with a potty training child, or to get up and pace the aisle with an overtired baby. Once you reach cruising altitude, you can also take advantage of the floor space to set your tote bag full of toys or your diaper bag.

On the downside: the arm rests are fixed on these rows, and the trays are small and too close to work with a baby or toddler on your lap. There is no under-seat storage, and you may be too close to the movie screen to enjoy the show. As well, bright and flashing light from a projected movie may annoy sensitive sleepers, especially those in bassinets mounted at the bottom edge of the screen. The disturbance can be minimized for babies by draping a lightweight blanket over part of the bassinet, but toddlers and preschoolers may not sleep a wink in such proximity to the screen—even babies with car seats in rear-facing positions are likely to lean out far enough to catch the projector lights (or distracting glimpses of them). And finally, bulkhead rows are usually opposite the food preparation areas or lavatories, so extra traffic and noise can also be a problem for light sleepers and, without a row of seats as a privacy buffer in front of you, you may feel more exposed when breastfeeding.

So consider your situation carefully before you reserve these seats. With baby snoozing in the bassinet, you may be able to fly the long haul more comfortably. But think twice if your child is easily over-stimulated, and you will regret not having under-seat stowage each time you have to access the overhead bin, or if your child's car seat is pushing the limits for width and you may need to lift an arm rest to accommodate it.

Best Bet Seats With...

Infants – Window seats on non-bulkhead rows afford the most privacy for nursing, and peace and quiet for sleeping babies. If you want to use an airline bassinet for a long-haul flight, however, you may have to settle for bulkhead seating. Call the airline to ask where bassinets may be used in the particular aircraft you'll be in.

Older babies – Your baby may need more wiggle room now, and if he thrives on smiles and coos from passersby, the bulkhead row of a large airplane may be just the place for him. But if you seek peace and quiet, and hopefully a nap from your child, try seats near the rear of larger aircraft, where side seats taper down from three to two if possible. These highly coveted seats give you extra space between the window seat and the window, while the center seats in this portion of the aircraft are usually the last to be assigned and some are often left empty—until other passengers seeking more space or an extra seat claim them (this could be you). If you will be on a smaller plane with lavatories only in first class and in the aft, try for seats near the front of the aircraft as most of the coach passengers will have to pass to the back of the plane to use its lavatories.

Toddlers on laps – The bulkhead row will give you more space to maneuver, and without the constant temptation to your child of flopping down the tray incessantly or pulling on your forward-neighbor's hair. Once in the air, you can set a tote bag of toys and books at your feet where you'll be able to access them more easily than you would on other rows. However, on long flights the two of you may not fit behind the armrest-mounted tray during meals. For long-haul flights on a large aircraft, it may be best to request the seats near the rear as described in the last section.

Toddlers in seats – The bulkhead row offers three great advantages here. 1) Your forward-facing toddler will not be able to kick a seat in front of him. 2) On smaller aircraft, you will be served drinks and snacks much sooner than the passengers in the rear. 3) It is easiest to pop out of your seats for quick access to the lavatory during potty training, especially on larger aircraft when these seats place you right next to the lavatory. However, be prepared that your child may keep a running commentary on everyone else using the potty!

Preschoolers – Once your child begins flying without a car seat and has mastered potty training, she can sit virtually anywhere on the aircraft other than emergency exit rows. However, she may still prefer to sit near the window for the entertainment value and to have you as a buffer between her and the other passengers on the aircraft.

- *Chapter 15* -
Countdown to Take-Off

REQUIRED DOCUMENTS FOR AIR TRAVEL

In your pre-parent life, you may have whisked off to the airport with little more than a carry-on bag in your hand, your driver's license already in your wallet, and your e-ticket awaiting its printing for you at the airport kiosk. You may need to reprogram your thinking for air travel with your child, and not just because of the amazing increase in baggage.

Domestic Air Travel

Your child does not need photo I.D. for flights within the U.S. unless he is traveling alone as an unaccompanied minor (not generally allowed before 5 years of age). You should, however, travel with a certified copy of your child's birth certificate—especially if your child is under 2 years old and will be flying in your lap free of charge or in a seat at a reduced rate based on her age. Often times, agents will not ask to see the birth certificate unless they are uncertain whether the child may be 2 years old already. If you were not asked for a birth certificate for a previous flight, it could be different the next time around. And once your child begins walking, it could be a tough call for agents with limited exposure to children. Be forewarned, the delays and chaos that can result from not having the proper paperwork when requested are simply not worth the risk. Although a lap child does not need or receive a ticket for the flight, she must have an "infant boarding pass," which will be issued upon check-in.

International Air Travel

In the past, children traveling with their parents to most destinations within the Western hemisphere have not needed passports—but not anymore. All airline passengers that travel to or from Canada, Mexico, Central and South America, the Caribbean, and Bermuda are required to have a valid passport. As before, your child will need a passport for air travel to any other countries as well. Information on obtaining passports for infants and children begins on page 96. Parents not traveling together with their child should be sure to read the next point.

Important note: Children flying with only one parent or guardian
In order for one parent to cross the border with a child without the other parent, he or she will need a notarized letter of permission or power of attorney from the absent parent. This applies even when crossing the U.S. border to Canada or Mexico. If you have sole custody of your child, you will need to present the applicable verification—a custody order, death certificate, adoption decree, etc. A sample letter can be found on page 100.

CARRY-ON CONSIDERATIONS

When you are traveling with a baby or toddler, how you've packed your carry-ons—and how many carry-ons you pack—can make all the difference between a comfortable flight and a catastrophic one. The more items you can check-in upon arrival the fewer items you will have to lug through the security line, run through the X-ray, and carry all the way to your gate.

Your car seat and a diaper bag of some sort may already be necessary carry-ons. Your stroller may also play a critical role in getting your child and some of her gear to the gate (it can carry the child, diapers and/or a daypack, or possibly even the car seat), and you may also need it to help her sleep during a layover or simply to help keep her contained while you use the restroom or collect your checked baggage. That's already three items to get through security, plus yourself and your child. Now, take off those shoes.

Clearly, it pays to simplify your carry-ons as much as possible. Yet you don't want to find yourselves wanting for snacks, toys, changes of clothes, or other essentials as a compromise. How do you strike the right balance for your flight?

Carrying On Liquids and Gels

The amount of other liquids or gels you are allowed to carry into the cabin for your flight—or whether or not you're allowed to carry any at all—may be subject to change due to heightened security alerts or concerns about certain airports or regions. For the latest policies or restrictions concerning carry-on baggage, check www.TSA.gov/travelers.

When only travel-size quantities of liquids and gels are permitted in the cabin, you should be able to bring onboard a quart-size clear plastic bag (with slide-lock top) containing various liquids and gels in quantities of no more than 3 ounces each. All products should fit easily into the closed bag and lie flat on the X-ray conveyor belt. Many items from your child's travel kit (page 44) are already the appropriate size for this restriction and may prove quite helpful during your flight. You may want to pack the other items from your travel kit in a checked suitcase, but carry a "modified travel kit" into the cabin if that is an option.

In the event of a ban on liquids or gels: Even when a complete liquid ban is in effect, parents traveling with a baby or toddler are still generally allowed to bring a reasonable amount of infant formula, expressed breast milk, and/or liquid baby foods into the cabin (as much as is needed for the flight and a possible delay). You can call your airline if you have specific questions, but if lines are busy, try www.TSA.gov/travelers for the latest information.

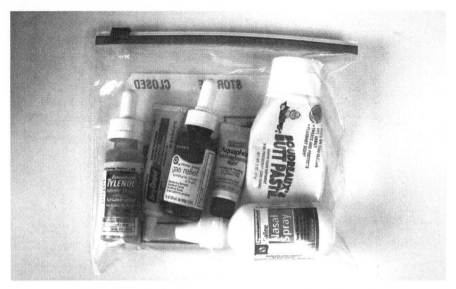

Sample modified travel kit for carry-on with 3 oz. liquid restrictions:

- Infants' Tylenol, 1 fl. oz.
- Infants' gas relief drops, 1 fl. oz.
- Small tube of diaper crème, 2 oz.
- Small tube of teething gel, .33 oz.
- Sample tube of healing crème (from doctor's office), .25 oz.
- Saline nasal spray, 1.5 fl. oz.

Carrying On Diapers

You will obviously need enough diapers with you en route to cover your entire time spent traveling between home and your destination, plus a few extras for good measure. Then add a few more in case a flight delay finds you camped out at the airport for untold hours. As one father discovered while stranded overnight in an airport with two toddlers, even airport shops (and restaurants) close for the night. Now add the corresponding number of baby wipes, and your diaper bag may already be bursting at the seams.

As I prepared for my first long-haul flight with my daughter, I loaded up the largest diaper bag we had (Winnie the Pooh meets the Hummer) with plenty of diapers and wipes, that extra change of clothes, a couple of receiving blankets, small toys, her travel kit, and a few other things to help pass our travel time. I proudly called it, "Angelina's Carry-on," slinging the 25 lb., almost-completely-zipped bag over my shoulder. I'm not sure how many passengers I blessed with Angelina's Carry-on that first time we sidled down the aisle to the lavatory, but imagine my surprise, once inside, when I couldn't shut the door—not without some serious shifting and wiggling. What was worse, Angelina's Carry-on didn't fit beneath a seat and had to be housed in the compartment above our neighbor's heads (not terribly convenient for any of us).

"Angelina's Carry-on" quickly transformed into a small backpack that fit neatly beneath the airplane seat in front of us (or at our feet during the cruising portions of flights on the bulkhead rows), and beside it fit the "diaper purse." The diaper purse has just the essentials we might need in the lavatory. The strap goes over my shoulder and crosses my body to where the bag sits conveniently at my hip, where I can reach into it one-handed as I tend to her on the changing table or on the toilet seat. Having the changing mat, diaper, and crème steadily at my hip with one hand free at all times has proven invaluable in many situations that did not provide a place to set a diaper bag, and especially as Angelina sprawled longer and longer across the changing tables or danced her toddling two-step upon the toilet seat. The new messenger-style "diaper slings" can be worn in this manner and are often styled so that even dads will wear them without complaint (one is even called "the Diaper Dude").

Carrying On Backpacks and Totes

Backpacks may be easily worn through the airport and help keep hands free; they also generally fit well beneath airplane seats. But you may want to reconsider using one for the items you'll want to access frequently in flight, like toys, since you will be bending over and trying to maneuver the zippers each time, opening the pack nearly all the way between you and your neighbor's feet to find the one or two items you seek. In the mean time, other items may spill out the sides. You may fare better with a simple tote bag for toys, snacks, reading materials, etc. One light in color will make it especially easy to see the items inside, and there will be no zippers or Velcro to make noise if you need to access it as your child sleeps.

As for the items packed inside, you can subdivide and conquer by using clear, slide-lock food storage bags (or other containers) to group like items in your carry-ons. It makes it much easier to find what you need en route (toys here, snacks here, eating utensils and bib here, diapers and wipes here, travel kit there). Plastic storage bags also make it easy to pack a fresh change of clothes very compactly (and keep it fresh) by squeezing the extra air out of the bag as you zip it. And be sure to pack an empty one for soiled clothing.

Carrying On Car Seats:

Whether or not you are planning to use your child's car seat on your flight, there is one very important reason you will want to carry it to your gate: safety. Car seats are made to withstand the forces of one accident, one time, after which the manufacturers advise replacing the car seat and most insurance companies foot the bill. Molded of plastic, a car seat's integrity can be compromised quite easily (even by age, which is why car seats are assigned expiration dates). If you turn your car seat over or remove its cover to see where the harness straps feed through, you might be surprised to see how thin the plastic is at these important places. And just the strain of a "fender bender" can create cracks so thin you cannot see them with the naked eye but should they be stressed as they would be in an accident, the seat may fail when you need it most. With that in mind, you can probably understand why it is best not to subject your car seat to the rigors of an airport baggage system or risk having 75 lb suitcases dropped on top of it. But how to get it to the gate, along with the rest of you?

Infant carrier car seats that "ride" on strollers or stroller frames are fantastic for travel, but will likely be outgrown by your child some unpredictable time before his first birthday, at which point you'll have to switch to a larger car seat which can be much trickier to get to your gate. If you have a stroller with two separate handles, see if you can lengthen the straps of your car seat and loop them over the handles. If not, you may be able to wear the car seat over your shoulders by lengthening the straps. If that doesn't work, you may want to consider getting a car seat backpack carrier like the Pac Back or any of the various car seat carrying cases that include backpack or shoulder carrying straps (especially if you'll be traveling alone with your child or with more than one child).

Some models of Britax convertible car seats can be attached to the GoGo Kidz Cart which makes it possible to wheel your child right to the gate in his own car seat, and possibly right down the aisle of larger aircraft (different models work with the Roundabout, Marathon, Decathlon, Boulevard, and Wizard). If you'll be traveling much by airplane and/or taxi, you might also consider the Sit'n'Stroll car seat that converts to a stroller (can be used from birth to 40 lbs, rear- and forward-facing).

CHECKING BAGS AND BABY GEAR

The first order of business is to know your airline's baggage restrictions and limitations. If you are flying with a lap child, check if your airline grants lap children any checked baggage (see airlines table). Generally, a collapsed stroller and/or car seat checked at the gate do not apply toward your baggage allowance.

Also, be aware of the airline's weight limit for checked items. The standard 70 lbs. per bag of the past has been reduced to 50 lbs. by some airlines (e.g. Delta and United), and although it may be far simpler for you to transport one suitcase at 59 lbs. rather than two separate, lighter suitcases, it may cost you an extra $25 or so at check in to do so. To avoid surprises, visit your airline's Web site to see their baggage policy or call their toll-free telephone number (both are listed in the Airline's Table). It may work best for your family to use multiple suitcases that can "piggy back," so you are able to roll, for example, two or three separate pieces with only one hand.

Also, be sure to tag all items you will check—including the stroller, car seat, etc.—before you leave for the airport. This will save you from scrambling for pens, airline tags, etc., while juggling all your items through the line at check-in.

Checking a Car Seat

Not recommended—see carrying on car seats for details. If you still must check a car seat, be aware that airlines don't always provide plastic bags for checked car seats (and other unsuitcased items), so be sure to tighten and fasten the u straps, and stow away any loose LATCH equipment or tethers to help prevent your car seat from catching in the baggage system. You may also want to consider getting a car seat carrier case (generally a zipped fabric bag with handles) to help protect your car seat and keep it clean.

These carriers also provide a great place to store any jackets or sweaters you'll want to access on arrival, but won't need in flight.

Checking a Stroller

If for some reason it is easier for you to check your stroller in on arrival, rather than at your gate, keep in mind that it will be far more vulnerable traveling through the airport baggage system than it is when left (and later retrieved) at the gate. Again, you may want to use a carrying bag or case to help protect your gear. If your stroller didn't come with a "travel bag," manufacturers often sell model-specific bags you can purchase separately, or you can choose from a variety other stroller bags made to fit the standard sizes.

Checking a Play Yard

Play yards can be very helpful in providing a safe space for your child in un-childproofed settings, but if you just need a place for your baby or toddler to sleep, you may consider other solutions before hauling one to the airport. First of all, if you'll be staying at a hotel, resort, or vacation property, ask if a crib is available for you to use (for a fee or for free) during your stay. You may also be able to rent a play yard, along with any other equipment that would be of help, at your destination (more on this in the pages ahead).

If neither of those options works for you, you may prefer flying with a baby or toddler travel bed. Often called "travel trundles," these mini beds provide some cushioning for children with raised edges to help keep them from rolling out, and they fold nearly flat and zip closed for travel (also great for train travel). Some brands even include carrying straps or extra pockets for storage, and the infant models may even fit in the bottom of your suitcase. For infants, portable co-sleepers like the Snuggle Nest, which goes in the center of a large bed between parents, are also a convenient option. If you must ultimately bring your play yard along for the trip, make sure to pack it as carefully as possible. You may want to remove any wheels ahead of time to prevent them from breaking off in the baggage system. The carrying sacks they come with often don't always completely cover the ends, in which case you may want to use heavy duty garbage bags and strong tape to ensure no pieces will be lost.

PLANNING YOUR IN-FLIGHT ENTERTAINMENT

Rather than bombard your child (and possibly your neighbors) with every toy you could possibly fit into the carry-on, plan a strategic rotation of toys and books to keep things interesting—and under control, and leave a second set of different items in the checked bag for a change later on.

As an example, if your flight will include one meal (whether served to you or by you), decide ahead of time which activity would be best for the time before eating—stacking blocks on the dinner tray, playing with puppets, etc. After the meal, it might be a good time to enjoy an audio book together, or to read some favorite stories that often precede naptime. Older children may enjoy a special new coloring book just for the trip, or the chance to decorate airline napkins with portraits of their neighbors in coach. Portable DVD players are also helping many families travel happier these days. Whether it's the calming intrigue of Baby Einstein for a baby, Dora's greatest hits for a toddler, or the exciting promise of a feature film for a preschooler, everybody seems to enjoy a good movie during a flight.

On long-haul flights, you will need to plan for some amount of physical activity for your child as well—which is not easy when new FAA regulations keep passengers in their seats virtually the entire flight. Babies may benefit from some of the routine exercises you probably do at home already—riding the bicycle, playing patty cake, etc.—and these can be done on your lap, on the floor of the bulkhead row, in the travel bassinet, or on a spare seat (if such a thing exists on your flight). If your child is old enough to walk independently or while holding onto your hands, she could benefit from the chance to stretch her legs as much as you could, so try to work in a lap around the aircraft together when you make trips to the lavatory.

On your return journey, be prepared to mix it up a little. Pack the earlier flight's books and toys in your checked suitcase, and bring alternates onboard. Your child may even like to choose which items to bring onboard—especially after he's learned what to expect from the earlier flight.

Lastly, don't forget this traveler's motto: "The best toys are found." It's amazed me how fascinating the illustrated flight safety brochures can be to small children, and the plastic cups, and the crinkly packets of pretzels, and the reading lights, and the in-flight magazines, and just the fellow passengers who may be all too happy to play peek-a-boo or smile and wave at your child (we'll hope).

PREPARING TODDLERS AND PRESCHOOLERS FOR THE FLIGHT

Security screenings can be a little unnerving for any of us, but for a toddler or preschooler it can be especially disconcerting. Help your child know what to expect at the airport, including lengthy lines for check-in and security, as well as what you will all need to do to pass through security (e.g. Yes, even the teddy bear must pass through the X-ray machine—but it's a quick ride).

Although airplane noise can soothe some children right to sleep, the roaring engines and the exciting sensation of lifting off the ground may frighten more sensitive children. Ear pressure is another good topic to discuss in advance, including how our ears will all need to pop, and what we can do to help. The more you can discuss these kinds of details in advance, the more confident—and more content your child will be when traveling by air.

Discuss the amount of time you will spend in the aircraft during your flight and how you will spend this time. Older children may enjoy contributing their own ideas, too, as you discuss possible books and toys to bring, snacks, games, etc. If a meal will be served in flight, talk about the procedure of getting served and eating at your seats (and how it may require a little patience waiting for the food to come—and to return the trays).

For those in potty training and beyond, the aircraft lavatory may be a little intimidating. Again, help your child know what to expect ahead of time, including the need to wait, as is often the case, and to tell you as early as possible when he feels the urge. Also, discuss modifications you may make to the aircraft toilet—a folding travel seat you can practice using at home, or perhaps even a travel potty you may set on top of the toilet lid, like the "Inflate-a-Potty." In early potty training, it may be simplest and safest to use diapers or disposable training pants during the flight, especially in the event that turbulence or other conditions may require all passengers to remain seated at length.

- *Chapter 16* -
At the Airport and
On the Plane

CLEARING SECURITY WITH SMALL CHILDREN (AND A SMALL MOUNTAIN OF GEAR)

Many a parent has tried to slip through the scanner with a sleeping infant in his sling or stroller—unsuccessfully. Be prepared to put all of your gear, and I do mean all of it (collapsed strollers, infant carriers, car seats, slings, frontpack carriers, etc.), onto the X-ray belt—right along with your shoes and anything else that would normally go through the scanner.

Since higher security measurements have been implemented in recent years, U.S. airports now require that all infant carriers, e.g. Baby Björns, Snugglys, and slings, as well as infant carrier car seats, be separated from the passengers and run separately through the X-ray scanner. Likewise, children need to come out of their strollers, and the strollers should be collapsed and placed on the conveyor belt. However, when unwieldy tandems, twins, and other oversized strollers arrive on the scene, they are generally sidelined and scanned by hand if they cannot fit through the X-ray on the conveyor belt (you will want to budget for extra time).

With all of your bags, gear, shoes, and jackets placed on the conveyor belt, you will then stroll through the scanner with your baby in your arms. Once children can walk by themselves, they will be expected to do so through the scanner. You or your partner may want to go first to help encourage them to pass through and alleviate any anxiety about what awaits on the other side, but if you are traveling alone, you may want to send your child first in case you beep and require further scanning.

Just how you can get everything removed, collapsed, and scanned while tending to your child is a wonder—and you may still find yourself wondering how to do it many, many trips from now. Even knowing you will need to remove your sling or frontpack carrier, it may still seem perfectly logical to wear your baby and leave your hands free for toting baggage and loading items onto the conveyer belt—until you find yourself scrambling on the other side of the scanner to get the sling back onto yourself once again, one-handed while holding your baby, as an army of hurried travelers stampedes over your bare feet, trying to collect their own gear on the other side of the scanner (your shoes are somewhere under the diaper bag, or stroller, or car seat).

After struggling through airport security a number of times with my daughter in and out of various carriers and strollers, I thought I'd finally figured out how to streamline our family's passage through the scanner. With Angelina nestled into my elaborate "wrap" of some 19 ft of fabric, I explained to the guard, "It's just fabric, see? There are no buckles or clasps or anything—just fabric." I didn't see how this was any different from walking through the scanner fully clothed with my baby in my arms, but he did. So there I stood at the front of the growing line, trying to untangle some 19 feet of fabric from around my legs and hips as the guards chuckled, and my fellow passengers grew anxious about catching their flights.

Your simplest solution may be to leave your child in his stroller until the last possible moment—and bring a stroller that folds with one hand if possible. On the other side of the scanner, you can nab your stroller first and place your child in it right away. If needed, you can even wheel her out of the path to park next to a security guard as you collect your other belongings from the conveyor belt.

In some parts of the world, you will find airport security to be a bit more child-friendly than you will in the United States. You might get away with pushing your sleeping child through in his stroller or wearing her in a sling, and getting manually scanned with a wand. Of course, there is usually an additional price for this treatment—a few extra moments of your time as agents dote upon your child, ask twenty questions about his age and disposition, and inevitably stroke his cheek.

If you are traveling solo with your child or with more than one child (or if you just feel precarious trying to juggle your carry-ons and your child), do not hesitate to smile at the first security person you encounter and say assertively, "I will need some assistance." Sometimes you may need to ask more than once, or more than one agent, whereas other times the agents may jump at the chance to help. Either way, the extra help may be even more appreciated on the other side of the scanner as you try and regroup (the people behind you will likely appreciate it as well).

Remember, the fewer items you have to shuffle at security, the better. You may feel inundated already with just the items for your child, so the less you have to carry or slip on and off for yourself the more manageable the procedure will be. Consider these tips for traveling parents:

- Pack your jacket and wear a sweater instead.
- Only travel in slip-on shoes (no laces, no buckles).
- Do not wear a belt when traveling, or keep it in your carry-on until you've passed through security.
- Pack your watch and only necessary jewelry in your carry-on to put on after clearing security.
- Use a backpack or over-the-shoulder bag that you can sling on and off easily and will keep your hands free to contend with other items.
- Consider letting your diaper bag double as your purse, and/or
- Wear a neck security wallet to keep your boarding passes and ID handy while keeping your hands free.
- Avoid wearing your baby in a frontpack carrier or other type of carrier that requires two hands to remove and/or resume wearing.
- Consider taking twins or young siblings in separate travel or umbrella strollers, rather than in a cumbersome double stroller.
- For the latest information about airport security requirements, visit the Transportation Security Administration online at www.tsa.gov, or call them at 1-866-289-9673.

10 Ways to Entertain Your Tot in the Terminal

If you dread spending time awaiting your flight with your toddler, or surviving a layover with your preschooler, fear not. Airports can be far more interesting to a child than they are to the rest of us. In fact, when my brother-in-law recently panicked, unsure of how to keep his three- and four-year-old entertained on a rainy afternoon, he asked them where they would like to go, "To the movies? To the mall?" They both exclaimed excitedly, "To the airport!" And off they went. Here's a sampling of some of the fun to be had inside the terminal.

- Ride the escalators.
- Ride the elevators.
- Play "I see a blue coat, I see a black coat" (or some version of "I spy with my little eye").
- Count backpacks.
- Have a picnic at a vacated gate.
- Watch the airplanes taxi and take off.
- Watch the airplanes descend and applaud the smoothest landings.
- Fill water bottles for your flight at a water fountain.
- Befriend airline personnel also awaiting your flight with questions like, "How many times have you flown on an airplane?" and "Have you ever seen Santa Claus up there?"
- Get some quality physical activity in like practicing yoga, doing calisthenics, or dancing the Hokey Pokey at a vacated gate—that's what it's all about! If you're traveling with a baby, put down a blanket and let her roll, rock, or crawl, practicing all her latest moves.

The Great Preboarding Debate

Most airlines offer preboarding for families with children under the age of 5. With your infant still in your arms, you may happily march ahead of the crowd of other passengers, making way to your seats down open aisles with plenty of overhead storage to choose from. But as your child gets older, you may stand at the gate scratching your head, asking the flickering florescent lights overhead, "To pre-board or not to pre-board?" It's a good question and one worthy of careful consideration.

When to preboard:

- If your child is slow to adapt to new situations, pre-boarding can be a good way to help him adjust to his new surroundings and make himself comfortable before take-off.
- If you are flying with a car seat (especially for the first time), pre-boarding might allow you the extra time and attention from the flight crew to help get settled into your seats.
- If you are flying a carrier that does not have pre-assigned seating (like Southwest), pre-boarding may be the only way to ensure your family gets seats together and ones that will be appropriate for car seats.
- If you are flying alone with your child, pre-boarding will help ensure you get the assistance you need folding your stroller at the gate, storing your baggage, installing your car seat, etc., all while taking care of your child.
- If you are boarding a large aircraft or traveling on a very full flight, pre-boarding will help you get to your seats expeditiously without getting trapped in a slow-moving line of passengers struggling to store their carry-on baggage—possibly bumping you or your child in the process.
- If you are traveling on a large airplane with a lap child and have seat assignments near the rear (where any remaining seats will most likely be found), you may want to board early to "squat" on an extra seat near yours in case you can claim it—or make a trade with someone for another vacant seat.

When not to preboard:

- If you have an extremely active child, it might be best to let her burn off her energy outside of the aircraft and not board until the last moment possible.
- If you have a toddler that will be traveling on your lap, it may be best for the whole family to wait until the last moment possible to settle into your seats.

Using a Car Seat (CRS) on Aircraft

According to FAA regulations, infants (children under 2 years) flying in purchased seats rather than on laps must be secured in their car seats as they would be in an automobile. As for children 2 to approximately 4 years and weighing less than 40 lbs, the FAA "strongly recommends" the use of an FAA-approved CRS (Child Restraint System, which is airline-speak for "car seat"), though it is not required. However, some airlines may request that you hold a smaller child that doesn't have a car seat in your lap during takeoff and landing. If you are undecided about bringing your car seat on board, keep these benefits in mind:

- Children are safest flying and landing in their car seats.
- Children are often more comfortable in their car seats than on a lap or in the airplane seat.
- You will likely be more comfortable with your child riding in his car seat, especially if you plan to eat during the flight.
- You may both be more likely to snooze during the flight.
- Your car seat will be best protected from damage traveling in the cabin.

To be certain your car seat will be accepted by the airline, look for red type on the label that clearly says, "This restraint is certified for use in motor vehicles and aircraft." If your child's car seat does not have this statement on its label, be prepared to have your car seat checked for you at the gate. Some toddler car seats that later convert to belt-positioning booster seats do not include this statement on the label, but may explain in the user's manual that the seat is approved for use in aircraft as a car seat only—so be sure to have your manual tucked into its storage place as you travel in case there is any question.

Otherwise, car seats may be used on aircraft similarly to how they are used in automobiles throughout the U.S.:

Children under 20 lbs – a rear-facing car seat

Children 20-40 lbs – a forward-facing car seat

Children over 40 lbs – a forward-facing car seat with a suitable upper weight limit for use as a car seat with the harness, not as a booster.

In some cases, your airline may even be able to provide you with a CRS for your child during flight. For example, British Airways and Virgin Atlantic now offer a limited number of CRSs for its seated passengers under 2 years old—jolly good if you'll be riding the tube or train on your vacation and won't otherwise need a car seat.

Installing Your CRS on the Airplane

A CRS can be an obstacle to other passengers en route to the lavatory or, more importantly, when exiting in event of an emergency, so be sure to mention it when you reserve and/or reconfirm your seat assignments. You will need to place the CRS in the least obtrusive seat possible—either a window seat or in the middle of a center row on a larger airplane. A CRS cannot be used on an exit row. Your CRS installs with the airplane seat belt just as it would with the lap belt of an automobile, though you may find it helpful or even necessary to turn the buckle so that it may be opened away from the arm rest after your flight.

Although the FAA advises that a CRS no wider than 16 inches should fit in the coach section of most aircraft, the truth is that virtually no car seat fits the bill. Even the popular Graco Snugride infant car seat measures just over 16 inches at its widest point. Among the narrowest of convertible (rear- and forward-facing) car seats, is the Radian folding car seat by Sunshine Kids, which measures just 17 inches wide at its base and is approved for use in aircraft. The Graco CarGo is a forward-facing toddler car seat that converts to a booster, which also measures 17 inches wide (like most car seats that convert to boosters, it doesn't have aircraft approval stamped on it, though it is mentioned in the user's manual, which you'll want to bring along in case there's any question). The streamlined Britax Roundabout convertible car seat measures just over 18 inches wide, yet you'll see plenty of them on airplanes (including ones provided by aforementioned airlines).

If you have one of the more commodious car seats for your child, be warned that those comfy car seat armrests or side pockets that may be a plus in the car may simply not fit on an airplane. What can you do? As long as you're seated in a non-bulkhead row, you should be able to help increase your "wiggle room" by lifting the airplane seat armrests.

Why No Booster Seats Onboard?

Booster seats are not approved for use on aircraft, as they are made to properly position shoulder belts on children, and are not supposed to be used with lap-only belts as found on aircraft. Children over 40 lbs are not required to have additional restraint beyond the aircraft's seat belt.

A Note on the New CARES "Safety device"

The FAA recently approved a new flight "safety device" designed as an alternative to car seats for children over 1 year old and weighing between 22 and 44 lbs. The CARES device (Child Aviation Restraint) is basically a harness that goes around the adult airplane seat back and attaches to the passenger lap belt. It helps protect against "turbulence and other incidents" by converting the airplane's seat belt into a safety harness. Weighing just 1 lb. and packing into its own 6" stuff sack, it clearly has its advantages over hauling a car seat through the airport. However, it is not meant to be used in automobiles. If you will be flying often and without other need for a car seat, this may be a good option, though it is not necessarily as comfortable for very small children as a well-fitted car seat might be, especially on long flights. More information about CARES can be found online at www.kidsflysafe.com or call 1-800-299-6249.

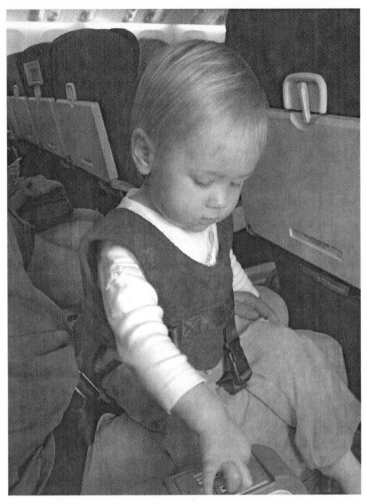

Flying high in a Baby B'Air flight safety vest.

LAP CHILD SAFETY

Because turbulence is unpredictable and is the leading cause of injuries on commercial aircraft, lap-held babies are among the most frequently injured passengers on turbulent flights. At this time in the U.S., the Baby B'Air flight safety vest is the only safety device specifically designed for lap children and tested for use on aircraft (frontpack infant carriers and slings are not permitted for use in aircraft seats by the FAA). This little red vest straps around the child's waist and crotch, with a strap attached to the back that loops around your adult aircraft seat belt. Note that it is not approved by the FAA for use during takeoff, landing, or taxiing as it is designed to help with turbulence, not the motion or risks associated with landings. Nevertheless, it is a far safer alternative to merely holding your child on your lap, and certainly makes it easier to relax during your flight (you can even nurse your child while using it).

Some foreign airlines, may offer you a special safety belt for your lap child that simply goes around her waist with a second loop to go around your own seat belt. A few airlines, like Austrian Air and British Airways, may even require you to use one of these safety belts for your lap child (interestingly, these have been banned for use on U.S. carriers). Again, international airlines vary widely on these practices, so ask for details when you book your flight.

WHAT ABOUT ALL THOSE GERMS?

The prospect of hundreds of air passengers, some inevitably sick with colds and possibly worse, coming together in cramped conditions with little vents spewing forth recycled cabin air can be especially disconcerting for parents traveling with babies and small children.

The good news is that the air itself that is circulating—and re-circulating—in your aircraft may actually be healthier than the air in your child's day care, preschool, or even at the library. Most commercial aircraft now re-circulate the cabin's air every three to five minutes through state-of-the art HEPA filters. In a 20/20 special report by ABC News, an air filtration expert reported that these HEPA filters can capture up to 99.9% of small bacteria and viruses — even SARS and bird flu virus.

Although the cabin *air* may be relatively free of illness causing viruses and bacteria, the surfaces inside the airplane and the airports may be a different matter. Germs like to travel, too. If you had a microscope handy you could follow them on their course through the airport to their connecting flights as well. They tend to hitch-hike from one surface to the next via droplets of moisture, particularly those coughed and sneezed onto hands that share railings, elevator buttons, arm rests, trays, and lavatory doors.

What's your best defense? Wash your hands, and often. Better yet, keep a travel-size pack of antibacterial Redi-Wipes handy in your diaper bag or carry-on to use when washing hands isn't an option—especially after changing diapers in the lavatory where it may be impossible to safely wash your hands while your child is on the changing table. You can also use the wipes to quickly wipe down the armrests and trays at your seats as you settle in for your flight.

EAR PRESSURE, PAIN, AND RELIEF

Most parents embarking on their first flight with an infant or toddler fear, more than anything else, whether their children's ears will adjust properly to the changes in air pressure. The good news is, Mother Nature is on their side. Except in certain situations, the body is well equipped to adjust to such changes almost automatically—we swallow, we yawn, we chew, and we chat, all of which helps our middle ears to adjust to changes in the cabin air pressure.

Complications that may prevent the ears from adjusting properly or in time to prevent pain from developing can include swelling or mucus in the Eustachian tubes from a cold, allergies, or a recent ear infection. If your child has experienced any of these ailments leading up to your flight, you may want to consult your doctor to make sure "all ears are in the clear" and find out about any precautions or remedies he might recommend in case ear pain is still a problem during your travels.

When ear discomfort occurs in flight, it is usually most pronounced during the descent portion rather than the ascent. Just think of past airplane ascents, drives through mountain passes, or rapid elevator ascents in tall buildings when your own ears may have begun to "feel funny" until they popped. With a healthy, functioning Eustachian tube, this is not generally painful, although a child unfamiliar with the sensation may be uncertain how to respond, and the added engine noise during takeoff may also frighten some children (your own calm example and soothing voice may help here).

On the other hand, when ear pain does occur during descent, it can be quite painful—enough to make any of us want to cry, especially babies and small children. (Perhaps this is Mother Nature's last-ditch effort to help—even crying helps equalize ear pressure!) The pain should only be temporary, though the crying and distress may continue for a while. But if your child experiences ear pain during descent, and it continues well after landing, be sure to contact your doctor's office.

In any case, remember you have a number of tools at your disposal to help encourage your child's ears to adjust to the changing air pressure in the cabin. First of all, encourage your child (and all members of the family) to stay well hydrated leading up to the flight, as this will help thin any mucus that may be present in the Eustachian tube and prevent blockages or reduce restrictions. As well, any of these methods may help during take-off and landing:

- Breastfeeding
- Bottle feeding
- Cup feeding
- Sucking pacifiers
- Chewing on a teething toy
- Snacking
- Licking lollipops
- Talking
- Singing

We have marveled at the power a simple cup full of water has over an infant in distress; even when breasts and bottles would not be had, a small cup or even a bottle's cap filled with water was a fascination that beckoned our daughters each to sample and sip their way to instant relief. Just be sure you have what you need before the airplane begins its descent and you can no longer access overhead baggage or move about the cabin.

Children 1 year and older may also be helped by EarPlanes, the soft, hypoallergenic silicone "filters" that can be inserted into the ears to help regulate pressure during flights (Doctor-recommended, Navy Pilot-approved). They also reduce noise, which may help set some children at ease as the airplane gets much louder during take-off and landing.

Finally, try to relax. And help your child to do the same. Not only can stress and tension get in the way of ear pressure equalization, but any

223

signs of stress you exhibit may cause your child to feel distressed as well. If this scenario builds ("Come on, PLEASE DRINK your juice!"), you may not be sure if your child is crying from ear pain or because of other anxieties.

DEALING WITH DIAPERS, DINING, AND SUCH

Changing Diapers at 30,000 Feet

For many parents contemplating a flight with an infant or small child, how to handle diapering en route is a top concern. I wish I could tell you not to worry, that you can rest assured that your plane's lavatory will be equipped with a changing table, and that flight attendants won't tell you to get back in your seat because of a risk of turbulence—though the risk of a blowout is imminent. But life is full of surprises, and so is air travel with children.

Whereas some airlines such as JetBlue offer a changing table in every single airplane in their fleet, others such as Frontier Airlines do not currently offer a single changing table in any of their aircraft. But whether or not there is a changing table in a lavatory onboard is often more an issue of the aircraft model than of the airline you will fly. A good rule of thumb is that, if your aircraft will have three or more lavatories onboard, chances are good that at least one will come equipped with a changing table. Ask your flight attendant if you aren't certain where it is.

Parents faced with diaper changes on aircraft not equipped with a changing facility have made use of their seats, the floor, the top of the toilet, and even their own laps in some cases. Needless to say, none of these situations is ideal. If you've flown on many long flights, you know how messy the lavatories can become as the hours pass, and how little space a toilet lid affords a reclined baby or toddler. Be sure to come equipped with plenty of antibacterial Redi-Wipes and a large piece of flannel-backed vinyl to protect your seats from your baby—or your baby from the lavatory. Once your child can stand securely, it may be easiest (and most sanitary) to let her stand on the toilet seat or floor and change her diapers in the vertical.

If you have the good fortune of flying aboard a plane with changing tables, be prepared to work without elbowroom. Chances are you will be most efficient by taking only the essentials into the lavatory with you. An over-the-shoulder purse or fanny-pack may actually be handiest for your in-flight changes, as it will keep a couple of fresh diapers, wipes, and crème handy at your hip without getting in your way or requiring (non-existent) space on the (almost assuredly wet) counter or toilet seat. We've also found a gallon-size zipped plastic bag works well, but you'll have to find a place to set it.

Also, be sure to bring a plastic bag along in your diaper bag for storing dirty diapers until you reach your destination (lavatory trash space is limited, as is the air supply). The larger, sliding zip storage bags can be quite useful for this purpose as they make it easy to squeeze out extra air to save space and seal away odors quite effectively. They are also fairly durable and can be reused.

And one final warning: If you find yourself with a dirty diaper in your hand, don't even think of passing it off to a flight attendant. As members of the food service, they are not permitted to handle human waste—not even from the cutest humans they've ever had the pleasure to serve. Instead, ask them where you can dispose of the diaper yourself.

Dining on the Aircraft

Breastfed babies have it easy when dinner is up in the air, but their bottle-fed friends and solid-food seniors may have a more interesting time of it. Larger airlines will almost always warm bottles for passengers, especially on longer flights. But if you haven't confirmed this detail with the airline ahead of time, don't count on it (see airlines table for reference). Otherwise, you can bring your own large travel mug onboard and request hot water (as available for tea), or bring along a thermos that will fit your child's bottles (the hot water may keep long enough in the thermos for a second use). Take great care with the hot water around your child, and if possible, warm the bottle while your partner takes her for a diaper change or a walk around the cabin.

Strained or blended baby foods are still permitted in your cabin baggage, so long as they are in sealed jars and you are indeed traveling with a baby or a toddler (you will need to present them at security). As we quickly learn, baby foods can be quite messy regardless of where they are eaten. Some clever parents may color coordinate their child's meal to her travel attire ("Her favorite color is carrot!"), and others will opt for less visible faire, like bananas or pears. Jarred baby foods that are blended with oatmeal or rice have a slightly thicker consistency, which makes them a little easier to keep contained.

Children flying in their own car seats may face the wrong direction or be too far (and/or too high) to make use of the tray—unfortunate since they could pass much time feeding themselves and using the tray for activities. But if their car seat has regular (non-sloping) arm wrests or an overhead shield, you can bring along a portable tray that will attach and provide these services. The "Taby Tray" is made specifically for use with car seats and has a raised edge on all sides and a depression for cups. Another handy product may be the "Drink Deputy," which can attach to your child's car seat at one end (or overall strap, etc.) and her baby bottle or sippy cup at the other to keep it from falling to the floor and possibly rolling under your seats. (More about these and other helpful products in Great Products and Gear for Travel, page 47.)

Be aware that fewer and fewer airlines are providing meals on domestic flights, though some offer food for purchase on longer flight segments or flights that fall right at the typical meal hour. If you are considering taking a domestic flight during a mealtime, you may not want to count on purchased meals, even if they are offered on your flight—it's hard to know what exactly will be offered on the flight, or if your choice will still be available by the time the cart makes its way to your seat, especially if you are seated at the back of the aircraft (they don't generally plan on all passengers buying food, so quantities are limited). If your child is a picky eater or has food sensitivities, you may be packing along her meal regardless. Be sure to check the Transportation Security Administration at www.TSA.gov for the latest on what you can and cannot bring onboard aircraft (e.g. jarred baby food may be all right, but packaged applesauce may not be).

International long-haul flights, thankfully, still provide meals for passengers included in the ticket price. Be sure to find out if your airline offers toddler or children's menus (or baby food, etc.) and put in your request well in advance. The airlines table can help you see which carriers offer these perks.

WHAT TO DO IF IT ALL GOES WRONG

It's a great feeling to end the flight with a crew of smiling flight attendants and passengers praising your child for being such a great little traveler, and you for raising such a great traveler. The older couple in row three may even turn their heads in surprise to say, "Oh, we didn't even realize there was a baby on this flight!" I hope it happens to you. But even when your child is an accomplished traveler, there may be times it simply doesn't go so well.

Teething pain can strike at any time in the first couple of years. A sudden new awareness of unfamiliar surroundings. An inexplicable dislike for strangers. Growing pains. Gas. The inability to sleep in airspace no matter how exhausted. And no matter what the reason, it seems there is always a chorus of strangers explaining to you that her ears haven't properly adjusted. It is stressful enough in times when you can't seem to sooth your child at home, but when tapped in an airplane full of fellow travelers it can be especially unpleasant.

Heightened security regulations may make it even more difficult to ensure a smooth flight, especially if you are not allowed to bring liquids onboard, including such helpful things as saline nasal drops for dry/stuffy noses, infant's and children's liquid pain relievers, or infant gas relief drops. For the time being, however, there is nothing to prevent you from bringing onboard a supply of chocolates and ear plugs for your fellow passengers as a show of your goodwill. Here are some other tips for dealing with difficult situations that might present themselves during a flight:

- Bring two dry extra washcloths onboard, one for dipping in a cup of ice water to help with teething (and keep the mouth busy), the other to moisten with warm water from the lavatory to help clear a stuffy little nose.
- Avoid feeding your child any gassy foods (and yourself if you're breastfeeding) for at least 24 hours before your flight.
- Bring a supply of Hyland's Calms Forté 4 Kids onboard to help relieve restlessness and irritability. Unlike the liquid form of most medicines for babies and small children, this homeopathic remedy is in the form of dry tablets so it can be carried into the cabin even at

times when liquids are banned. Since the tablets dissolve almost instantly under the tongue, they can be given to toddlers and preschoolers, and also to babies with your pediatrician's guidance.

- Keep a crying baby in motion, walking laps around the aircraft. Even if the motion fails to calm her, changing locations will at least spread the burden of noise among the passengers!
- Create a canopy over your child with a blanket tucked into the seat-back tray at one end, and behind your head rest, child's car seat, or your shoulder at the other end. It may help block out distractions and light, while helping your child feel more cozy and secure.

When all else fails, don't despair. Remember in the greater scheme of your vacation, the flight is just one little piece of the puzzle, which you will most likely be laughing and rolling your eyes about in the months to come. At some point, the flight will be over and, with any luck, you'll never see the other passengers again. But in case any of them really rub you the wrong way, you might offer the following:

"She heard they were getting warm cookies in first class."

"We tried to give her drugs for the flight, but she just said no."

And to the real stinkers:

"She's afraid of grown-ups who don't smile at her."

- *Chapter 17* -
Special Situations

FLYING SOLO WITH BABY

A ny time you will be crossing the border with your child, but without the other parent, you will need a notarized letter of consent from the absent parent, or evidence that you are the child's sole legal guardian (see a sample letter of consent on page 100). But regardless of your destination or the duration of your flight, flying alone with children presents challenges far greater than paperwork.

For example, how do you get your carry-on bags, stroller, and possibly a car seat—oh, and your shoes, and your coat onto the X-ray scanner while you juggle your child (and now they ask to see your boarding pass and photo I.D. for a second time)? How do you fold your stroller at the gate with your child in your arms? What do you do with your baby while you use the lavatory? And how do you install the car seat while wrestling your toddler and situating your carry-on bags? And if you're flying with a lap child, how will you eat your dinner when there may not even be room for the tray and your child in your lap?

Anything else to consider? How about negotiating baggage claim in an army of strangers slinging their heavy suitcases off the track? Traveling alone with a child requires the swift dexterity of an octopus. But believe it or not, people do it all the time. They survive, and you can, too. Here are a few strategies that may help:

- Curb-check your checked baggage if possible to avoid the hairpin turns and longer wait of the line inside the airport. An extra fee may apply (around $2 per item usually), but it could be well worth it.
- Carry infants and babies in a simple over-the-shoulder sling that will slip off easily to go through the X-ray just before you walk through the scanner with your child (remember, you cannot wear any kind of infant carrier through the scanner).
- Keep toddlers and older children in their collapsible strollers until you have finished loading all other items onto the X-ray belt. On the other side, collect your stroller first and strap-in your child before collecting your other gear.
- Extend car seat straps and slip them over the handles of your stroller if possible, or narrow-shouldered parents may be able to loosen the straps to wear over the shoulders like a backpack. The "Pac Back" and other backpack carriers are also available to help parents carry car seats and keep their hands free.
- As you approach security, tell the first guard you see, "I'm going to need some assistance please," and expect it (and ask the second guard you see, too, if you must). A security guard should help you get your items into the X-ray, and one will hopefully help you collect them again on the other side.
- Keep your travel documents and those of your child, boarding passes, and your cash and credit cards in a necklace-style travel wallet. They will be easy to locate and access each time they are needed en route (even while you have a child in your arms), and will slip under your sweater or shirt otherwise for far greater security and convenience than carrying a purse or placing them in a carry-on.
- When using airport restrooms, use the handicapped stall where there is plenty of room for your child to sit in his stroller and for you to park any extra gear.
- In aircraft lavatories, have small children stand or sit on your lap. Babies can go into your over-the-shoulder sling, but remember flight crew will not allow you to hold the child in the sling during take-off or landing (and some will not permit it as you sit in your seat).
- Throughout your flight, don't hesitate to ask a flight attendant if you need help with anything, from assistance in installing your child's CRS to getting your bag into the overhead bin. Your seat

should come equipped with a flight attendant call button—don't be afraid to use it.

FLYING WITH TWINS, MULTIPLES, OR MULTIPLE CHILDREN

Flying with More Than One Lap Child

Airlines do not allow more than one lap child per adult traveler, so if you are traveling alone with twins (or if your offspring outnumber you and your spouse) you will need to purchase at least one child's seat and plan to bring your car seat onboard (chances are you'll be glad to have extra space).

Generally airlines do not allow for more than one lap child per seat row due to a limited number of oxygen masks, some of which may also need to be shared with cabin crew in the event of an emergency. This can vary by aircraft, so be sure to call and discuss your possibilities with the airline. In some cases, the family with twins may sit in the bulkhead row where there are sometimes extra oxygen masks. But most often, parents with more than one lap child sit in consecutive rows.

Reserving Airline Seats for Multiple Children

Call your airline as soon as possible to notify them of any (and all) lap children that will be flying with you, as well as the number of car seats that will be coming on board with your family, and try to get seat assignments if available. When purchasing seats for small children, remember that there are restrictions as to where child restraint systems (car seats) can be placed on the aircraft. On larger aircraft, parents with two seated children may opt for the center row where Mom and Dad can sit at each aisle and keep the children to the center seats (out of the aisles). As always, be sure to call your airline 24 to 72 hours in advance of both outbound and return flights to reconfirm your seat assignments, as some airlines will reassign unconfirmed seats at check in ("Would you prefer a window seat—or an aisle?")

FLYING WITH A SPECIAL NEEDS CHILD

Traveling with Mobility Devices

You will want to call your airline ahead of time to ask about its specific policies and procedures regarding mobility devices. The following is true of most major airlines around the world, but again, you should confirm any critical details with your airline.

Most major airlines:

- Accept and transport wheelchairs, including folding, collapsible, non-folding manual, and electric/battery-powered wheelchairs, as well as electric-powered carts.
- Have room for one collapsible wheelchair onboard (in addition to overhead and under-seat storage space where some collapsible wheelchairs may also fit).
- Accept non-collapsible and electric wheelchairs as checked baggage at the ticket counter or gate.
- Require at least 48 hours' advance notice and earlier check-in (usually 1 or 2 hours) when checking battery-powered wheelchairs and carts as extra time may be needed to prepare the chair for loading (provide written instructions or special tools if available). Some batteries are also subject to dangerous goods handling, which could take extra time. In some cases, the airline may need to contact the manufacturer for special instructions.
- Allow you to bring walkers and other assistive devices that may be collapsed small enough to fit in overhead bins and underneath seats into the cabin without counting toward your carry-on limit.
- Allow you to gate-check strollers, which may be easier and faster to use in airports while getting to your gate and making connecting flights at other airports.

Security Screenings

If your child has special needs, including medical equipment or mobility devices, be sure to plan for a little extra time at security checkpoints. As you approach the screening area, alert the security guard as soon as possible and explain that your child has special needs or devices, including any hidden disabilities that may affect his screening (e.g. a mental disability, hearing impairment, or if you have checked your child's wheelchair and he is riding in a stroller). This officer may help you or may contact someone else to help you with the screening process.

What you can expect during your child's screening:

- You will not be separated from your child during the screening, whether it occurs right at the metal detector, to the side, or in a private area.
- Infants will remain connected to their apnea monitors while they are screened.
- If you choose to carry your child through the metal detector, you will be responsible for removing him from his mobility aid. (The security officer will not do this.)
- A security officer will help you get your carry-on items onto the X-ray belt if needed (ask for help if you need it).

How you can help the screening go smoothly for your special-needs child:

- Tell your child what to expect ahead of time to minimize any anxiety during the process.
- Tell the officer all relevant information about your child's condition and medical devices.
- Explain what your child's abilities are, e.g. if he can walk through the metal detector or if he will need to be carried, or if he can stand slightly away from his equipment for a hand-wand inspection.
- If needed, the security officer can conduct a pat-down search of your child in his mobility aid and visually inspect the equipment.

- Tell the security officer if the child is likely to become upset and offer suggestions on how to minimize an outburst.

FLYING FOR AN INTERNATIONAL ADOPTION

Adopted Children Flying to New Homes in the U.S.

These children do not need (and cannot yet be issued) a U.S. passport as they must first clear immigration upon arriving in the U.S. Generally, internationally adopted children arrive under one of two visas (the IR-3 or IR-4 depending on the particulars of their situation), and qualify for U.S. citizenship upon entry. Based on the Child Citizenship Act of 2000, children arriving with an IR-3 visa automatically acquire U.S. citizenship and should be issued a Certificate of Citizenship without needing to file any additional forms. Those with an IR-4 visa are considered legal permanent residents, but must file for proof of citizenship. In both cases, the adopted children will need their proof of their U.S. citizenship to apply for a passport before flying outside of the United States again. For more information, call Overseas Citizen Services at 1-888-407-4747 or the U.S. Department of State Visa Office at 1-202-663-1225.

Airlines' Minimum Age Policies

The majority of commercial airlines require infants to be at least 1 week old before flying. Here are some of the exceptions:

- Alaska Airlines – No minimum age
- American Airlines – 48 hours
- British Airways – 48 hours
- Delta – 1 week OR letter from physician required
- Easy Jet – 2 weeks
- Jet Blue – 3 days (with letter from physician if under 2 weeks)
- Korean Air – 2 weeks for international flights (1 week domestic)

Special Discounts and One-Way Adoption Fares:

Some airlines offer programs to assist adoptive families by providing lower airfares with little notice, one-way infant fares, and other perks to meet the needs of this special situation. Be aware, however, that a last-minute deal from another agency (with restrictions and little or no flexibility) may still beat the flexible, "special" airfare offered by the airline—which is based on a full-price, last-minute ticket, unrestricted ticket price. So if you are flying at the last minute, it could be worth it to double-check before committing to your reservation.

As an example of what an adoptive fare program may provide, Northwest and KLM Royal Dutch Airlines have created a Special Delivery program that offers adoptive parents and their children:

- Low airfares with flexibility
- No advance purchase required
- Available up to the last seat in main cabin
- No penalties for cancellation or changes
- Open returns and stopovers are permitted

The program is valid for families adopting children from any of the 100+ international destinations they serve, including Asia, Africa, Europe, India, and the Middle East. To qualify, you will provide some of the basic information you have already received during the adoption process, which can be registered online at www.nwa.com or by calling them at the number listed below.

British Airways 1–800-AIRWAYS

NWA/KLM International 1-800-322-4162

United & Lufthansa 1-800-538-2929

PART VI
TRAVELS BY TRAIN

- *Chapter 18* -
Deciding to go by Rail

ADVANTAGES OF TAKING THE TRAIN

O nce you've officially spent too many hours cramped in an airplane with your child, waiting for the drink cart to pass again before you can finally dodge to the lavatory aft (hopefully before the next round of turbulence) to change a diaper that needed attention well before take-off, or listening to him protest from the back seat of the car that another fifty minutes—or five, for that matter, are not okay with him, well, the prospect of traveling by train may become truly enticing. You can:

- Wave goodbye to the car seat.
- Avoid lengthy airport lines.
- Go for a walk whenever you please.
- Forget about turbulence.
- Explore the various train cars and facilities.
- Watch the scenery change with each passing mile.
- Keep your mind on the adventure, not the traffic and road signs.

For travel in Europe, rail trips may become even more sensible when you consider that children can ride most trains free until their fourth birthdays (and beyond in some countries)—and for half the cost of the adult ticket thereafter; compare that with flying or filling up with expensive petrol! Not to mention, lap children are not at risk of turbulence when riding on trains as they are on airplanes.

As well, riding a train with a baby can be much easier than driving or flying, as you can hold and rock, and bounce or walk your child as you please. For the toddler or preschooler, riding the train may even be the most exciting part of your vacation—be it an hour-long scenic excursion train or a cross-country rail odyssey. Which brings us to an important point: Unlike flying, train travel isn't only a means of getting to and from destinations with suitcases in tow. You can ride a historic steam locomotive to visit a legendary logging camp in the redwoods, or take a vintage parlor car for an afternoon jaunt along the shore, pit-stopping for a picnic lunch, sand castle, and souvenirs (see Twelve Scenic Day Trips by Train for details and more ideas).

Have more time for the train? Take a day-trip to the bustling heart of Manhattan or Montreal, or say good night in one European capitol and awaken in the next. However you envision your great rail experience with your family, this section of the book will help you make it happen.

THE CASE FOR TRAVELING BY TRAIN WITH TWINS OR MULTIPLE CHILDREN

For parents traveling with twins or multiples, there are additional advantages to traveling by train, especially when compared with the option of flying:

- Seating is often more flexible for train passengers (excluding reservations-only trains and some busy trains during peak hours) and there are no restrictions for how many lap children may be seated in a row.
- Restrooms are generally larger on trains than they are on airplanes (even handicapped facilities are available on most Amtrak trains), which makes it easier to manage more than one child versus the cramped aircraft lavatory. Handicapped restrooms onboard most trains have room enough for a stroller, so you can keep one child strapped in while attending to the other, if need be.
- Most trains will allow you to check far more gear than traditional airlines will, which can be very helpful when you are bringing TWO of everything (or three, or four, or…).
- Long distances are covered far more comfortably by train than by a car crowded with multiple car seats and mountains of gear.
- Family sleeper cars will give your brood much privacy and space to set up changing, napping, and eating stations without interference from other passengers or their seats. One parent may even nap with a child or children in the quiet compartment while the other(s) enjoy the café or view car. (Or when it's play time in the sleeper, one parent may catch winks in an unreserved seat in coach.)
- Children ages 2 and older may travel less expensively by train than by airplane—a difference that really adds up when purchasing multiple children's tickets. For example, children 2 years and older travel half-price on Amtrak in the U.S. and on VIA Rail in Canada, whereas children's discounts are being phased-out by most airlines. As mentioned earlier, in Europe children also travel free on their parents' laps until their fourth birthdays (and beyond in some countries).
- When booking a sleeper compartment, you only pay one accommodation price (the sleeper supplement) for the whole

family, regardless of how many passengers. Since the price includes meals for everyone for the duration of your trip, the more mouths you need to feed on your trip, the more valuable this benefit will be.

Five Tips for Great Train Trips with Babies and Small Children

1. Bring a sling or child carrier for babies and young toddlers to help you keep your hands free as you move about the train, especially in case you need to brace yourself as the train starts into a curve or as you carry back goodies from the snack car.

2. Plan for a meal or snack en route even during shorter rides to make it an extra special occasion and help stabilize blood sugar levels. You can splurge in the dining car, if available, or just get a hotdog in the snack car. Or pack your own lunches of favorites to look forward to. When you arrive, no one will be hungry or have to go in search of food!

3. Bring a lightweight stroller with a shoulder strap. Not only will it help you climb stairs everywhere you will find them (and not escalators or elevators or ramps), it will help you immensely as you get on and off the train holding your child or your child's hand—or while pushing commuters out of your way in case of a crowded station. When your child is ready to nap or tires of walking—or you tire of carrying him, you'll be glad to have the stroller with you. (See suggested models at TravelswithBaby.com.)

4. Choose destinations with great public transportation and centrally located stations so that you can avoid bringing the car seat along or needing a rental car or taxis.

5. Pack good travel gear. It is tempting to bring the kitchen sink, but with good travel gear, you won't need it. For example, inflatable bed bumper rails pack down to practically nothing but can be used with hotel beds or sleeping berths for babies and toddlers. (Find more ideas in Great Products and Gear for Travel, beginning on page 47.)

GET STARTED: TWELVE SCENIC DAY TRIPS BY TRAIN

If you're not accustomed to traveling by train, a scenic excursion train ride can be a great initiation and a fun outing for the whole family. Throughout the United States, opportunities abound to take private rail lines for just an hour or an afternoon. What's more, many of these rail lines feature restored rail cars and locomotives that make the trip even more special as they venture through some of the most spectacular scenery in the nation. Here are just a handful of the great scenic rail opportunities that await your family across the U.S.

1. ALASKA: Alaska Railroad – Anchorage (and other points)

1-800-544-0552 www.akrr.com

Board the Glacier Discovery Train mid-morning in Anchorage and head off toward what is called by many the most beautiful stretch in Alaska. First, you will travel two hours along the Turnagain Arm of Cook Inlet, where Beluga whales, Dall sheep, eagles, and moose are often sighted. Make quick stops at Girdwood and then Portage, where you may choose to connect to a Prince William Sound wildlife and glacier cruise before your return trip to Anchorage. Or stay onboard all the way to Grandview and see three spectacular glaciers from the comfort of your heated rail car: Trail Glacier, Bartlett Glacier, and Spencer Glacier. On your return trip, you will travel by the segment from Portage to Anchorage by motorcoach, arriving in time for a late dinner. You may bring your lunch and snacks with you or buy them onboard in the snack car. You may also board at other points along this route with adjusted fares. Other routes and packages are available, including journeys with overnight accommodations at hotels or cabins along the way. Some packages and extensions include cruises, wilderness jeep safaris, riverboat journeys, Arctic Circle air tours, helicopter hiking, salmon bakes, and more. For the Anchorage to Grandview Glacier Discovery route, children under 2 years are free, children 2 to 11 years are $50, and adults are $99.

2. ARIZONA: Grand Canyon Railway – Williams, AZ

1-800-the-train   www.thetrain.com

Day-long excursions take you from Williams to the Grand Canyon Village and back, by way of a Wild West Shootout. These vintage diesel engines run year round and some historic steam engines also run spring through early fall. Once at the Grand Canyon, you can shop and explore on your own or take their optional motor coach tour of the rim. Five classes of train travel are available. Coach rates: children under 2 free, ages 2 to 10 are $25, youth 11 to 16 are $35, adults are $60. The new Polar Express train operates November through early January, with evening departures including hot chocolate and cookies with the telling of the children's story *The Polar Express*, while Santa Claus and his reindeer greet everyone at the destination: The North Pole. Polar Express tickets are only available by phone; children 2 to 16 are $12, adults are $24. Packages including lodging at Williams are available.

Note: For a complete vacation by rail, take Amtrak's Southwest Chief, which runs daily between Los Angeles and Chicago, and stops at Williams, AZ (more info in Chapter 19, Amtrak's Notable Routes and Highlights).

3. NEW MEXICO: Cumbres and Toltec Scenic Railroad – Chama (and Antonito, CO)

1-888-CUMBRES   www.cumbrestoltec.com

Authentic Denver & Rio Grande steam locomotives charge along this historic, narrow-guage railroad, and negotiate a steep 4% grade as they travel the Cumbres Pass (you may recognize the train and scenery from movies including Indiana Jones and the Last Crusade). As you travel along the border between Colorado and New Mexico, watch for eagles, hawks, mule deer, antelope, coyotes, mountain lions, and range cattle. Six hours round trip, including a 1-hour stop at Osier with buffet lunch included in your fare. Children under 2 years are free, children 2 to 11 years are $31, Adults are $62. Trains run May through October, with itineraries originating from either Chama, New Mexico, or Antonito, Colorado. On Thursdays in mid-summer, the "Cinder Bear Express" train runs a shorter route (4.5 hours) especially for children, with a picnic lunch at Cumbres included.

4. GEORGIA: Blue Ridge Scenic Railway - Blue Ridge

1-800-934-1898 www.brscenic.com

Enjoy a 3.5 hour excursion along the white waters of the Toccoa River, through the Chattahoochee National Forest and historic Murphy Junction. A 1.5 hour stopover at the border cities of MacCaysville, GA and Copperhill, TN, allows you to enjoy lunch and ice cream, shopping, and stretching your legs in these quaint sister towns. The train is comprised of restored passenger cars from the 1920s and 1930s, plus others, including open-air cars. Also offered: Holiday trains and Rest and Rail packages that include discounted rail tickets with a cabin rental. Fees vary by season: children 2 and under are free (without seats), ages 2 to 12 are $11-15, adults are $22-30.

5. IDAHO: Thunder Mountain Line – Horseshoe Bend

1-877-IDA-RAIL www.thundermountainline.com

The popular Horseshoe Bend Route takes you along the scenic Payette River to the historic settlement of Banks along what was once an old wagon road. Choose from vintage 1950s parlor and passenger cars, or open platform cars, and visit the bar car for a snack. Many other routes and special event trains are offered, including the Black Canyon sunset train (2.5 hours), Cabarton Flyer (2.5 hours), Cascade Limited (4-hour ride one-way + 1 hour return by bus), Wild West train (2.5 hours with shootout), and holiday trains. For the Horseshoe Bend Route, children under 2 are free, ages 2 to 12 are $15, and adults are $24.50.

6. MASSACHUSSETTS: Cape Cod Central Railroad – Hyannis

1-888-797-RAIL www.capetrain.com

Pass by cranberry bogs, woodlands, and marshes on a 2-hour ride from Hyannis to the Cape Cod Canal in vintage 1940s and 1950s rail cars. In addition to this basic scenic "Fun Train" ride, you may also choose the Rail/Sail combo, where you take the train in one direction, and then catch an old-time Maine coastal steamer replica for a one-hour tour of Hyannis Harbor out to the Kennedy Compound. Also offered: Family Supper Train, Brunch Train, and special events trains, including lunch with Santa. Children under 3 ride the Fun Train for free, children 3 to 11 are $13, adults are $17.

7. NEW YORK: Upper Hudson River Railroad - North Creek

1-518-251-5334 www.uhrr.com

Halfway between Saratoga Springs and Lake Placid, you can board a historic rail coach with great views of the river and Adirondack Mountains (fall foliage is especially nice). The four and a half hour journey includes a 30-minute stop for picnicking or visiting the Caboose Café or gift shop. Runs seasonally with some special events, including "Robbery Trains." Children 2 and under are free (without seats), ages 3 to 11 are $10, adults are $15.

8. NORTH CAROLINA: Great Smoky Mountains Railroad – Dillsboro and Bryson City

1-800-872-4681 http://gsmr.com

The Fontana Trestle route takes passengers on a 2-hour round trip from Bryson City to the Fontana Lake Trestle, which spans 780 feet at 100 feet above the water (you may recognize it from various movies shot here like The Fugitive). These trips are usually timed for a spectacular view of the sunset on the lake. Other routes and special event trains are offered, including Natahala Gorge route (4.5 hours from Bryson City), The Tuckasegee River (4 hours from Dillsboro), plus the Polar Express, Little Engine that Could, Day out with Thomas, and more. For the Fontana Trestle Route, children under 2 years are free, ages 2 to 12 are $18, and adults are $38.

9. OREGON: Oregon Coast Scenic Railroad - Tillamook County

1-503-842-7972 http://ocsr.net

A restored 1910 Heisler steam locomotive chugs along Tillamook Bay from Garibaldi to Rockaway Beach at the Pacific coast, where you can make a quick sand castle and stomp in the surf, or enjoy an ice cream cone before your return. 1.5 hour round trip, including layover. Late May through September, including an evening 4th of July Fireworks Spectacular. Children under 2 are free, children 3 to 10 are $7, adults are $13.

10. PENNSYLVANIA: Pioneer Lines Scenic Railway – Gettysburg

1-717-334-6932 www.gettysburgrail.com

Also dubbed the "Gettysburg Express," this 16-mile narrated journey takes you past the First Day of Battle, Seminary Ridge, and other sites of historical importance. 1 hour 15 minutes. Children 3 and under are free on laps, children 4 to 12 are $9, adults are $16.50. Many other train rides are offered as well, including Fall Foliage, Abe Lincoln Trains, and Holiday Trains with Santa Claus.

11. RHODE ISLAND: Old Colony Railway - Newport County

1-401-624-6951 www.ocnrr.com

Enjoy a 10 mile round-trip ride along Narragansett Bay in either a 1904 open platform car in fair weather or an 1884 parlor car heated on the chillier days by a pot belly stove. Or go first class in a separate parlor car, where all passengers ride in wicker chairs arranged to face the bay. Travel through the old navy base and look out on the sailboats and the natural beauty of the Newport shore. Sundays only, open year round with 11:45 a.m. and 1:45 p.m. departures. The ride is 1 hour 20 minutes round trip. Adults are $7.50, children are $5.00, first class is $11. Special packages are available for St. Patrick's Day festivities (don't miss the Newport St. Patrick's Day Parade), including box lunches, optional tours of the Newport mansions (Vanderbilts, etc.), and an Irish supper.

12. WEST VIRGINIA: Potomac Eagle Scenic Railroad, Romney

1-304-424-0736 www.potomaceagle.info

Enjoy a 3-hour narrated ride along the South Branch of the Potomac River, where historic farms are glimpsed between a mix of hardwoods and evergreens. Bald eagle sightings are said to occur on over 90% of these excursions, and if you are lucky you'll catch one—with your camera, of course. Vintage 1940s and 1950s passenger cars wend their way through this scenic narrow mountain valley. All-day trips are also offered, with photo stops and a mid-day rest in Petersburg. In September, the Hardy Heritage Days and Historic Homes Tour combines a 3-hour tour of historic homes with your rail excursion. For the 3-hour trip, children under 6 years ride free, ages 6 to 16 are $10, and adults are $30.

- Chapter 19 -
All Aboard Amtrak

AMTRAK'S NOTABLE ROUTES AND HIGHLIGHTS

Beginning in the 1940s, the once glamorous and romantic passenger trains across the country began to suffer from competition against new air travel options and a boom in ownership of private automobiles. The steady decline of U.S. passenger rail services continued for nearly 30 years until 1970, when congress passed the Rail Passenger Service Act. The act created Amtrak, the United States' nationwide passenger rail network, in an attempt to revive passenger rail service across the country.

Today, Amtrak serves approximately 68,000 passengers per day in 46 states (Alaska, Hawaii, South Dakota, and Wyoming do not have Amtrak service). Trains cover 22,000 route miles across the continental U.S. and include scenic viewing cars, sleeper cars, auto trains, and twenty high-speed Acela Express trains that can travel up to 150 m.p.h. Following are some of Amtrak's most notable routes and highlights, each with a handful of their cities served and onboard amenities. Amtrak's interactive Route Atlas is available online at www.amtrak.com, with easy links to station information (including additional stops not listed here) and more details for each route.

ACELA EXPRESS: Boston – New York – Philadelphia – Washington D.C.
Travel up to 150 m.p.h with limited stops helping you speed between cities

in record time. Service is hourly during peak commute hours. Most discounts (including children's) do not apply during week days. Overhead storage bins, plus additional stowage for strollers or oversized items near exits of most cars. Approximately 7 hours total run one way. Café car onboard and electrical outlets at all seats.

THE ADIRONDACK: New York, NY – Poughkeepsie – Albany – Ticonderoga – Montreal, Quebec. Daily trips from NYC to Montreal, through the Hudson Valley wine country, the Adirondack Mountains, and along the shore of Lake Champlain. Travel in either direction with a morning departure and arrive at the final destination city in time for dinner. Approximately 10 hours total run. Snack car, reserved coach seats available.

AMTRAK CASCADES: Eugene, OR – Salem – Portland – Tacoma – Seattle – Vancouver, B.C. Travel up the Willamette Valley, cross the Columbia River Gorge, and enjoy views of the Cascade and Olympic mountain ranges. Eugene to Seattle is approximately 6.5 hours by train; Seattle to Vancouver B.C. is by connecting bus service (final 3.5 to 4.5 hours). Multiple daily departures. Train amenities include lounge, checked baggage at staffed stations, bistro car, feature movies, reserved coach seats, roomettes, family bedrooms, and bedrooms. Additional info at www.amtrakcascades.com.

AUTO TRAIN: Washington D.C. (Lorton, VA) – Orlando, FL (Sanford). This option makes it really easy to check your car seat—just leave it in the back seat of your car (if you choose to bring your car). The Auto Train takes you and your car nonstop from the D.C. area to Florida (passengers must have a vehicle in order to take the auto train). Approximately 16 hours 30 minutes one way, overnight each direction. Reserved coach seats, roomettes, bedroom suites, bedrooms, and family bedrooms are available. Lounge, dining car, and entertainment onboard.

CALIFORNIA ZEPHYR: Chicago, IL – Omaha, NE – Denver, CO – Salt Lake City, UT – Reno, NV – Emeryville, CA (San Francisco). Daily departures whisk you from the Windy City through the heart of the Rocky Mountains, with views of Colorado's Gore, Byers, and Glenwood Canyons.

Then it's on to the Sierra Nevadas, and finally the San Francisco Bay (Thruway bus service from Emeryville to downtown San Francisco). Total trip one way is approximately 51 hours and 20 minutes. Reserved coach seats, roomettes, bedrooms, bedroom suites, and family bedrooms are available. Also onboard: dining car, sightseer lounge car.

CAPITOL CORRIDOR: Auburn, CA – Sacramento – Davis – Emeryville (San Francisco) – Oakland – San Jose. Multiple daily trains take passengers from the Sacramento Area to and through the San Francisco Bay Area by way of scenic wetlands dotted with numerous egrets and wildlife. All trains on this route are equipped with a limited number of bicycle racks where you can stow your bike—or bulky stroller if you please. Total trip one way is approximately 3 hours 14 minutes. Snack car, bicycle rack, and quiet car onboard.

CAPITOL LIMITED: Washington, D.C. – Pittsburgh, PA - Cleveland, OH – Chicago, IL. Travel through the Potomac Valley, past historic Harpers Ferry, over the Alleghany Mountains, then up and over toward the Great Lakes until arriving at Chicago. Daily departures. Total trip one way is approximately 18 hours, overnight service each way. Reserved coach seats, roomettes, bedrooms, bedroom suites, and family bedrooms are available. Also onboard: dining car and lounge car.

THE CARDINAL (HOOSIER STATE): New York, NY – Philadelphia, PA – Washington, D.C. – Charlottesville, VA – Cincinnati, OH – Indianapolis, IN – Chicago, IL. The Cardinal runs between New York and Chicago 3 days a week, and the Hoosier State line runs the segment between Chicago and Indianapolis daily. On the Cardinal, you'll enjoy views of West Virginia's white water as can only be glimpsed by train, plus the Shenandoah Valley, the Alleghany and Blue Ridge Mountains, and the Ohio River. Total trip one way is approximately 26 hours 30 minutes (Note: For faster, less-scenic service between Chicago and NYC, take the Lakeshore Limited). Reserved coach seats, Viewliner roomettes, Viewliner bedrooms, and Viewliner bedroom suites are available. Lounge car/dinette onboard.

CAROLINIAN / PIEDMONT: New York, NY – Philadelphia, PA – Baltimore, MD – Washington, D.C. - Raleigh, NC – Richmond, VA – Raleigh, NC – Charlotte, NC. Travel through a Who's Who of historic towns on the Carolinian, with daily service between Charlotte and New York City. The Piedmont makes additional daily trips between Raleigh and Charlotte. Total trip one way on the Carolinian is approximately 13 hours 30 minutes (no overnight service). Reserved coach and business class seats, with snack car onboard.

CITY OF NEW ORLEANS – Champagne - Memphis, TN – Jackson, MS – New Orleans, LA. Travel through the heart of the U.S.A., tracing the trail of its musical heritage all the way to New Orleans, the birthplace of Jazz. Watch for photo ops en route of picturesque farms, cityscapes, plantations— and possibly even Elvis. Daily departures with overnight service. Total trip one way is approximately 19 hours. Reserved coach seats, roomettes, bedrooms, bedroom suites, and family bedrooms are available. Dining car and lounge car onboard.

COAST STARLIGHT: Seattle, WA – Portland, OR – Eugene – Klamath Falls – Sacramento, CA – Oakland – Emeryville (San Francisco) – Santa Barbara – Los Angeles. The "Sightseer Lounge," with its floor-to-ceiling windows, helps you enjoy unparalleled views of snow-covered mountains, forests, valleys, and the Pacific Ocean as you travel this route. Total trip one-way is approximately 35 hours. Reserved coach seats, roomettes, bedrooms, bedroom suites, and family bedrooms are available. Also onboard: dining car, sightseer lounge car, and kiddie car where children can meet and play.

CRESCENT: New York, NY – Washington, D.C. – Greensboro, NC – Atlanta, GA – New Orleans, LA. Travel from the Big Apple to the Bayou by way of the nation's capitol, Blue Ridge Foothills, and scenic towns of the deep South. Daily departures with overnight service. Approximately 30 hours one way. Reserved coach seats, Viewliner roomettes, bedrooms, and bedroom suites are available. Dining car and lounge car onboard.

DOWNEASTER: Portland, ME – Dover, NH – Exeter – Boston, MA. Travel along the New England shoreline through coastal marshes, villages, and quaint colonial cities. Multiple daily departures. Approximately 2 hours total run one way. Reserved coach seats available. Snack car and bicycle racks onboard.

EMPIRE BUILDER: Chicago, IL –Milwaukee, WI – St. Paul, MN – Grand Forks, ND – East Glacier Park, MT – Spokane, WA – Portland, OR – Seattle, WA. Follow major portions of the Lewis and Clark trail as you set out across the Mississippi, travel over the plains and atop the spectacular Gassman Coulee Trestle. Then on through Glacier National Park. At Spokane, you may venture north to Seattle, or travel down the Columbia River Gorge to Portland with views of Mt. Hood. Daily departures with overnight service (two nights). One way is approximately 46 hours. Reserved coach seats, roomettes, bedrooms, bedroom suites, and family bedrooms are available. Dining car and sightseer lounge car onboard.

EMPIRE SERVICE: New York, NY – Poughkeepsie – Schenectady – Syracuse – Niagara Falls, NY. Escape from New York (City) through the Hudson River Valley and travel on to the Finger Lakes region. You'll pass by way of Buffalo on to Niagara Falls. Frequent daily trains. Approximately 7 hours total run one way. Reserved coach seats are available. Snack car onboard.

ETHAN ALLEN EXPRESS: Rutland, VT – Albany, NY – New York. Spring wildflowers and fall foliage especially dazzle travelers along this route through the Hudson River Valley and on through the wilderness of upstate New York and Vermont. In winter months, a motorcoach connection can take you on from Rutland to Okemo. Multiple daily departures. Approximately 5 hours 30 minutes total run one way. Reserved coach seats are available. Snack car onboard.

MAPLE LEAF: New York, NY – Albany – Buffalo – Toronto, ON. Similar to the Empire Service Route, with most of the same New York stops, you will travel up through the Hudson River Valley to the Finger Lakes region, and near Niagara Falls (stopping on both U.S. and Canadian sides). As you cross the Canadian border, the route becomes officially operated by Canada's VIA rail and a passport is strongly recommended—and will be required for this crossing as of June 2009 (until then photo I.D. plus proof of citizenship is acceptable). Approximately 12 hours 30 minutes one way, traveling from morning with evening arrival (no overnight). Reserved coach seats are available; snack car onboard.

PACIFIC SURFLINER: Paso Robles, CA – San Luis Obispo – Santa Barbara – Ventura – Los Angeles – Anaheim – San Diego. Travel the coastline of southern California, from its "Sideways" wine country (PRB) to Disneyland (ANA) and right into San Diego's Old Town (OLT). Approximately 5 hours 45 minutes one way with multiple daily departures. No reserved seating. Café car and bicycle racks onboard. Multi-ride passes are available.

REGIONAL: Boston, MA – Providence, RI – Hartford, CT – New York, NY – Newark, N.J. – Philadelphia, PA – Baltimore, MD – Alexandria, VA – Williamsburg – Newport News. With several daily departures, the Regional is an easy way to travel between the hearts of cities and historic outposts throughout the northeastern U.S. Entire route one way is 12 hours 30 minutes. Reserved coach seats are available, snack car onboard.

SAN JOAQUINS: Oakland or Sacramento, CA – Emeryville (San Francisco) – Martinez – Merced (Yosemite) – Fresno – Bakersfield. Take this route from either the San Francisco Bay Area or Sacramento through California's agricultural center, the San Joaquins is your ticket to many great sites and attractions, including Yosemite National Park. Spring through fall, you can board a luxury motorcoach right at the Merced (and sometimes Modesto) train station, which will take you for a 2-hour scenic drive right to the Yosemite Park Lodge (enter station code YOS as your rail destination for Yosemite; your park entrance fee is included). Or ride to the Martinez station and board a Thruway motorcoach for a quick ride that drops you off right at the main entrance to Six Flags Marine World (use station code VMW).

SOUTHWEST CHIEF: Chicago, IL – Kansas City, MO – Dodge City, KS – Lamy, NM – Albuquerque, NM – Flagstaff, AZ – Williams Junction, AZ – Los Angeles, CA. Travel the celebrated "Atchison, Topeka, and Santa Fe" route out west through historic Indian regions and captivating canyons. Cross the Mississippi on a double-decked swing bridge completed in 1927, see the prairies named for Spanish silver (la plata), and follow the Red Cliffs of New Mexico and travel through a canyon that's only a few feet wider than the train. Arrive at the southern rim of the Grand Canyon where you can take a Thruway bus to the Grand Canyon Railway with its scenic tours and lodgings. Or stay on to the end point at Los Angeles. Total run one way is approximately 40 hours. Reserved seats, roomettes, bedrooms, bedroom suites, and family bedrooms are available. Dining car and sightseer lounge car onboard.

RATES, PRICING, AND PASSES FOR AMTRAK JOURNEYS

Amtrak ticket prices may vary widely for the same journey due to a number of factors, including how far in advance you make your purchase, availability of seats or rooms on your dates, and any special offers that may be underway at the time of booking. The easiest way to search and compare fares is to visit www.amtrak.com, where you can also check the latest special offers and weekly deals that may save you up to 90% on travel, generally within the next month.

Remember that if tickets are available for purchase or pick-up (via Quik-trak kiosk or agent) at your station of departure, you should plan to do so or else you will have to pay an extra service fee for purchasing your tickets onboard. When departing from an unstaffed station, where no tickets may be purchased (or one where the electronic Quik-trak kiosk is out of service and no attendant is on duty), you will have no choice but to purchase your ticket onboard and will pay no extra service fee for doing so.

One bit of advice when purchasing unreserved seats: If you have no need for a reservation on the route and dates you plan to travel, or if reserved seats are already sold out, and you can find a lower ticket price for your same journey on other dates—buy it. Tickets for unreserved seats are valid for one year from the time of purchase, and may be used on any train traveling the route, regardless of the actual price paid!

Amtrak Pricing for Infants and Children

Infants – Children under 2 years travel free on their parents' laps.

Children – Children 2 to 15 years old, accompanied by an adult ride for 50% of the adult's ticket price.

This pricing applies to all Amtrak tickets for U.S. journeys, except for weekday travel on two eastern lines used heavily by commuters: the high-speed Acela Express (Boston to Washington, D.C.) and Metroliner service (New York to Washington, D.C.). These discounts do apply, however, to these routes during weekends. The child's discount may also not apply to some rail passes, like the North American Rail Pass, where fixed prices apply for children (infants on laps are still free).

Infant and Child Fare Rules

Limitations also apply to the number of free infants and discounted children that may travel per paid adult. The fine print can be confusing, so if you are traveling with twins, or multiples, or multiple children, here is a quick guide:

1 adult may travel with... 1 free infant

1 adult may travel with... 1 free infant, 1 infant at 50% (riding on child's ticket)

2 adults may travel with... 2 free infants

2 adults may travel with... 4 children at 50 % each

1 adult may travel with... 2 children at 50% each... and/or 1 free infant

2 adults may travel with... 4 children at 50% each... and/or 2 free infants

Rail Pass Options

If you'd like to plan a multi-stop journey, or travel with greater flexibility, Amtrak also offers a small number of rail passes and flat-rate fares, including:

- **North America Rail Pass** – 30 days of travel in the U.S. on Amtrak and in Canada on VIA Rail, with unlimited rides and stopovers. Sleeping car accommodations are an additional charge. Seniors, children, and students save 10% on this pass.
- **California Rail Pass** – 7 days of travel within California over a consecutive 21-day period. Eligible trains include the Capitols, San Joaquin, and Pacific Surfliner corridor trains, most connecting Thruway services, and the Coast Starlight between Los Angeles and Dunsmuir, California. Seat only, sleeping accommodations are extra. Adult and discounted child tickets.
- **Florida Rail Pass** – Available to permanent Florida residents only. One year of unlimited travel throughout Florida, without blackout dates, and no reservations are required.
- **Explore America Flat-rate Fares** – 45 days of travel within your choice of one, two, or three zones within the continental U.S. Prices vary by season and number of zones purchased. See www.amtrak.com for zone maps, routes, and pricing.

Be aware that some Amtrak passes require you to make reservations for each segment you will travel, in addition to carrying your pass. See pass pricing details, restrictions, and any updates to these pass plans at www.amtrak.com, or call 1-800-872-7245.

Other Discounts Available from Amtrak

If your party includes any of the following, you may be eligible for additional discounts. Note that some discounts may not apply to the weekday Acela Express or Metroliner routes, or possibly the Auto train, and most will only apply to the individual ticket holder's ticket (e.g. the AAA member himself).

- AAA members save 10%
- NARP Members (National Association of Railroad Passengers) save 10%
- Veterans with a Veterans Advantage card save 15%
- Active duty US military personnel, their spouses and dependents, save 10% Students with Student Advantage card save 15%
- Seniors 62 years and over save 15% on tickets (not sleeper supplements) and get 10% off the North American rail pass.

SEATS, SLEEPERS, AND ONBOARD AMENITIES

Amtrak Seats and Sleeper Compartments

Although seat types vary by train and route, even Amtrak's short-haul coach train seats are still more spacious than airline coach seats (your baby or toddler can probably sit between you and your mate), and offer space enough on the floor in front of you to set your baby in her infant carrier or put down a small blanket to let your toddler play.

Unreserved Coach Seats are available on certain short-distance trains. They will still be larger than coach seats on aircraft, recline, have trays and reading lights, and most will have leg rests. On some trains, you may also have the option of table seating, with four seats facing each other and a large table in the center—a great option for families who can break bread, play games, color, and converse more easily facing each other than they would across the aisle. When traveling by day on a short-distance train, ask your conductor if there are any of these seats on your train.

Lower Level Coach Seats must be made available first to elderly and disabled travelers, but they do offer some advantages for travelers with babies and small children as well. First, it is easier—and safer—to board the train and get settled into your seats with your carry-on bags stowed without having to negotiate the steep stairs of Amtrak trains (you can always explore the train later without your hands full). Second, the handicap-accessible restrooms on this level are where you'll find the diaper changing stations.

Coach seats on overnight trains are spacious and feature a deep recline with a leg rest—plus fold out trays and individual reading lights. You will enjoy more legroom, more elbowroom, and more of a view from your large window than you could hope to on an airplane. Some newer coach cars also feature 110 outlets at the seats, but this is still not considered standard for coach seats. Check for amenities on your particular train online at www.amtrak.com or call 1-800-USA-RAIL to inquire.

The Superliner Roomette (formerly called "Budget Sleeper") is a great option when your child is still small enough to sleep comfortably beside you and doesn't need much room to play. By day, your private compartment has its own picture window and two wide seats with a table. At night, your attendant transforms it into two twin-size bunks, complete with pillows and linens. Passengers with a roomette are considered first-class passengers, and all meals during their journey are included. You will share a restroom with only the other passengers in your train car, as well as shower facilities (towels and soap provided in your room). See photo on page 258.

A Family Room is less expensive than the traditional room for 2 adults (Superliner Bedroom), but it does not include its own private bath. Instead, it offers more space for playing, visiting, and sleeping. By day, your room provides two wide, reclining seats and a table (same as the roomette), plus a sofa, and views from two picture windows. Come nightfall, your room converts to two adult-size bunks and two smaller beds for children. Passengers with a family room are also considered first-class passengers, and all meals during their journey are included. Bathroom and shower facilities are shared, as described for the roomette.

The Superliner Bedroom is designed primarily for two adults, but can accommodate two adults and a small child if desired. It has three seats by day with two bunks at night (the lower bunk is slightly wider and may work for co-sleeping with your child between you and the wall). These cars include a private toilet, sink, and shower in the compartment, but at the expense of much space.

The Superliner Bedroom Suite is ideal if you will be traveling with friends, grandparents, or just a big family of your own. The "suite" is simply made up of two interconnecting Superliner Bedrooms, for a total of two separate rooms, each with its own private bathroom and shower. It is designed for four passengers, but can accommodate up to six. By day, each room has a large sofa with reclining sections and an easy chair. At night, the sofa converts to a bed and an upper berth folds down from above. Be sure to reserve your suite WELL IN ADVANCE as there are a limited number of rooms that may connect on each train, and any of them may be reserved as individual rooms. Unfortunately, there is no cost savings for booking two rooms as a suite, so you will ultimately pay the same price as you would for two separate rooms. Suites can only be reserved by telephone at this time: 1-800-USA-Rail.

Traveling by day in our private Superliner Roomette. This seat becomes one half of the lower bunk by night.

A Note on Amtrak's (Amazingly Expensive) Sleeper Options

Before you get too enamored with the idea of overnight travel in a sleeper car on Amtrak, you should brace yourself for the "sleeper supplement" you will pay in addition to your passenger fare or rail pass. This is where your rail costs may suddenly skyrocket. As mentioned earlier, passengers with sleeper accommodations on Amtrak are traveling first class, with complete hot meals served in the diner, soap and towels and shower, a daily newspaper, bottled water, and nightly turn-down service. Sure, it's no overnighter at an all-inclusive beach resort in Cancun, but your checkbook might not see any difference.

Consider a trip on Amtrak's Coast Starlight, traveling overnight from Emeryville, California to Portland, Oregon in low season. With advance planning, tickets for 2 adults and one child riding one way on this train, in reserved coach seats, is only $167 for the three travelers (priced at time of writing and most certainly subject to change). Now, to add one of these sleeper options, you would pay an additional:

$245   Roomette

$462   Family bedroom

$298   Bedroom

Given the current departure and arrival times, the only meals included at these rates would be breakfast and lunch. And guess what? You've still got to get home again. Oh, and did you want to stay at your destination, too? Chances are you can think of a few other ways you'd rather spend $462 for one night's accommodations and a couple of meals with your kids.

So it's not hard to see why more families aren't traveling Amtrak for overnight adventures across the U.S. Unfortunately, at present, Amtrak doesn't offer a more affordable second class sleeper option, as is so popular in Europe and in some other countries. For now, you must choose between overnight coach seats or first class compartments—or more practically, do your rail travel by day and spend the night at a hotel.

But imagine how nice it could be to have a private, secure compartment with bunks for your family, with the option of bringing your own food and snacks onboard, or purchasing food at your discretion from the snack or dining cars. And just think how much you could save turning down your own bed at night! (Heck, you could probably even splurge to buy yourself a newspaper if you needed one.)

If more economical sleeper options—or other improvements to the Amtrak system—would make your family more likely to travel by train in the United States, you may want to send your comments or suggestions to Amtrak (easy email form available at www.amtrak.com on the Contact Us page). Or consider supporting the National Association of Railroad Passengers (NARP), the only national organization speaking for the users of passenger trains and rail transit. A $45 tax-deductible family membership earns you two member cards and a 10% discount for both travelers on most Amtrak trains (visit www.narprail.org or call 1-202-408-8362).

Amtrak's Onboard Amenities

Each train is different, so to be certain of any critical onboard amenities for your journey, check with an Amtrak reservations agent by phone or look up your train's specs online at www.amtrak.com. Although you can expect roomy reclining seats with reading lights and trays on virtually all Amtrak trains, you may also be able to enjoy some of the following amenities:

Electrical outlets: 110-volt electrical outlets can be found in most First Class, Business Class, and sleeper cars. Some of the newer coach cars feature outlets at the seats as well.

Lounge, dinette, and café cars: You can expect at least one of these less formal dining options on most of Amtrak's trains, except on a small number of very short-distance trains. Get coffee, donuts, hot dogs, and the like, to eat at your seat, or possibly at a small table in this car.

Dining cars: Long-distance trains feature full-service dining cars, where you will most likely be asked to make reservations for your preferred lunch and/or dinner times. Reservations can be made from 11:30 a.m. to 3 p.m. for lunch, and from 4:30 to 9:00 p.m. for dinner, and you can simply tell the attendant passing through your car which time you prefer. If you have booked a sleeper car or roomette, your meals are included in your fare; otherwise, you will pay extra. Remember, if you are traveling with an "infant" even with overnight accommodations, your child is not guaranteed a space at the table, so to avoid eating with your child on your lap, book an earlier seating when the dining car will be less crowded. Ticketed children can order from the children's menu.

digEplayer™ for rent: You can now rent a portable, digital entertainment device with 7" screen and headphones at select Amtrak stations. The digEplayer is preloaded with movies, TV shows, music videos, music, and Amtrak travel guides. Ask for the "Family digE" to get one loaded with new release movies, or the "All-kids digE" for new release and classic children's movies. Rental prices range from $12 to $40, based on trip length.

Changing tables: Changing tables are available in most handicap-accessible restrooms found on the lower level of Amtrak Superliner trains and in select cars on older trains. Ask the conductor where you can find an accessible restroom if you are unsure where to look.

Showers: Showers are available to passengers with Roomette and Sleeper reservations. Facilities are shared only with other passengers traveling in their same car. Soap and towels are provided.

Bicycle racks: Some Amtrak trains include cars with bicycle racks just inside the doors. You may use this area to lock up your bike, place cumbersome strollers (even doubles—don't be shy), and other oddly-shaped or oversized items.

AMTRAK'S BAGGAGE POLICIES

One of the great advantages of taking the train for families with small children is the incredible amount of stuff you can bring with you. While the same 50 lbs. per bag weight limit now common for air travel is the norm for bags traveling by train, consider this: each ticketed passenger may carry on two suitcases of 50 lbs. each, AND each passenger may also check three suitcases of the same weight! But wait, there's more…

Accepted Carry-On Baggage:

- Two pieces per passenger, 50 lbs. max each, not to exceed 28" x 22" x 14"
- Additional personal items such as briefcases, purses, laptops
- Additional "infant paraphernalia," including strollers, diaper bags, and car seats

Guidelines for Checked Baggage:

- Three pieces per ticketed passenger, 50 lbs. max each, not to exceed 36" x 36" x 36"
- Up to three additional bags may be checked, at $10 each
- Special items, including baby carriages, bicycles, golf bags, and skis are accepted as checked baggage, but may cost $5 for a special handling fee.

If you plan to check bags, first make sure your departure station actually checks baggage. This shouldn't be a problem at the larger stations, but some small depots and unstaffed stations do not offer this service. www.amtrak.com has details for all of its stations, including baggage service and hours. You can also call their toll-free number to inquire: 1-800-USA-RAIL. Bags must be checked in no less than 30 minutes prior to departure, and be clearly tagged. You will need to present valid photo I.D. to check your bags, and keep track of your claim check for pickup at your destination.

As for carry-on bags, just remember that space is limited, especially when trains may be at their fullest during peak times and seasons. When riding in standard passenger cars, you may need to store your bags in the space above your seats if the oversized baggage racks are already full, so carry on smaller suitcases that are sure to fit (and won't break your back). Space is also at a premium in sleeper cars and roomettes, so it may prove a far greater convenience to check everything you won't need during your journey.

Baggage Handlers and Handcarts

Uniformed "Red Caps" provide free baggage assistance at most major Amtrak stations (tips are appreciated, of course), and will provide you with a claim check for any checked baggage. Self-service handcarts are also available at most stations, free of charge.

AIRPORTS SERVED BY AMTRAK

A handful of U.S. airports are served by Amtrak, at least by a connecting Thruway bus. These connections can be helpful if you'd like to connect to Amtrak from an airport, or plan your journey to coincide with a one-way flight. When checking schedules and fares to or from these airports, use the station code shown in parentheses after each airport name below to be sure your Amtrak fare includes service all the way to or from the airport. Note: if you are planning to connect for a flight departure, be sure to plan your arrival time earlier than you would otherwise need to be at the airport as trains, like airplanes, do sometimes experience delays—especially in winter weather.

Baltimore Washington International Airport, MD (BWI).

Free bus transfers are available to and from Baltimore Washington Airport. Connect with the Acela Express, Regional, Metroliner, and Vermonter trains.

Burbank / Bob Hope Airport, CA (BUR)

Catch either the Pacific Surfliner from the airport, or take an Amtrak Thruway bus from this airport to Bakersfield, where you can catch the San Joaquins. You may also take the Pacific Surfliner (or Metrolink commuter train) from this airport to reach downtown Los Angeles.

Oakland – Coliseum Airport, CA (OAC)

This Amtrak station is connected by a pedestrian bridge with the Oakland Coliseum / Airport BART (Bay Area Rapid Transit) station, where you can catch an AirBART bus to the Oakland international Airport ($2 exact change or BART ticket). Connect here with the Capitol Corridor.

Milwaukee General Mitchell International Airport, WI (MKA)

The station is located at the western edge of the airport, with a free shuttle bus running between the two. This station is served by the Hiawatha line.

Newark Airport, N.J. (EWR)

Ride a monorail between the Newark Airport Stop station and airport with your fare included in the price of your Amtrak ticket (when the airport listed as the final destination on your ticket—other passengers purchase $5 monorail tickets from a vending machine). Connects with Keystone and Regional trains.

Palm Springs Airport, CA (PSP)

Amtrak Thruway bus service connects the Palm Springs Airport (PSN) with the North Palm Springs train station (PSN) where you can board the Sunset Limited.

Van Nuys Airport, CA

Connecting bus service at the Van Nuys rail station (VNC) and Van Nuys Airport Bus Stop (VNF). Catch the Coast Starlight or Pacific Surfliner.

REQUIRED DOCUMENTS FOR U.S. RAIL TRAVEL

Domestic Rail Travel

Passengers under 18 years are not required to carry travel documents or I.D. when not crossing borders. Passengers 18 years and over must have valid photo I.D. when:

- Obtaining, exchanging, and refunding tickets
- Storing baggage at stations
- Checking baggage

- Asked for I.D. onboard as part of a random ticket/I.D. check per federal Transportation Security Administration guidelines.

A current state or provincial driver's license, military photo I.D., or Canadian provincial health photo I.D. card is acceptable.

Border Crossings and Foreign Nationals

U.S. and Canadian citizens crossing their shared border are urged to carry valid passports, though it isn't required until the new land-crossing portion of the Western Hemisphere Travel Initiative goes into effect. Until then, you may present proof of citizenship (e.g. certified copy of a birth certificate) and valid proof of government-issued I.D. (e.g. driver's license). Citizens of other countries must carry a valid passport and any applicable visas. As when traveling out of the country by air, sea, or automobile, children traveling with only one parent must have a notarized letter of consent (see page 100).

- *Chapter 20* -
Catching VIA Rail in Canada

CANADA'S NOTABLE ROUTES AND HIGHLIGHTS

VIA Rail is Canada's primary passenger rail system, with trains running vast distances across the continent, from Prince Rupert on the Pacific Ocean to Halifax on the Atlantic Coast, and from sub-arctic Churchill on the Hudson Bay (the world's polar bear capital) to Windsor at the southern tip of the Ontario peninsula (drive north and you're in Michigan). It can take you to the hearts of Canada's cosmopolitan cities, or to destinations so remote that no station even exists (a "special stop" can be wherever you please, but must be reserved at least 48 hours in advance).

THE CANADIAN travels from Toronto, ON to Vancouver, B.C. by way of Edmonton and Jasper, and the Canadian Rockies. Total run is 3 days.

THE SKEENA takes you from Jasper National Park in the Canadian Rockies to Prince Rupert with an overnight layover in Prince George (book your own hotel room). Total run is 2 days, including layover.

THE SNOW TRAIN EXPRESS leaves Edmonton for Jasper on Friday evenings and returns on Sunday nights. Fare includes travel in a panorama viewing car and a meal onboard the train.

THE HUDSON BAY (Winnipeg – Churchill) takes you to the tundra in comfort and *warmth* to the small city of Churchill, the self-proclaimed Polar Bear capital (great viewing opportunities).

THE MONTREAL-TORONTO LINE travels between downtown areas of both cities, with local and regional transit connections at both Montreal Central Station and Toronto's Union Station, greatly simplifying your travel between the two destinations.

RATES, PRICING, AND PASSES FOR VIA RAIL

VIA Rail tickets can be compared with airline tickets, where you opt for varying degrees of flexibility and save accordingly. Generally, you have the choice between Regular Fares, Discounted Fares, and Supersaver Fares, each providing a greater level of savings and less flexibility in making changes to your ticket. There are a limited number of Discounted and Supersaver fares available for each journey as well, so they tend to sell out close to the departure time. It is also well worth checking the special offers online at www.viarail.ca. Promotions sometimes include free travel for children, free upgrades, and discounts on select routes.

VIA Rail's Pricing for Infants and Children

Infants - Children under 2 years travel free on their parents' laps (may occupy seat when available). You must call 1-888-VIA-Rail to provide your lap child's name after booking your reservation.

Children - Children 2 to 11 years travel at half price in Comfort Class (Economy), and for 25% off the adult ticket price in other classes (e.g. Sleeper class).

Students - Children 11 to 17 years get student discounts of 35% off Comfort class fare or 10% other classes of service.

VIA Rail's Rail Pass Options

Although children do get a standard discount on each of these passes, it is not nearly the 50% savings they receive on point-to-point tickets in Comfort class (Economy), so be sure to compare costs for your journey if you'll be traveling with a child 2 years or older. If you'll be traveling a great deal with a lap child, however, one of these passes may be your best option.

Canrailpass – 12 days of unlimited travel in Comfort class (Economy) within a 30-day period. Make as many stops as you like during your travel days, and add up to 3 extra days if you like. Valid on all VIA routes.

Corridorpass – 10 days of unlimited travel in southern Quebec and southern Ontario.

North America Rail Pass – 30 days of unlimited travel on all Amtrak and VIA Rail routes.

Other Discounts Available from VIA Rail

Full-time students – Regardless of age, full-time students with an ISIC (International Student Identity Card) can receive student fares for travel throughout the VIA Rail system.

Seniors – Travelers 60 years and over receive a standard 10% discount on Comfort class fares, even in conjunction with other special offers. No standard discount is given for Sleeper class, however.

VIA Rail's Classes of Service, Seats, and Sleepers

VIA Rail offers two basic classes of service: Comfort class and Sleeper class. Comfort class (Economy) is essentially coach seating—the lowest priced, most basic option available, and you will find it offered in all regions. No meal service is included in this fare, but you may purchase food onboard where available and reserve seating in the dining car where you will pay additionally for your meals.

All passengers with "bedded" accommodations, be they basic berths or private bedrooms, are traveling Sleeper Class. In most cases, this means your meals will be included during your journey, and you will also have access to shared shower facilities (except in deluxe rooms, which include a private shower). Note that VIA Rail's bedrooms all include a private toilet and sink, which not only makes them rather expensive, it also greatly reduces the available floor space (to little more than leg room for the seated passengers).

If you'll be traveling with an active child who needs room to roam, it may be far more practical to reserve sleeping berths rather than a bedroom. With an upper and lower berth reserved, you will actually have cushy seating for four by day, plus any additional open seats that may be found around you (and no walls closing you in).

Comfort Class Seats – Wide, roomy seats with head rests, reading lights, and fold-out trays. On most routes, seats recline and a pillow and blanket will be provided for overnight travelers.

Sleeping Berths – Passengers traveling with sleeping berth reservations travel by day on upholstered sofa-like seats that face each other (each seat is wide enough for two and so is quite comfortable shared with a child). At night, these seats convert to a lower berth (or bunk) with a privacy curtain. An upper berth folds down from above, with its own privacy curtain, but it has no view from the window. Lower berths cost slightly more than upper berths. Each berth is the size of a single bed, but may be shared by an adult and child or even by two adults. Six total berths (upper and lower) are located in a car. Unlike most couchettes found in Europe, there is no locking door to secure the compartment, just a privacy curtain for your bed. Restrooms and shower facilities are shared with the other travelers in your car.

Single Bedroom or "Roomette" – Unlike Amtrak's Roomette, this option features only one single bed, though you may share it. Also unlike Amtrak's Roomette, it includes a private toilet, sink, and mirror. However, the compartment is scarcely larger than the bed itself (6' 5" x 3' 7"), so only share this with your mate *and* child if you like to sleep tight—*really* tight—and won't need extra room for playing.

Double Bedroom – Enjoy two arm chairs by day (side by side, facing the bathroom with the window to one side) and two bunks by night, with your own toilet, sink, and mirror. A small closet, fan, and electrical outlet are also included. Shared shower with fellow passengers in your car.

Triple Bedroom – By day it offers two armchairs and a sofa. At night, it converts to two lower bunks and one upper. A small closet, fan, and electrical outlet are also included. Shared shower with fellow passengers in your car.

VIA RAIL'S BAGGAGE POLICIES

Carry-On Baggage
On most VIA trains, you may carry onboard 2 pieces of baggage. The Halifax-Montreal line and certain Montreal-Quebec trains limit passengers to only 1 carry-on per passenger.

Checked Baggage

Where offered, you may check three bags or items per ticketed passenger (ticketed children included). Certain trains may allow you to check even more items, depending on the route.

AIRPORT SERVICES

AirConnect Airport Service in Montreal

VIA Rail provides a free shuttle service between its Dorval train station and Montreal-Trudeau International Airport. The shuttles run every 20 minutes, with AirConnect stops clearly market outside the exits of both domestic and international airport terminals. You can also travel from the city center to the airport for free; just stop by the AirConnect counter at the Central Station and get a free pass to ride between Central Station and Dorval, and then take the AirConnect bus to your terminal.

From Montreal- Trudeau International Airport to the train:

Complimentary AirConnect shuttles depart Montreal-Pierre Elliott Trudeau International Airport for VIA Rail's Dorval train station every 20 minutes. Just look for the AirConnect stop outside both domestic and international terminal exits.

Between Dorval station and Central Station: Take your bags to the AirConnect counter and collect your free pass to ride the next train to Montreal's Central Station (approximately 15 minutes). No reservation is required.

- *Chapter 21* -
Train Travel in Europe

RIDING EUROPE'S FAMILY-FRIENDLY RAILS

You could say that Europe was made for rail travel, with its sophisticated and streamlined rail service delivering travelers to the smack-dab center of city after city, even chunneling under water to whisk travelers from the mainland to Great Britain. It's efficient. It's affordable. And it can be a great way to see Europe whether or not you're traveling with a baby or very small child.

Since rail travel is a way of life for the majority of people in Europe, you can expect information and facilities to be abundant and fairly accommodating. Families, especially, can enjoy these major perks of train travel in Europe:

- Children may travel on trains free until at least 4 years (list follows), and older in some cases
- Two parents traveling together at all times (or any 2 adults) save with the Selectpass Saver rail pass, which also entitles them to first class travel
- Second-class sleeper cars (couchettes) are an option and are much more affordable than the sleepers available in the U.S.

- Centrally located train stations and better public transportation can eliminate the need for rental cars, taxis, or car seats at most destinations.
- Paying a child's fare will entitle your family to an extra sleeping berth in the couchette car, which not only means more space for you, but fewer other passengers. If traveling with 2 paid adults and 2 paid children where a 4-berth couchette is available, you can have the entire compartment to yourselves.

But if you're thinking that rail travel is hands-down the cheapest way to travel in Europe, you'd be wise to check your itinerary first—and check with the European budget airlines that may be able to whisk you cross-continent in far less time, and possibly for far less money, including www.easyjet.com, www.ryanair.com, and www.virgin-express.com.

That said, it is hard to beat the convenience of arriving at the city center versus an airport in an outlying suburb, or avoiding lengthy airport security lines and carry-on restrictions. Traveling by train also allows you to see much more of the territory you cross, including villages and other points of interest where you may be able to get out and stretch your legs or eat lunch before catching a later train to continue on.

EUROPEAN RATES, PRICING, AND PASSES

Free Travel for Infants and Children

Infants - For train travel throughout Europe's international rail network, children under 4 years old may travel free on a paid adult's lap, or in a shared sleeping berth or sleeper compartment. Within some European countries, children may also ride free up to 5 years or 6 years, as noted in the list of "Children's Discounts" that follows.

Children with rail pass-holding adults - In a few European countries, older children may also travel free when their parents have qualifying rail passes and an optional family card or pass. In Great Britain, one child under age 16 may travel free with an adult BritRail Pass holder who also carries a BritRail Family Pass—free on request when you purchase the individual country rail pass in advance of your trip (or for a fee when purchased after arrival in the country). In Switzerland, the same applies to adult Swiss Pass holders carrying a Swiss Family Card, also free on request when you purchase the individual country rail pass in advance of your trip. Note that these family discounts are not available with rail passes that combine multiple countries (e.g. the Select Pass).

Children of adults with point-to-point tickets - In Germany, children under 14 ride free whenever named on one adult's point-to-point ticket, so a German rail pass may actually be a less attractive option for families traveling with older children.

Children's Discounts for Rail Travel

Children 4 to 11 years travel for 50% of the adult ticket or rail pass price for international travel in Europe. For travel within individual countries on national networks, children exceeding the free lap child age, as listed below, travel for 50% of the adult ticket price, except where they may travel free, as described in the previous point.

Children 4 years and older must have their own point-to-point tickets or rail passes for International rail travel within Europe. Within individual countries, the minimum age required for a child's ticket can vary across Europe. Depending on where you will travel, it may be most economical to purchase point-to-point tickets for domestic travel only where needed. For international tickets, children may travel free on a parent's lap until they are 4 years old, and for a child's fare (generally 50% of the adult ticket price) from 4 to 11 years. Rail passes for children are priced at 50% of the adult first class or Saver pass fare. In some countries, however, one child up to age 16 may travel with a rail pass carrying adult for free! See details in the following section: European Rail Passes Favored by Families.

Point-to-point tickets within individual countries:

Country	Free until age	Child's fare
Austria	6 years	6 to 15 years
Belgium	6 years	6 to 11 years
Bulgaria	6 years	6 to 11 years
Croatia	4 years	4 to 11 years
Denmark	6 years	6 to 15 years
Czech Republic	6 years	6 to 11 years
Finland	6 years	6 years to 16 years
France	4 years	4 to 11 years
Germany	4 years	4 to 14 years
Greece	4 years	4 to 11 years
Great Britain	5 years	5 to 15 years
Hungary	6 years	6 to 13 years
Italy	4 years	4 to 11 years
Luxemburg	6 years	6 to 11 years
Macedonia	4 years	4 to 11 years
Netherlands	4 years	4 to 11 years
Norway	4 years	4 to 15 years
Poland	4 years	4 to 11 years
Portugal	4 years	4 to 11 years
Rep. of Ireland	4 years	4 to 15 years
Romania	4 years	4 to 11 years
Serbia	4 years	4 to 12 years
Slovakia	6 years	6 to 11 years
Slovenia	6 years	6 to 11 years
Spain	4 years	4 to 11 years
Switzerland	6 years	6 to 15 years

RailEurope (www.raileurope.com) is a good resource for comparing rail passes and scoping out the various accommodations and their prices on the popular overnight trains. However, if you are trying to consider your various options, including sightseeing and pit stops along the way, and plan a detailed adventure for your family by rail, the German rail ubersite www.bahn.de is a much better place to get started (be sure to click the button for English). This site will show you every train you need to take to get from Moscow to Madrid, not to mention any necessary transfers by bus, metro, or even by foot. However, pricing information for journeys outside of Germany may not be available on this site.

For single-country journeys, or itineraries that venture just beyond the border, you should be able to get helpful information including ticket and reservation (when necessary) prices on the country's own rail Web site. Some will even allow you to purchase and print your tickets at home, saving you time at the rail station, not to mention panic attacks if the ticket machines are jammed. Here are a few of these sites to get you started:

> Britain/The U.K. – www.britrail.com
>
> Germany (and well beyond) – www.bahn.de
>
> France – www.voyages-sncf.com
>
> Italy – www.trenitalia.com

Rick Steves' travel guidebooks also provide invaluable information, including suggested itineraries, pit stops, and practical rail travel advice (www.ricksteves.com).

European Rail Passes Favored by Families

There are many types of rail passes you can choose when traveling to or through Europe. If you will be there for an extended period of time, you may want to explore all of your options more closely. For most families on vacation with a baby, small child, or with multiple children, these may be the favored options.

No pass at all – If you're like many families with small children, you don't plan to travel between very many destinations to begin with. It may be more cost effective for you to buy point-to-point tickets to your destination(s), especially in Germany where children up to 14 years may travel free when named on accompanying adult point-to-point tickets, but pay 50% for German rail passes.

BritRail Passes – When you purchase any BritRail Pass in advance of your trip (but not a rail pass combining Britain with other countries), you can opt for a free BritRail Family Card. With this card, one child age 5 to 15 years may travel with each BritRail Pass-holding adult free. Additional children (outnumbering the adults in the group) are 50% of the adult fare. The BritRail Pass is also valid on the Heathrow Express and Gatwick Express airport trains, and entitles pass holders (and families) to special Eurostar fares.

Swiss Pass Holders – As with BritRail Passes, children under 16 years may travel free with Swiss Pass-holding parents and a Swiss Family Card. The Swiss Family Card is also free on request when you purchase your Swiss Passes in advance of your trip.

Rail & Drive Passes – Combine a rail pass with a car rental in one package. Available with some individual country passes (Spain, Germany, Italy, France, or Great Britain), or with Eurail and Scanrail Passes.

Saverpass - If you will be two adults traveling together at all times, be sure to look at the Saverpass options that will let you do so at a savings, and with first class status. Children under 4 years will travel free on your first-class lap, and older children may have their own Saverpasses for 50% of the adult price (except in Britain or Switzerland where they can travel free with your adult Saverpass and Family Card).

European Classes of Service

First class cars have fewer seats and better upholstery. For parents, this translates to more space for luggage and lap children, and often a cleaner travel environment. When traveling first class on "premier" trains, a meal is sometimes included. If you travel with a Saverpass, you are entitled to ride in first class.

Second class cars accommodate far more passengers, and seats are generally fixed in place (no reclining). If you are traveling on point-to-point tickets, second class will be your least expensive option.

European Train Seats and Sleeper Compartments

Coach seats – On European trains, coach seats generally refer to seats situated on either side of an aisle, much like on an airplane. In first class, these seats may be larger and there may be only one seat on one side of the aisle with two on the other to compensate for the use of space.

Compartment seats – On many trains in Europe, you'll find compartment seating, where a corridor passes along one side of the train car, with doorways into individual compartments. These compartments may seat up to six or even eight people. With unreserved seating, you may walk along and choose the least crowded — or empty compartment.

Couchettes – These are usually the second class option for lying down flat to sleep on an overnight train. Like compartments (which some of them are by day), you will walk down a corridor at one side of the train car with couchette compartments on the other side. Couchettes may contain up to six bunks stacked three high on each side, so be sure to arrive early to ensure you get a lower bunk—hopefully both lower bunks for the greatest comfort and convenience while traveling with your child. A pillow and blanket are provided. You may be sharing the couchette compartment with strangers, but the compartment door should lock for general security at night.

Sleepers – These may be offered as first class accommodations, usually with beds for 1 or 2 people (and sometimes a very small optional 3rd bed suitable for a child), or as second class accommodations, with beds for 2 to 4 people. In either class, there is usually a sink provided in the compartment, an outlet, reading lights, and linens. Where "deluxe" first class sleeper accommodations are available, they may include a private toilet and shower as well.

EUROPEAN AIRPORTS WITH RAILWAY STATIONS

These major airports have built-in train stations, which can help whisk your family to the city center or help you get on your journey most efficiently. Ending your rail journey at the airport of your return can also be quite helpful, without need of taxi or shuttle, or the car seat.

Amsterdam Schiphol (AMS)	Barcelona Prat (BCN)
Berlin Schönefeld (SXF)	Birmingham (BHX)
Brussels National (BRU)	Copenhagen (CPH)
Düsseldorf (DUS)	Frankfurt am Main (FRA)
Geneva, Cointrin (GVA)	London, Gatwick (LGW)
London, Heathrow (LHR)	London, Stansted (STN)
Malaga (AGP)	Manchester (MAN)
Munich, Strauss (MUC)	Paris, Charles de Gaulle (CDG)
Rome, Fiumicino (FCO)	Stockholm (ARN)
Stuttgart, Echterdingen (STR)	Vienna, Schwechat (VIE)
Zurich (ZRH)	

PART VII
TRAVELS BY CRUISE SHIP

- Chapter 22 -
Before You Book Your Cruise

THE CASE FOR CRUISING AS A FAMILY

A family vacation aboard a major cruise ship is for many the ultimate, all-inclusive dose of rest and relaxation. For parents that want to escape it all, lift nary a finger for meal preparation, eliminate the risk of getting lost on the way to the next destination, and never be more than a moment away from some form of entertainment, a snack, a restroom, or even a doctor—cruising is where it's at. Those who have planned any kind of trip with a baby or small child can appreciate the ease and simplicity a well chosen cruise vacation may offer.

Top Reasons to Cruise as a Family

- **"All-inclusive" pricing** – you can plan to eat often and well, without guilt, even when ordering multiple side dishes to appease a picky toddler. And when cruising abroad, your price will be locked in, in spite of exchange rate fluctuations that could cause a land-based vacation budget to jump.
- **Convenience** – All of the restaurants and facilities are an easy walk from your cabin.

- **Safety of a closed community** – between ports, you know that everyone on board is a ticketed passenger or hired staff, and there are miles of deck to stroll and explore without need of crossing streets or dodging cars. And while you are onboard, you don't even need to carry a wallet with you — most things are included, and any extras are charged to your room.
- **Multiple destinations** – see a number of different destinations without the need to repack or schlep baggage, and without the frustration of losing extra time in transit, stuck in seats. If you sign up for any of the ship's organized excursions, you can even be escorted right from the gangway to the best highlights at your port, complete with a guide.
- **A drop-off nursery or children's program** – you can leave your child in the qualified hands of registered staff onboard while you explore an exotic port, go on the dive trip, enjoy a late show, or decompress in the steam room.
- **A doctor in the house** – you have the added comfort of knowing a doctor is onboard, should you need one, along with a small supply of prescription drugs and over-the-counter remedies (antibiotics, ear drops, etc.).
- **Exotic and remote locales** – you can satisfy your appetite for adventure by visiting regions you might not feel so comfortable exploring independently with a baby or small child, with safe water and food onboard, secure accommodations, and a registered organization ensuring you're safely at home each night.

But before booking that next best bargain cruise you see advertised, make sure the cruise line really provides all the pluses you're hoping for — including an environment where your family will feel comfortable and welcome. Remember, not all cruise lines cater to families with babies or small children. Some don't even allow children younger than 12 years onboard, and others may allow only a limited number of children or infants on each sailing.

Cruisers Beware: Some Cruise Lines Do, Some Don't...
- Offer discounted pricing for infants and/ or children
- Allow babies on board, or children under certain ages
- Limit the number of child passengers onboard

- Provide family-friendly cabins
- Offer flexible dining options or children's menus
- Provide babysitting, childcare, or children's activities

As you shop for an enticing itinerary and the perfect price for your cruise, you'll want to be sure you also get the best possible amenities and perks for your family—and in an atmosphere that will be comfortable for everyone. In other words, you'll first want to know which cruise lines are the best match for your family's needs. And even though 24-hour pizzerias, children's programs, and high chairs are lovely, the single-most important factor for many families will be price—and the bottom line for families with children can vary dramatically depending on a cruise line's passenger rate policies and special promotions.

PRICING FOR INFANTS AND CHILDREN

Unless otherwise noted, the cruise prices you see advertised are quoted as a per person rate, based on two people traveling together and staying in a room designed to fit no more than two passengers. Most cruise lines charge a fee for an additional person, a third- or fourth-passenger rate, even if that person is not yet eating solid foods and shares a bed with his parents. Third- and fourth-passenger rates are generally less than the primary passenger rates, but as you can imagine, they can make the cost of cruising with a baby jump—without giving you any additional cabin space or the benefit of her 5-course dinner plan. So, the option of having your child cruise free or at a discounted rate should be carefully considered.

At present, two cruise lines always allow infants (children under 2 years) to cruise "free," meaning for only the cost of port taxes and government fees: Norwegian Cruise Line and Cunard Line. Disney Cruise Line always allows children under 3 years to cruise at a drastically discounted flat rate based on the length of cruise (and not by accommodations). For example, the infant fare for a 3- or 4-night cruise with Disney would be about $30 total, plus the applicable port taxes and government fees.

However, free or discounted passage for your child will not necessarily mean the best savings for your family. You may still get your best *total* price from a cruise sale (e.g. last-minute offer) where the rate for the first 2 passengers is already substantially lower than what you might pay for regular adult fares where children are given special rates. So it can definitely pay to price out multiple cruises for your entire family before making your final decision.

Children under 2 years always cruise "free" with:
- Norwegian Cruise Line www.ncl.com 1-866-234-0292
- Cunard Line www.cunard.com 1-800-7CUNARD

Children under 3 years always cruise at a discounted rate with:
- Disney Cruise Line www.disneycruise.com 1-800-951-3532

A handful of other cruise lines run special promotions with discounted rates for children that are better than the standard 3rd/4th passenger rates, but these offers only apply to certain sailing dates or itineraries. Depending on the offer, the discount may include infants under 2 years or all children up to 17 years. Since these deals are not always advertised, you may want to check the cruise lines' Web sites for possible upcoming children's specials, and make note of the specific sail dates and ship names. The discounts should be automatically reflected in your quote from a cruise specialists or online agency, so long as you are prompted for the children's ages at the time of the cruise. Here are your best bets for bargain sailings with your child.

Best-bet cruise lines for children's discounts and special offers:

Carnival Cruise Lines www.carnival.com 1-888-Carnival

Costa Cruises www.costacruise.com or 1-888-249-3978

Disney Cruise Line www.disneycruise. com 1-800-951-3532

Holland America Line www.hollandamerica.com 1-877-SAIL-HAL

MSC Cruises www.msccruisesusa.com 1-800-666-9333

Norwegian Cruise Line www.ncl.com 1-800-327-7030

OTHER CRUISE DISCOUNTS

Depending on the cruise line, point of embarkation and some other factors, you may be able to get an additional discount on your cruise. When getting a cruise quote on line or over the phone, you may be asked for additional information to see if you qualify for any of these possible discounts. Some possible discounts include:

Past passenger discount – if you have cruised with the same cruise line in the past

Resident's discount – sometimes having residency in a certain state may qualify

Military discounts – several major cruise lines offer discounts to active members of the U.S. military. Some cruise lines also extend these discounts to retired members and veterans as well.

Interline discounts – Airline employees may qualify for discounts on select sailings with certain cruise lines.

Police, fire fighters, and teachers – Occasional discounts may be offered

Group discounts – Most often your group will need to book a minimum of eight cabins to qualify, but occasionally (in the low season) fewer cabins will qualify. This can be a clever way to plan family reunions or cruise with several other friends or family members. You will need to call the cruise line or a cruise specialist to discuss requirements and group discounted rates for your select sailing.

MINIMUM AGE REQUIREMENTS

Although many cruise lines are welcoming babies and toddlers on board with open arms and ample amenities, cruise lines still vary widely in their policies regarding the minimum ages required for infants and small children. While some cruise lines, such as Royal Caribbean and Peter Deilmann, have no minimum age requirement whatsoever for children, Clipper Cruise Line does not allow children under 9 years to sail, and Viking Cruise Line insists cruisers be at least 12 years old (and so they are not included in the cruise lines table).

Other cruise lines, such as Celebrity and Princess, effectively discourage children from cruising on most itineraries by charging full-price third and fourth passenger rates (no children's discounts) and limiting the number of children onboard each cruise; Crystal, Radisson, and Silverseas specifically reserve the right to limit the number of children under age 3.

The itinerary may also affect whether or not an infant may cruise. For cruises calling on more than one country, there is often a minimum age requirement of 6 months, and most exotic cruises (e.g. South America, Asia, etc.) will require infants to be at least one year of age. Minimum age requirements are included for each cruise line in the cruise lines table.

Depending on your child's temperament and your own vacation wishes, there is one other factor that could determine whether or not she is old enough for the cruise vacation you envision: Is she old enough to qualify for the onboard babysitting or children's activities? For many parents, this may make or break a cruise deal; if you're one of them, consult the cruise table for details about babysitting with each of the major cruise lines.

BABYSITTING AND CHILDREN'S PROGRAMS

Be warned: A cruise line that says it offers "babysitting" does not necessarily provide babysitting for babies! Most cruise lines offer childcare–be it in the form of babysitting or children's activity programs—only for potty trained children (no pull-ups or training pants), and for those over 3 years old. If you are depending on shipboard childcare to get the most out of your cruise, you'll want to be sure you choose a cruise line that will accommodate your needs.

Onboard Babysitting

Babysitting onboard cruise ships can be divided into three categories: formal drop-off nurseries, private in-room babysitting, and group babysitting. Disney, Cunard, and Carnival offer childcare for the youngest cruisers, caring for infants as young as 12 weeks. Norwegian will care for children 2 years and older, but requires parents to carry a beeper and come change the diaper themselves if needed (while in port, at least one parent must stay on ship to do so). A handful of others are also noted in the cruise lines table.

- **Formal drop-off nurseries** called "Flounder's Reef" can be found on each of Disney's ships (12 weeks to 3 years, hourly fee). Cunard's QE2 also has a nursery, which is staffed with certified British nannies (12 months to 7 years, complimentary).
- **Private in-room babysitting** is offered on very few cruise lines and is usually subject to crew member availability, so book ASAP: Celebrity (6 months to 12 years), Crystal (6 months to 12 years), Holland America (no age specified), and Royal Caribbean (6 months to 12 years).
- **Group babysitting** is far more common on cruise ships and is usually offered during late night and port visiting hours: Carnival (4 months to 11 years), Celebrity (3 years + toilet trained), Costa (3 years minimum), Holland America (3 years to 12 years), Norwegian (2 years to 12 years), Princess (3 years to 12 years), Royal Caribbean (3 years to 12 years).

For any of these babysitting options, be sure to check hours of availability and book as far in advance as possible to avoid disappointment. More details about babysitting in the Cruise Line Table.

Complimentary Kid's Programs

Children's programs have been added to many cruise lines to help give children a chance to socialize and stretch their imaginations, sometimes with arts or crafts, games, dance lessons, or special activities related to the itinerary. While Royal Caribbean includes a program for children 6 months to 3 years to attend *with* parents, most programs are designed for children to attend without their parents. At this time, those cruise lines offering supervised (ie. "drop-off") activities for the youngest sailors to attend without their parents include:

- **1 year and older:** Cunard
- **2 years and older:** Carnival, Norwegian
- **3 years and older:** Celebrity, Costa, Crystal, Disney, Holland America, Princess, Royal Caribbean

More details about children's programs are provided in the cruise lines table.

DINING OPTIONS AND OPPORTUNITIES

Traditionally, cruise guests would be assigned one of two dinner seatings, and would have to report to the formal dining room at their appointed time. This option still exists on many cruise ships, and if you want to take advantage of the gourmet dining onboard, this may be your only chance to do so. But more and more ships are offering additional flexible dining options as well, a great help to the family that struggles to get out the door on time, or has a picky eater in tow, or a toddler who struggles to sit through a five-course meal. Here are some of the dining options and opportunities available from some cruise lines that may help make your family's cruise all the more enjoyable.

Flexible dining – Most large cruise ships now offer additional flexible dining options, like buffets or pizzerias that open earlier and let you come as you are and sit where you please whenever suits you. Norwegian and Disney offer multiple round-the-clock dining options with complete flexibility for families. This may serve your family well for most or all nights of your cruise, but if you want some time to enjoy the full-meal deal in the dining room (even Disney offers adult-only restaurants as a reprieve), be sure to check what babysitting options the cruise line offers before booking with them.

Child-friendly dinner times – Another innovative solution for the dinnertime dilemma has come from Carnival. They offer an earlier dinnertime (5:45 pm) each evening for children 2 years and older where they dine with other kids in their age group and youth counselor hosts (while mom and dad hit the Jacuzzi). After dinner, the kids join in more activities with their age group while Mom and Dad can dine alone. Norwegian's youth counselors also take participating children to dinner one night of each sailing (and possibly more times on longer cruises).

Room service – Having your dinner delivered to your door can also be a delightful way to enjoy the evening's meal… while your baby snoozes in her bed… or your toddler practices the delicate art of using silverware. Some cruise lines will charge additional fees for this service, whereas some others will include room service in the price of the cruise—a serious value if this option works well for your family.

High chairs – Even in the formal dining rooms on ships, you can expect a high chair to be provided for your child if needed. However, strap and tray configurations are not always ideal, so if your child is an escape artist or has special needs, you may want to consider bringing a portable dining booster you know and trust. In peak family travel times, there may also be more competition for high chairs, and they will be doled out on a first-come first-served basis. Hook-on chairs that mount to the table's edge take up little space while traveling, but beware that they should not be used on tables with table cloths—what you are most likely to encounter in a ship's (formal) dining room.

Bottles and baby food – In formal dining rooms and shipboard restaurants where you will be waited on at your table, feel free to ask for bottles or baby food to be warmed for your child. Regular milk will be available, but bring your own formula if you'll need it. In most cases, waiters will be more than happy to accommodate your special requests, and will be more than happy to receive your special appreciation at the end of your cruise (do be sure to tip). In self-serve buffets and less formal eateries, you may need to ask for a mug of hot water (as for tea) to warm things yourself.

Table food for toddlers – Casual café-style dining may provide some good options for your toddler, like pasta, bread, yogurt, fruit, pizza, or French fries, but don't be afraid to make special requests in the dining room.

Anything on your menu that sounds remotely like it may interest your child—mashed potatoes, rice, steamed vegetables, soup—is fair game. Feel free to ask for side orders, even served in a bowl, without salt or sauce, or whatever suits.

Children's menus – If you choose a cruise line that offers a children's menu, rest assured that your child will have his fill of pizza, chicken nuggets, French fries, grilled cheese sandwiches, and the like, as you might expect from a children's menu at any restaurant.

A NEW PARENT'S GUIDE TO CRUISE LINES

Deciding which cruise to take can be daunting for anyone, but the stakes are even higher when bringing a baby or small child along for the ride. You are not only committing to where you will vacation, but where and how you will eat, sleep, and entertain yourselves in one fell swoop. Don't risk choosing a ship that isn't a fit for your family—where you might push your stroller through casino after casino only to wind up in the blaring discothèque with nowhere left to go but your cabin, or spend your nightly 5-course meals cringing as your toddler tosses breadsticks at your distinguished dining companions. Instead, use the following table to size up which cruise lines are the best match for your family's high seas adventure. As you'll see, there are plenty of cruise lines ready to accommodate families with babies and small children—even where pricing is concerned. At a glance, this table will help you quickly size up which cruise lines may be best for your family now, and in the years ahead.

Crib notes: All of these cruise lines state that they can provide a crib on request, though the number available on each cruise will be limited. Since they are all are available on a "first-reserved first-served" basis, be sure to reserve yours ASAP.

TABLE 2: A NEW PARENT'S GUIDE TO CRUISE LINES [2]

Cruise Line	Min. age	Child discount[3]	In-room babysitting	Drop-off babysitting	Free children's programs	Flex dining	Child menu	Room service	Playroom
Carnival www.carnival.com 1-888-CARNIVAL	4 mos.	No	No	4+ mos. $6/hr	2 yrs +	Yes	Yes	Yes	Yes
Celebrity www.celebritycruises.com 1-800-647-2251	None	No	6+ mos. 2 child max, $8/hour	3 yrs+ Potty trained $6/hr	3 yrs + Potty trained or w/ parent	Yes	Yes	Yes	Yes
Costa www.costacruises.com 1-888-249-3978	3 mos.	Select itineraries	No	3 yrs + Free	3 yrs + Potty trained	Yes	Yes	Yes	3 yrs + or w/adult
Crystal www.crystalcruises.com 1-800-804-1500	6 mos.	50% min. fare up to 12 yrs w/ 2 adults	6+ mos. $7.50/hr	No	Select sailings, 3 yrs +	Yes	Yes, + baby food	Yes	Yes

[2] Please bear in mind that some details may be subject to change, so always confirm critical information at time of booking.

[3] Child discounts only apply when traveling as the third or fourth passenger with two fare-paying adults in same cabin.

Cruise Line	Min. age	Child discount[3]	In-room babysitting	Drop-off babysitting	Free children's programs	Flex dining	Child menu	Room service	Playroom
Cunard www.cunard.com 1-800-7CUNARD	6 mos. or 1 yr.[4]	Up to 24 mos. free[5]	No	1 yr + Free	Yes	No	Yes	Yes, 24 hours	1 yr+ or w/adult
Disney www.disneycruise.com 1-800-951-3532	12 wks.	Up to 3 yrs Flat-rate discount prices	No	12 wks to 36 mos. $6/hr (10 hr max per cruise)	3 yrs +	Yes	Yes	Yes, 24 hrs	Yes
Holland America www.hollandamerica.com 1-877-SAIL-HAL	12 wks.	Select itineraries	Yes, no ages specified, $8/hr	Yes, $5/hr "after hours" program, $8/hr other	Prinsendam is 5+ yrs All other ships 3 yrs + potty trained	Yes	Yes, + baby food $1 ea. by advance request	Yes, 24 hrs	Only Westerdam and Zuiderdam
MSC Cruises www.mscruisesusa.com 1-800-666-9333	3 mos.	Select itineraries	No	$18/hr, 3 yrs + potty trained	Yes, 3 yrs. + or w/parent	Only breakfast & lunch	Yes	Yes	Yes

[4] Cunard requires 6 months for cruises in North America, Europe, Caribbean, Mexico, Transcanal, Australia, and New Zealand. Children must be 1 year old for the following cruise destinations: Africa, South America, South Pacific / Hawaii / Tahiti, world cruises, exotic cruises (Asia / Orient / Antarctica / Indian subcontinent), Transatlantic / Transpacific.

[5] "Free" meaning no passenger rate, but government taxes and port charges still apply for each passenger onboard.

Cruise Line	Min. age	Child discount[3]	In-room babysitting	Drop-off babysitting	Free children's programs	Flex dining	Child menu	Room service	Playroom
Norwegian www.ncl.com 1-866-234-0292	No	Up to 24 mos. cruise free[6]	No	Yes, 2 yrs to 12 yrs "after hours" and in port, fee may vary	Yes, 2 yrs +	Yes	Yes	Yes, 24 hrs	Yes
Princess www.princess.com 1-800-PRINCESS	6+ mos.[7]	No	No	Yes, 3 yrs + potty trained, $5/hr	3 yrs. + potty trained	Yes	Yes, + baby food by request	Yes	Yes, under 3 yrs with adult only
Regent Seven Seas www.rssc.com 1-877-505-5370	6+ mos.	50% min. fare 11 yrs. and under	1 year +, $25/hr where available	No	5 yrs +, select sailings only	Yes	Yes	Yes	No

[6] "Free" meaning no passenger rate, government taxes and port charges still apply for each passenger onboard.

[7] Princess requires 6 months for Alaskan and Caribbean cruises, 18 months for exotic cruises, and 12 months for other cruises.

Cruise Line	Min. age	Child discount[3]	In-room babysitting	Drop-off babysitting	Free children's programs	Flex dining	Child menu	Room service	Playroom
Royal Caribbean www.royalcaribbean.com 1-866-562-7625	6+ mos.	No	1 yr +, $8/hr	3 yrs + potty trained, $8/hr	3 yrs + and potty trained, and 6 mos. to 36 mos. w/ parent	Yes	Yes	Yes	Yes
Silversea www.silversea.com 1-800-722-9955	1 yr	No	No	No	No	Yes	No	Yes	No

- *Chapter 23* -
Booking Your Cruise

STATEROOM TYPES AND CONFIGURATIONS

Your options for ship cabins or "staterooms" may vary widely. With large cruise lines, there may be numerous stateroom options available, ranging from the most economical interior stateroom to a sprawling multi-room suite complete with private butler service. As mentioned earlier, bathtubs are not considered the norm on cruise ships, nor are mini refrigerators, unless you are cruising with Disney Cruise Line or in a family cabin or suite that specifically states otherwise.

Interior Staterooms

Your basic interior stateroom features few bells and whistles, and is likely to be the headlining price advertised for the cruise. Keep in mind that it will have no window and will most likely have two separate beds unless otherwise stated. Interior cabins are generally the smallest offered, and the beds may even be bunk style to save space (and not for a crib), so make sure you have the specifics for this type of stateroom on your particular ship before reserving it. Often the cruise line's Web site or online agency will have helpful pictures of most ships' basic cabins (if you're not seeing them elsewhere, try www.vacationstogo.com).

Oceanview Staterooms

A room with a view may be far more valuable to a family cruising with a baby or small child that will likely be spending more time in its cabin than some other passengers, not to mention, oceanview cabins are generally larger than interior staterooms. Oceanview cabins may have either a small porthole window or a larger window, depending, and often include more floor space—possibly even a pull-out sofa. When traveling as a family, it can be well worth the extra cost to upgrade to this cabin type if possible, especially if you would like to have a portacrib in your cabin. Sometimes cabins with an "obstructed view" or "partially obstructed view" are listed at a discount—be sure you have details about just how obstructed the view may be to avoid disappointment (lifeboats, columns, etc.). If you are on a tight budget, however, this may be a good option to help increase your floor space.

Deluxe Stateroom

What this means may vary by ship, but generally it includes greater square footage for your cabin, which may be especially helpful if you will be using a portacrib or need extra space for a child to play. It may also mean nicer furnishings and more of them, and you are more likely to find a king-size bed option in these rooms. Often a sofa with a pull-out bed is also included, which means more seating by day and an extra bed (if you need it) by night.

Verandah / Balcony

Having your own private balcony off your cabin can prove invaluable during nap times. You and your mate can step outside to fresh air and conversation, or a good book, and continue to enjoy the views as you cruise. If you are picky about your view, or nervous about having deck access with your little adventurer, visit the cruise line's Web site to see photos of these cabins, or call to request a brochure. Some older ships have open bars spread wide apart to maximize the view, but most have added plexiglas to optimize safety. Some newer ships feature balconies with solid, clear walls that are far safer with small children and provide an even better view.

However, some cabins may have a verandah made of a solid white wall—sturdy, but it blocks half the view from your cabin.

Triple / Quad + Occupancy

A variety of staterooms (any of those mentioned above) may provide sleeping spaces for three or even four people, but how they do so is especially important to know if you'll have a small child using one of the beds. In interior staterooms and some of the other smaller cabins available, the third and / or fourth bed is usually a bunk that folds down from above (not practical for a toddler, so you and your mate can arm wrestle for it). In oceanview or deluxe rooms, it is more likely to be a sofabed. If you are planning to use a portacrib or travel bed in your cabin instead of a third bed, you will be more concerned with how much floor space you will have to work with. Generally, cabins with sofas / sofabeds will give you the advantage of extra space allotted for the sofabed.

Suites

One-bedroom suites can be found on most ships, and some two-bedroom suites can be had as well. Although you most likely will not have a kitchenette as you might in a hotel, you are more likely to have a mini-refrigerator in your cabin, and possibly even a wet bar. All of these details will vary from ship to ship and by stateroom category, so check with your cruise specialist for any deal-breaker details before you book this cabin.

Family Staterooms and Family Suites

Some newer ships (including those from Carnival, Royal Caribbean, Costa, and Disney Cruise Line) offer cabins with beds for four or more people. Unless otherwise stated, these only include one bathroom, but there is more floor and storage space regardless. A few cruise lines, like Celebrity and Disney, offer family staterooms with privacy curtains or partitions between sleeping areas. Disney family suites have two bathrooms and include a bathtub.

Connecting Staterooms

A limited number of interconnecting staterooms can be found on most newer ships, but you will want to make your reservation before they sell out. This is also a great option if you'd like to travel with grandparents or friends—and the second bathroom, which you most likely would not have in a suite, may come in handy at times.

GETTING THE MOST ROOM FOR YOUR MONEY

Whatever the cruise line, more space may be had for a price. But chances are you'll have plenty of other things to spend money on during your cruise. Here a few extra tips for helping you get the most space for your money.

- Carnival offers some of the largest standard staterooms available, with interior staterooms up to 185 square feet—keep that in mind as you compare prices with other cruise lines.
- You might also watch for free cabin upgrade promotions to help stretch your dollars. These and other "free bonuses" often crop up for last-minute cruises advertised online.
- If you're very claustrophobic, consider the cost of booking two interconnecting staterooms with low 1st and 2nd passenger fares for the first cabin and the 1st passenger + single supplement for the other—two such cabins may cost less than a suite booked for three or four passengers.

For more detailed information about square-footage specifics and family-friendly staterooms, check out the reviews by Cruise Critic.com (www.cruisecritic.com), and visit the Web sites of the cruise lines to see pictures of the cabins you are considering. Vacations to Go also has helpful pictures of ship cabins, deck plans, dining info and more (www.vacationstogo.com).

Close quarters: If your cabin is large enough to accommodate a portacrib, you may no longer be able to walk around your bed.

SELECTING YOUR CABIN'S LOCATION

When booking a cruise online, especially, you are often given the opportunity to choose which cabin you would like for your selected options and price category. As you peruse deck plans, try to think of the ship as a whole, not just the individual levels with cabins you are considering. Keep in mind:

- **Where are the elevators?** Not only will elevators nearby create extra traffic by your door, but you will also likely suffer through the conversations of strangers waiting for the elevators.
- **What's upstairs?** A theater, dance floor, or casino may provide unwelcome noise—and late into the night.
- **What's out the window?** If you're booking an ocean view cabin, watch for footnotes that may explain you will have an obstructed or partially obstructed view. If you are looking at cabins on one of the upper levels, also watch out for rooms that may be on a deck with passersby outside.

- **Why go below?** The lower the cabin, generally, the lower the pricetag. You may also feel less motion riding low in the ship. But if you're looking at lower levels, steer clear of the fore and aft sections if possible. Although there's a chance the humming of engines at the rear may help soothe your child, it may also give you a headache. And when the anchor drops at the front of the ship, the jarring noises can wake small sleepers.
- **Why go higher?** Cabins, windows, and balconies are generally larger, and you have less of a trek to get to the restaurants, pool, and other facilities. You can also avoid lengthy waits for the elevator during peak times (dinner, shows) by taking the stairs instead.
- **Why aim for the middle?** Many cruisers think the middle of the mid-ship levels offer the best balance of convenience, quiet, and calm. Just watch out for the lifeboats that may be blocking your view outside.

MAKING SPECIAL REQUESTS

As you book your cruise, whether over the telephone with a specialist or through an online agency, you will hopefully be given the opportunity to make your special requests. If not, call the cruise line directly with your questions and requests regarding cruising with your child. This is the time to make it known if you'd like...

A crib / portacrib – All major cruise lines except Seabourn will tell you they can provide these, yet they only have so many onboard a given ship. So if you're counting on the cruise line to provide your baby's bed, don't take any chances. Make your request ASAP.

Baby food – If your cruise line offers baby food by request, by all means don't forget to put in your request. This isn't a standard staple on even the cruise ships that offer it, so give them plenty of advanced notice if you'd like to take advantage of their offer.

Bed rails – Only Disney Cruise Line offers these to passengers, and like cribs, the number available is limited. Put in your request ASAP.

Babysitting – Ships offering private or after-hours group babysitting require advance notice, so the sooner you can put in your request, the better. If you have an idea of which days or evenings you would like to hire a babysitter (based on your itinerary), ask how far in advance you can reserve the service, and don't take any chances.

Children's programs – Your cruise line may assume at the time of booking that, based on your child's age, he or she will be participating in the onboard children's program. However, during peak family travel seasons, space may be limited—particularly for popular children's events. Contact the cruise line well in advance to be sure your child will be able to participate.

- Chapter 24 -
Preparing for Your Cruise

RESEARCHING YOUR PORTS OF CALL

An exciting itinerary means little if you can't get off the ship and see the destinations firsthand. Whereas some ports will find you smack dab in the middle of the action, allowing you to stroll off the gangplank and into the action with your child at your side (or on your person), others may require a bit more planning and/or spending to get you and your family where you'd like to be.

For example, cruise ships calling on San Francisco dock adjacent to Fisherman's Wharf offer an easy walk to the Pier 39 attractions, including restaurants, cable cars, Alcatraz and Bay cruise ferries, the Aquarium of the Bay, and public transportation. Cruise ships calling on Rome, however, actually drop anchor in a different town called Civitavecchia and require about an hour's drive (one way) to get to Rome itself.

Port-specific information is sometimes available through your booking agency or the cruise line's Web site itself, though these resources tend to lean heavily on the sightseeing activities and encourage you to pay for the excursions offered by the cruise line—which may be your best bet in some situations. If you are docking in a remote location, or where tourist services are few and far between, or where your personal safety is best ensured by using the business affiliated with the ship, a shore excursion might be best.

Fortunately, a visit to www.cruising.org will help you find a wealth of information about port destinations worldwide, including the docking location, what is within walking distance, how to find and use the local transportation to get to the major attractions, activities and events, area maps, and even where to get medical assistance or exchange currency. It is well worth checking out your destinations on this site in advance, and also reading any advice they offer regarding taxis and local transportation.

Consider for each destination:

- Can you walk off the ship and see what you'd like on foot?
- If not, is public transportation easily accessible from the port, or will you need a taxi?
- Are there places where the shore excursions offered by the cruise line may be best—and worth the expense?

Sometimes, the size of the vessel also determines how closely you may dock to the port city you would like to see, so while certain smaller ships may dock within walking distance of some attractions, others may need to dock farther out and will require you to take a shuttle or taxi into town. When docking beyond a reasonable walk from the port attractions, most cruise lines offer reasonably priced shuttle buses to and from the town center, a far safer option than taking a taxi into town without a car seat. And when calling on some island destinations, like George Town, Grand Cayman or Santorini, Greece, your ship may actually drop anchor at sea and ferry passengers in on a smaller vessel—exciting stuff for the kids onboard!

CHOOSING YOUR SHORE EXCURSIONS

When cruising with toddlers and preschoolers, especially, you may prefer an itinerary with many destinations that are quickly reached by foot or by shuttle bus, and where you may enjoy the flexibility of your own schedule. For example, when docking at Barbados (Bridgetown), you can simply stroll off the ship and walk to one of the most beautiful beaches there—perfect for a family day at the beach, complete with lunch and a diaper change back on the ship. But where the attractions and major sights are not so conveniently located, organized shore excursions can offer definite advantages over going it alone:

- The time in port is used to your best advantage, going straight to the sites of interest
- The tour bus is ready and waiting with no need for lugging along a car seat
- An English-speaking guide tells you everything you need to know to appreciate the sites
- There is no worry of getting back to the ship in time for departure
- You know you are with a trusted tour operator on land

Before choosing any shore excursions for your family, you'll want to make sure there aren't any restrictions that may prevent your child from going with you. On more active excursions, such as rainforest canopy adventure tours, children must be at least 12 years old and 48 inches tall—no standing around taking turns holding your baby on these tours! However, on many if not most excursions, children and/or infants are allowed to come along for the ride, with infants riding on laps for free, and children sometimes paying a discounted rate (though not always).

Most cruise lines provide details of their shore excursions on their Web sites, including the physical activity level necessary to keep up with the tour, and recommended clothing or shoes, all of which can help you better gauge the suitability for your family. Cruise lines encourage advanced booking, which is a good idea for the most popular tours that may sell out before the ship sets sail. You, however, may feel more comfortable waiting until you are on the ship and can speak directly to the cruise activities director about which excursions she would—and wouldn't—recommend for your family. If you are considering checking your child into the kid's activity program or onboard babysitting while in port, be sure to make the arrangements as early as possible (e.g. stop by the purser's desk to make arrangements before the ship leaves port).

Tips for Excellent Group Excursions

- Carefully consider excursions that require more than a half hour of uninterrupted driving to get to the destination (in addition to other drive time between sights). You may have the benefit of a tour guide providing background and commentary as you make the journey, but if your child isn't content with the situation, no one may be able to hear it. Shorter driving segments with fresh air and changes of scenery are safer bets.
- Use a frontpack or soft backpack carrier for your child rather than a stroller, which may become a tripping hazard to others in your group as they stop sporadically to gaze and take photographs. Your stroller may also be difficult to use over the changing terrain—not to mention it could become an annoyance in the bus. A soft backpack carrier that doubles as your diaper bag/daypack may be a great option for older children, and saves space over the framed (hiking) variety.
- Rest assured your group will make pit stops, and be prepared to make the most of them. In the event of an untimely diaper change, don't be afraid to check in with your guide for advice on where to change it, and be willing to sit out one round to take care of business, rather than risk holding up the tour while you negotiate diapers and wipes.
- Respect your fellow travelers' rights to an excellent group excursion, too, by being ready and willing to "take it outside" if your child becomes audibly unhappy with a tour or has difficulty respecting the boundaries of a given destination.

TAKING TAXIS IN PORT

There are times and destinations where your family may prefer some flexibility in its day—or the leisure of enjoying just one or two sites. Taking taxis can be a cost-effective way to get your family to its destinations, and at some destinations, like Antigua, taxi drivers are hailed as the most knowledgeable local guides available and are highly recommended for sightseeing. However, car seats (and the lugging of them) may be an issue, and going without is not recommended.

Your best bet may be to hire a "car and driver" for the day, whether it's one designated taxi driver who agrees to be your local guide (discuss the itinerary and price up front) or a local company that offers private sightseeing. You can strap in your own car seat and relax while someone else navigates, and you'll have an extra person to snap those family pictures with *all of you* in the shot. This is also a safer way to reach outlying destinations, as opposed to risking whether or not you will be able to get a return taxi when you need it, or finding yourself faced with drivers that insist your return trip will cost double: "You wanna get back to your fancy-pants ship or not?"

Hiring a car and driver may also be a less expensive than organized ship excursions in some cases, particularly if you have to pay full price for your child. At ports where taxis are considered to be risky, some cruise lines will also offer a private car and driver option. Or you can check www.cruising.org and for local sightseeing options including "car and driver hire" through a local agency.

If you take a taxi, be sure to have complete instructions in the local language as to where you want to go, or at least a map you can point to for clarity. But more importantly, have clear details of where you need to return to. Some cities have multiple docking locations or expansive harbors, so hard as it may be to believe, repeating the name of the harbor over and over again with an American accent, or saying "big boat" in the local language followed by the name of the cruise line, or even singing the theme song from "The Love Boat" may not be enough to get you back to your ship (just ask us).

Packing for Your Cruise

Packing Baby Essentials

If you'll be cruising for a week or more with a baby, it is not unreasonable to expect you will need an entire suitcase devoted to baby essentials. Really.

Cruise lines do not stock baby food, formula, diapers, or wipes onboard, except in very rare cases (you may find a few diapers on Disney ships). Also, you'll want to bring along any baby bottles or sippy cups, toddler utensils, bibs, and related paraphernalia you may need to help make it a comfortable voyage. Just remember, as your supply of diapers and baby food diminishes you'll be freeing up lots of room for souvenirs—which are much more fun to hunt for in port cities than diapers for your child.

You'd better bring it onboard:

- Diapers
- Swim diapers (if needed)
- Wipes
- Baby food
- Formula
- Bottles, nipples (or disposables)
- Sippy cups
- Toddler silverware, etc.
- Travel bottle of dishwashing soap, bottle brush
- Baby sun block
- Baby shampoo
- Preferred lotion
- Baby bathtub inflatable insert

Packing Your Carry-On Bags

You should arrive at your cruise ship no later than 2 hours before the departure time. The embarkation process itself may take around an hour, much of it reminiscent of waiting around an airport, though possibly with fewer comforts. During this time you will need to check in, check your luggage, and clear security.

Since your luggage may not be delivered to your cabin for a few hours, you will want to give some serious thought to what goes into your carry-on bags, which will accompany you to your cabin. Certainly anything you'll need for your first hours onboard should be there, but think of other things that can help kick-start your vacation, too. Depending on when and where you board, you may want sun block, swim suits, a favorite toy or game, or perhaps naptime essentials. Make sure you have:

- Enough diapers to last you through bedtime, just in case
- Corresponding amount of formula and/or baby food
- Changes of clothes for each passenger
- Any necessary bottles or sippy cups
- A favorite book or two
- Trusted lovey or security blanket
- Medications
- Toiletries
- Your trusty travel stroller

At the end of your cruise, you'll want to repack your carry-on bags just as thoughtfully, since the rest of your luggage will likely need to be packed and surrendered the night before you disembark (placing it outside your door). In case there are not enough porters for passengers, as is often the case, be sure you have enough diapers and essentials to last you through a couple of hours of disembarkation mayhem, as well. If you are heading straight to an airport, stock the outer pockets of your larger suitcases with refills of diapers, wipes, and other items you may need to replenish in your carry-ons and diaper bag before checking in for your flight.

Bringing Along Baby Gear

Car seats and strollers take up extra cabin space—yet having them along may be critical to enjoying your cruise. And having a portacrib provided by the ship may seem like a major convenience—but it may also be a major obstacle. Here are some points to consider when deciding what stays and what goes.

Stroller - The stroller may be helpful while visiting your ports, or not. Consider what kind of sights you will see and whether or not it might be easier to use a child carrier instead, or if she'll insist on walking most of the time anyway and the exercise would be beneficial. If you'll be joining a group for organized sightseeing, there may not be room in the bus or van for a stroller. Onboard, however, you may be very glad to have your stroller to help get your child to sleep, to use while feeding her in the cabin, to shade her while napping next to you on deck, or simply to keep her from getting into too much trouble in your un-childproofed cabin as you dress. We enjoyed watching our daughter practice walking while pushing her stroller backwards up and down the ship hallways and across the decks, and it was a comfy, secure place for her to sit (versus crawling and cruising free-range) while we enjoyed coffee on deck. If you do decide to bring a stroller, you will want to bring one that folds very compactly to take up minimal space in your cabin.

Car seat - You may be able to find safe transportation alternatives that don't require a car seat—or be able to rent one (along with a car) for the portions you do. In many cases, there is no need for a car seat once the cruise begins. You may be able to walk off the ship to explore your port by foot, or join an organized group to travel by bus or minibus—where you most likely wouldn't find seatbelts anyway. In the interest of cabin space, you might consider the Radian folding car seat which folds to a mere 6.5" thick to store nicely in your cabin closet. But if your destinations would most easily be explored by taking taxis, you might want to consider the Sit'n'Stroll convertible car seat and stroller, or a Tote 'n' Go DX travel vest for older children (both included in Car Seats, Accessories, and Alternatives, page 48).

Travel beds – Rather than use the portacrib provided by your ship, you may prefer to bring along a travel bed to save floor space in your cabin. Various options exist for infants, toddlers, and even preschool age children, which can be folded up and stored in your closet or drawer if needed during the day. (See Travel Beds and Sleeping Solutions, page 54.)

INDEX

Start your family's next adventure at

www.travelswithbaby.com

Visit us online at

www.travelswithbaby.com

You'll find even more helpful information and advice, a directory of useful links for planning your next trip, plus all the great products and gear mentioned in this book. You can also read more "Travels with Baby Tips" in my blog at TravelswithBaby.com.

Help make this a better book

I welcome your feedback and suggestions for future editions of *Travels with Baby*. Please address correspondence to Shelly Rivoli, Travels with Baby, P.O. Box 7696, Berkeley, CA 94707, or email shelly@travelswithbaby.com.

Want to share your tips with other parents?

Help other families have their best trips possible by sharing your own travel tips and experiences, including:

- Your recommended places to visit and stay—or stop and play—with babies and small children
- How you kept your child entertained during a long drive or flight
- A helpful product you've discovered and would recommend to traveling parents
- Anything else you think would help fellow traveling families.

You can submit your tips online at www.travelswithbaby.com or write to Travels with Baby, P.O. Box 7696, Berkeley, CA 94707.

Breinigsville, PA USA
05 May 2010
237451BV00001B/42/P